Crossing the Tracks

The New Press was established in 1990 as a not-for-profit alternative to the large, commercial publishing houses currently dominating the book publishing industry. The New Press is committed to publishing, in innovative ways, works of educational, cultural, and community value, which might not normally be commercially viable, and to operating in the public interest rather than for private gain.

Publication of *Crossing the Tracks* was made possible in part by a generous donation from The Edna McConnell Clark Foundation.

Published in the United States by The New Press, New York.
Distributed by W.W. Norton and Company, Inc., New York, NY 10110

Library of Congress Cataloging-in-Publication Data

Wheelock, Anne.
   Crossing the tracks: how untracking can save America's schools / Anne Wheelock.
     p. cm.
   Includes bibliographical references.
   ISBN 1-56584-038-0
   1. Educational equalization—United States. 2. Educational change—United States. 3. Ability grouping in education.
   I. Title.
   LC213.2.W44 1992
   371.2'52'0973—dc20   92-53728
                                       CIP

95 94 93 4 3 2 1

Book design by Mia Saunders

Printed in the United States

Crossing the Tracks

How "Untracking" Can Save America's Schools

Anne Wheelock
for the Massachusetts Advocacy Center

with a Foreword by Jeannie Oakes

To Cynthia Jean Sakofsky,
a memorable teacher,
Mamaroneck Junior High School,
1957–1958

Acknowledgements

In the process of preparing a book such as this, the writer becomes more a scribe than a creator, documenting the stories of schools and the teachers, parents, students, and citizens who are extending their thinking, talents, and time toward realizing deeply held convictions about democracy and schooling.

This book owes its greatest debt to the educators in schools across the country who responded to requests for information, spent hours with us on the telephone, wrote us letters, answered surveys and questionnaires, sent us videotapes, and allowed us to observe them at work creating the kinds of schools that daily meet the challenges of designing for all students an education worthy of the name. This book exists primarily because of their willingness to tell their stories. We thank them for helping us understand how they are working to mobilize resources and overcome hurdles to realize a vision of inclusive schooling where all children have a chance to succeed.

We could not have begun even to consider this undertaking without the generous support of the Edna McConnell Clark Foundation's Program for Disadvantaged Youth. We especially extend our appreciation to Hayes Mizell of the foundation. His advocacy for disenfranchised students over many years remains an inspiration to many who work on behalf of children.

This book relies on the expertise and advice of many experienced colleagues. We are especially grateful to Jeannie Oakes whose support and encouragement of our work from its beginning stages has sustained this project. Colleen Connolly, Dan French, Marcia Klenbort, John Lounsbury, and David Payton also deserve special appreciation. Their thoughtful guidance, suggestions, and comments reflected both their faith in us and the depth of their own commitment to high-quality, democratic schooling for young adolescents.

We are also grateful for the specific assistance of many other individuals. Jean Adenika, Georgia Christensen, Colleen Connolly, Jay Feldman, Marcia Klenbort, Wendy Hopfenberg, Jay MacLeod, Daniel Mayer, Elly Pardo, Janet Ready, Stephen Slaner, Tom Stone, and Leslie Talbot contributed detailed observations of effective hetrerogeneous grouping in classrooms, schools, and community programs. Ron Binckney, Steve Bing, Ann Coles, Suzanne Davenport, Emily Dentzer, Joan Eckengren, Ruth Eckstrom, Phyllis Hart, Leslie Hergert, Lyla Hoffman, Michelle Fine, Reva Gertel, Paul George, Holly Hatch, Anthony Jackson, Herbert Kohl, Sandra Lewis, Susan Markowitz, Phyllis McClure, Ruth Mitchell, Judy O'Rourke, Nancy Peck, Amy Pelletier, Joanne Pullen, Anna Sebastian, Dan Sharkovitz, Adria Steinberg, Susan Stetzer, Lee Teitel, Dale Weschler, and Diane Wood also directed us to important resources, sent timely information, or made comments at various stages. Each shaped the manuscript in a way that grounded our work more immediately in the realities of school life.

Michael Kennedy provided support and assistance of all kinds throughout the months of researching, writing, and editing this book. He deserves final but not least important mention, appreciation, and gratitude.

Foreword

Since the 1920s, most schools enrolling adolescents have offered a "tracked" curriculum—sequences of academic classes that range from slow-paced remedial courses to rigorous academic ones and an array of electives or exploratory classes in the arts, vocational subjects, and physical education. This tracked curriculum has seemed logical because it supports a nearly century-old belief that a crucial job of schools is to ready students for an economy that requires workers with quite different knowledge and skills. Thus, demanding academic classes could prepare students heading for jobs that require college degrees, whereas more rudimentary academic classes and vocational programs could ready students for less-skilled jobs or for post-high-school technical training.

Furthermore, the public has judged tracked schools that prepare for different work lives to be appropriate and fair, given the perceived differences in students' intellectual abilities, motivation, and aspirations. Thus, most people view a tracked curriculum with its "ability grouped" academic classes as both functional and democratic—an educationally sound way to accomplish two important tasks: 1) providing students with the education that best suits their abilities and 2) providing the nation with the array of workers it needs.

Increasingly, however, policymakers, national opinion leaders, and educators are concluding that tracking accomplishes neither of these tasks well, and they are adding tracking to the list of school practices that need to be "restructured." Clearly, tracking hasn't helped schools prepare students to meet the demands of the workplace, as is evidenced by the increasing disenchantment on the part of employers with students' knowledge, skills, and attitudes. Rapidly changing technology and out-of-date equipment limit the capacity of middle-level and high schools to prepare students with specific occupational skills. And, as more jobs require greater sophistication in terms of literacy, mathematical ability, and problem solving, schools are under fire for failing to provide entry-level workers with the competence based on academic ability and the capacity to think that many jobs require. The nation's former confidence that a tracked curriculum would ensure that non-college-bound students would leave high school ready for work has been shattered. At the same time, the tracks assigned to prepare students for college are also being judged as failing to make the nation's "best" students academically competitive with their peers in other countries.

Additionally, new conceptions and evidence about human abilities expose as fraudulent (or, at least, myopic) the claim that tracking is an appropriate response to differences in children's capacities and motivation. Educators, policymakers, and parents, as well, must now view intellectual ability as primarily a *social construction*, like race and gender, rather than as a genetic inheritance. That is, we are faced with overwhelming evidence that nearly every child is capable of achieving every worthwhile educational goal, regardless of gender, regardless of skin tone, and regardless of his or her scores on outmoded measures of intellectual ability. Increasingly, tracking is recognized as a school structure premised on an inaccurate and dysfunctional view that not every child is capable.

Pressure to eliminate tracking, however, is not based solely on disillusion with its effectiveness or the accuracy of its implied judgments about children's abilities. Typically, those who favor tracking meet these criticisms with promises of technological improvements—sometimes suggesting beefed-up curricula and teaching methods, more accurate placement criteria, or reconfigured tracking schemes. But, increasingly, the nation is losing faith in the "improvability" of many school structures; and more people are questioning the fairness and morality of any school structure that leads to immigrant, low-income, and minority youth more often taking low-level academic and vocational training, while middle- and upper-class whites more often enroll in the upper tracks that lead to college.

The matching of students to different tracks carried with it racial, ethnic, and social-class overtones *from the very beginning.* Early on in this century, low-level academics and vocational training were thought to be more appropriate for immigrant, low-income, and minority youth, whereas rigorous academic preparation was seen as better meeting the needs of more affluent whites. Few questioned the rightness of this pattern, just as few questioned the many other social and economic barriers faced by African-American and Latino minorities before the 1960s. But things have changed considerably, and today most educators and policymakers are deeply troubled by the fact that sorting students into "high" and "low" tracks severely limits the educational and occupational futures of low-income, African-American, and Latino students and, in racially mixed schools, perpetuates stereotypes of minority students as being less intelligent than white ones and constrains opportunities for meaningful interracial contact.

It is not surprising that these tracking "problems" have captured the attention of civil-rights groups and other advocates of school desegregation. In the last decade, NAACP Legal Defense Fund, the ACLU, and the Children's Defense Fund have all identified tracking as the most important "second generation" segregation issue. The U.S. Department of Education's Civil Rights Division has targeted tracking practices as an important consideration in determining racially mixed schools' compliance with Title VI requirements for categorical programs. However, what's striking now is that, because of the more general disillusionment with tracking, mainstream groups such as the National Governors' Association, the Carnegie Corporation, the College Board, and the National Education Association have added their voices to those calling for the elimination of tracking and ability grouping, and many states are beginning to frame "untracking" guidelines for their local schools.

This broad-based concern about tracking has brought with it hard, but reasonable, questions about what the alternatives might be to ameliorating tracking-related problems without compromising efforts to increase the quality and rigor of school programs or provoking white, middle-class families to flee from racially mixed schools. Increasingly, policymakers and practitioners want to know what good untracked schools might look like, and what reform strategies might foster such schools. It is important for judges who oversee desegregation cases to know whether educators in racially mixed schools can make further changes, such as untracking, that would provide minority students with greater educational opportunities.

Educators are not well prepared to answer these questions. Researchers who have focused on tracking and ability grouping have succeeded in describing the complex and problematic nature of tracking, but they have generated little research-based knowledge about more promising alternatives and how they might be integrated into schools. Nevertheless, schools across the country are plunging, headlong, into untracking, inventing new strategies and borrowing others from wherever they can. Until now, such schools have not only been without a knowledge base about how untracking can work, they have also been largely isolated from one another.

This book begins to fill these important gaps. The chapters that follow describe specific strategies for untracking, with examples of how these strategies vary across schools in different local contexts. What stands out in the stories of these schools is that, despite the considerable promise and "right-headedness" of the goal, untracking is a daunting task.

First, successful untracking requires changes in a myriad of school practices. The experiences of these schools makes clear that school organization, curriculum, and classroom practices are interrelated and mutually supportive; change in any one must be approached in the context of a set of mutually supportive reforms. That's because tracking is just one of many problematic school structures and practices. Tracking supports and is supported by much else that is wrong with schools—thin, skills-based curricula; passive, teacher-dominated instructional strategies; standardized, paper-and-pencil assessment, to name just a few. As a consequence, untracking requires far more than the development of new grouping and scheduling strategies. Simply mixing students into heterogeneous classrooms can't begin to provide diverse groups of students with the opportunities and supportive environment that they need in order to learn well. Neither can a *single* new technique pave the way. Training teachers in cooperative learning methods, for example, is typical of untracking efforts. As helpful as this teaching method is, teachers still confront disconnected subject areas, fragmented curricula, norm-referenced assessments, inadequate support for special needs, isolation from their colleagues, and so on. Untracking won't work unless these other practices are also reconsidered and made compatible with the new grouping structure. An outcome, now largely unanticipated, is that such changes should improve the quality of schooling for all children—even those now receiving the "best."

The array of practices invented and adapted by untracking schools provides enormously helpful illustrations for other schools. Nevertheless, these schools themselves should not be considered "models" to be copied, but, rather, purveyors of more general lessons. The critical lesson they teach is that creating a *culture of detracking* is more important than any particular organizational arrangements, curricula, or instructional strategies attempted by a school—as necessary as these are. This account of schools grappling with untracking shows that successful efforts move beyond an exclusively "practical" focus on programs and classroom strategies and attend to values and beliefs. Untracking schools restructure their thinking, which allows them to build political support for classroom cultures in which tracking no longer makes sense.

A second lesson from these schools, then, is that although new technologies are necessary, they are clearly insufficient to bring forth change. Alternative practices must *make sense* to educators and their communities before they can be fully implemented and sustained in schools. This making sense occurs when the values and beliefs at the core of tracking are challenged and replaced with new norms—norms that support heterogeneous grouping and classroom practices that such grouping requires.

Challenging norms is essential because the underlying assumptions of any practice provide the intellectual infrastructure that protects it from change. The norms that support tracking are conventional, if increasingly obsolete, conceptions of intelligence, as well as deep-seated racist and classist attitudes and prejudices. These norms—consciously and unconsciously—drive the day-to-day educational practices mentioned above. Tracking also conforms to the deeply ingrained bureaucratic notion that any process can be made more efficient when it's divided into hierarchical levels and specialized categories. Another norm that bolsters and legitimizes tracking is the American emphasis on competition and individualism over cooperation and the good of the community—a norm suggesting that "good" education is a scarce commodity available only to a few winners. Although the American system of public education was designed to promote the common good and to prepare children for participation in a democratic society, more recent emphasis has been placed on what a graduate can "get out" of schooling in terms of income, power, or status.

Obviously, efforts to untrack schools must reach beyond the technical, day-to-day functions of the school and address the way in which our society views such matters as human capacities; individual and group differences; fairness, efficiency, and competition; and the goals of public education today.

A third lesson drawn from these schools is that reformers must address pressures from the social-political milieu that holds tracking in place. Political concerns grow out of the norms that undergird tracking and, at the same time, have a strong influence on technical decisions at the school and district levels. The pressure placed on educators by savvy parents who want their children enrolled in the "best" classes is no doubt the most obvious such political factor. In most communities middle-class white parents, in particular, better understand the inequalities in a school's structure and know how to pressure the school into responding positively to their children. Parents of high-track students are clearly advantaged—both in terms of educational opportunities and status—by the current arrangement. And in a competitive system that offers only a small percentage of students slots in the high-track classes, these parents have few options but to push to have their children better educated than other children. Administrators rightfully worry that attempts to do away with tracking will lead to a loss of support from these involved parents and a lower enrollment of children from the most advantaged families. This latter concern has been fueled by advocates for high-achieving students and those who have qualified for state and local gifted and talented programs. These parents and others perceive the research on tracking and the response it has engendered as a serious threat to high-quality education for their children and constituents. They fear that untracking will sap the opportunities now available to high achievers. Because all schools need political support—not only for funding and physical resources, but also for credibility— a policy that allows some tracking (e.g., maintenance of separate gifted and talent programs) is often exchanged for the political credit that more advantaged and involved parents bring to a school.

The pressure from more affluent and better educated parents to keep schools tracked and to have their children placed and kept in the highest-level courses certainly reflects a competitive, individualistic attitude toward the purpose of schooling. But in racially mixed schools this view can take on another dimension. Because race, class, assessed ability, and track placements interrelate, heterogeneous ability grouping may mean racial integration in classes where none existed before. Fearing that minority-student enrollment leads to lower educational standards, white and wealthy parents often lobby for their children's enrollment in more racially and socioeconomically homogeneous gifted and talented programs or honors courses within desegregated schools. Most truly believe that their children will receive a better education in a homogeneous classroom. Given what we know about teacher expectations for students in different tracks and the resulting level of difficulty of the work that is assigned to students in those tracks, these parents are correct in their assumptions.

Successful untracking, then, will depend on building supportive communities both within and outside the school. This political dimension asks, "How might competing interests—such as advocates for the gifted, for the disadvantaged, and for minorities—redefine their roles and create a collective advocacy for all children?" Building such new communities will be an essentially political process and will require the political leadership of educators. Such support must emerge from reasoned and critical inquiry, based on research, self-study, and democratic values. And, it must be built on new norms—on new confidence in the intellectual capacities of all children and new confidence in the ability of schools to provide for all a far richer and more meaningful education than that now reserved only for those in the top tracks.

This book is an ambitious first step in our effort to understand and share the process of untracking. It should provide both inspiration and sobering insight to schools that are considering untracking. None of the schools whose stories are told here has resolved all of its tracking problems; many are still vulnerable to social and political forces grounded in old norms regarding race, class, ability, and competition for the "best" education. What matters here is that these schools, and those who read about them, should bear witness to the most essential lesson about altering schools in ways that serve all children well: At the same time that schools entertain new techniques, they must also recognize and be willing to confront the fact that tracking is simply a structural manifestation of norms deeply rooted in the culture of schooling and a reflection of the political forces driven by these norms.

Jeannie Oakes
University of California, Los Angeles

Contents

Part III: Strategies and Tools for Reform   63

1 • Involving Parents and the Community   65

2 • Expecting the Best   91

PART I
Introduction

To the Editor:

I think tracking is a good idea. Advanced students should be permitted to enter an advanced placement class, rather than be forced to remain in a class where other students are failing or getting low grades.

—Jeffrey Genovese, Allston, Massachusetts,
Boston Globe, 7 February, 1991

Dear Jeff:

My name is Amy Pelletier, and I am a first year student at Mount Holyoke College. I was in homogeneously grouped classes in seventh grade and changed to heterogeneously grouped classes (at Pioneer Valley Regional School in Northfield, Massachusetts) in eighth grade.

When the transition was first made, I did not really understand what was happening, and therefore saw little change. Then I began to notice that there were different students in all my classes. I was no longer "stuck" in the "high-level" rotation where I saw the same people all the time. By the time I graduated, I knew all the people in my class, not just their names, but something about them.

There was also a change in the style of teaching. Much more work was done in groups, rather than lecture. As a result, teachers were able to work more one-on-one with students. With this, students learned to be responsible to each other, not just to the teacher. I remember one particular project which required that our group read a short story, come up with a script, and make a movie. While I had no problem writing the dialogue, I did not know where to start in making the video. Luckily, the others in my group (from the "lower" levels) were very creative and knowledgeable when it came to acting, recording, and film editing. It is in these groups where people realized and learned to respect everyone's interests and talents.

Many people are worried about the effects of heterogeneous grouping on the "upper" levels, fearing that the "lower" level students will hold them back. I can honestly say I don't feel I was held back by any other student. After the transition, I did not see a change in the challenge of the class work. If a student was having difficulties, there were always alternative ways for the teacher to approach the subject. For example, in my senior English class we read *Dr. Jekyll and Mr. Hyde*. One student was having trouble getting through the book, and he was given the cassette matching the story, which allowed him to keep up with the class and participate in discussions. Another example is from my physics class where there were many different levels ranging from the top 5 percent of my class to the lower quarter. Our teacher combined mathematical problems and book learning with many hands-on activities. These projects included a rubber band race car contest and an egg drop contest. Ironically enough, the "lower" levels were far more successful than the "upper" level students in these assignments which applied our book knowledge to real life.

I recall that in the debate on the change to hetero-geneous grouping, many "upper" level students were afraid of becoming bored in their classes. However, I did not experience this. I believe this is where teachers must become more flexible in assignments, allowing students to do independent or extra work if they so desire. In my school, the opportunity for independent study is readily available and open to all students who find they have a particular interest and want to pursue it further. Independent projects provide opportunity for students to study more in depth, while fostering responsibility, creativity, and motivation.

Another concern is that the "upper" level student will have problems being accepted at top colleges and universities. I have not seen this to be true, however, since students from my class and the class before me are currently attending Georgetown University, Mount Holyoke College, Smith College, University of Vermont, Massachusetts Institute of Technology, and others.

I feel there is a great deal of discrimination among students grouped homogeneously. Not only do the "upper" level students look down on those in "lower" levels, but the "lower" students have many stereotypes for those in higher levels. These stereotypes are unfair since the level where students are placed is often determined by a standardized test which does not truly measure their capabilities. Heterogeneous grouping, on the other hand, lessens this discrimination by allowing students to interact with each other about these preconceived notions.

I believe that heterogeneous grouping is also more realistic in the long run. For example, colleges or universities generally run on a heterogeneous system, where people sign up for the classes they are interested in. On a broader scale, life in the "real world" involves dealing with people who are not at the same level as you. Therefore, I feel that heterogeneous grouping does not disadvantage any student academically, and the social and psychological gains are tremendous.

I hope that these thoughts have helped you dispel some fears about mixed-level grouping. Your worries are not uncommon; many students and parents experience them when there is discussion of this type of structural change. I wish you well and hope that you find the change as advantageous as I have.

Sincerely,

Amy Pelletier
May 2, 1991

From Tracking to Untracking:
A Paradigm Shift

America is rife with talk of school reform. The growing expectation that schools will educate all students at increasingly higher levels poses new challenges for educators, and many are responding by reorganizing school practices heretofore considered "givens." Among those practices are tracking and ability grouping.

What is tracking? Tracking involves the categorizing of students according to particular measures of intelligence into distinct groups for purposes of teaching and learning. Once they have been sorted and classified, students are provided with curriculum and instruction deemed suited to their ability and matched to spoken or unspoken assessments of each student's future. Research has dramatically demonstrated, however, that this practice has created as many problems as it was designed to solve.

Tracking does not result in the equal and equitable distribution of effective schooling among all students. Instead, on the one hand, it allocates the most valuable school experiences—including challenging and meaningful curricula, top-quality instruction, and high teacher expectations—to students who already have the greatest academic, economic, and social advantages. On the other hand, those who face the greatest struggles in school—and in life in general—receive a more impoverished curriculum based on lower assessments of their learning capacity. Over time, students at the lower levels move so much more slowly than those at the higher ones that differences that may have been real but not profound in the earlier grades become gigantic gaps in terms of achievement, attitude, and self-esteem. Furthermore, the sorting of students into groups of "haves" and "have-nots" contradicts the American educational credo that schools are democratic communities of learners whose purpose is to offer equal educational opportunity to all.

In the light of growing awareness of the real costs of tracking and greater familiarity with effective heterogeneous classroom methodologies, schools across the country are beginning to switch from practices that result in unequal access to knowledge to superior approaches designed to provide equal educational opportunity. We call this process "untracking." This book is about some of many schools, mostly at the middle level, that have begun this process. We call these institutions "untracking schools."

Untracking schools are those that are replacing the grouping of students by ability with mixed-ability classrooms. These grouping changes are made in tandem with shifts in curriculum, teaching approaches, and assessment strategies designed to enhance learning for more diverse groups of students. These schools also adopt routines and structures redesigned to extend expectations for success to all students and to foster a strong sense of the school as a community of learners. Moving into uncharted territory, untracking schools create new conditions for learning and teaching and, in the process, redefine their own character in relation to a true commitment to discover and nurture the genius in all their students.

As schools venture into the largely unmapped terrain of heterogeneous grouping, they encounter challenging questions that lie at the heart of public education: What is our mission? What do we want all our students to know when they leave our school? How are our grouping practices compatible with our mission and goals? What are the values that will guide us in developing alternatives? What kinds of curriculum and instruction can enhance new grouping practices? How will we assess student progress? How can we introduce change without sacrificing our best practices? How will we explain our changes to all the constituencies who have a stake in our school?

As educators come up with their own answers to these questions, the new practices that they adopt reflect a shift in the norms that underlie their daily routines. And as each school, in the process of untracking, begins to claim its uniqueness, it also shares characteristics with other schools including a new emphasis on:

- Releasing intelligence rather than quantifying it
- Nurturing effort rather than defining ability
- Building strengths rather than sorting according to weakness
- Developing dispositions and skills necessary for lifelong learning across all areas of knowledge rather than imparting particular information in a given subject area
- Balancing concepts with meaningful content
- Building on students' aspirations rather than circumscribing their dreams
- Recognizing students as members of a learning community rather than as products of an assembly line

What gives these schools their distinct personalities is the means by which they make these shifts, the strategies that they adopt, and the accommodations that they make along the way— all of which reflect the different contexts in which they find themselves.

The Scope of Tracking in Public Schools

In every school I've visited, there is a clearly delineated "top," "middle," and "bottom" group. There is an across-the-board comfort with the notion of ability grouping, and it dictates the critical process of aligning youngsters with instructional experiences and with one another. In almost every classroom I've visited, the teacher has given me a fairly direct signal as to how fast or slow, how gifted or average, or how facile or struggling the group is—and what effect this has on depth, pacing, and other instructional considerations.

—Peter Buttenwieser, "Notes from the field,"
for the Ford Foundation, 1985

Tracking and its various modifications have been accepted features of this country's schools for nearly a century. Coming into use at a time when growing numbers of immigrant children were enrolling in public schools, tracking was adopted as a legitimate means of sorting out those students who were viewed as having limited preparation or capacity for schooling from native children. By the 1920s, some schools had developed as many as eight distinctly labeled tracks—classical, arts, engineering, academic, normal, commercial business, commercial secretarial, and general—each representing particular curricula that in turn reflected assessments of students' probable social and vocational futures. And as Buttenwieser—who represented the Ford Foundation on visits to nearly one hundred secondary schools across the country—found, as recently as 1985, few high schools even considered reform of tracking.

Tracking and ability grouping characterize the organization of classrooms for even younger students, too. Approximately two-thirds of the principals of middle-level schools surveyed in 1990 by Jomills Henry Braddock II of Johns Hopkins University reported the use of whole-class grouping by ability in at least some academic subjects, and one out of five reported such grouping in all subjects. Braddock's survey also revealed that in all subjects but reading, whole-class ability grouping increased as students moved from fifth through ninth grade. These findings complement those of John Lounsbury and Donald Clark who, in a 1990 study of over a thousand eighth-grade classrooms, found that eighth graders are almost invariably grouped homogeneously for at least part of their school day, with 89 percent of the classrooms observed using some form of ability grouping.

In most schools, these practices are both well intentioned and convenient. Even educators who doubt the value of tracking are frequently unfamiliar with practices that work effectively with heterogeneously grouped classes. But nowadays tradition, convenience, and lack of compelling alternatives are no longer adequate reasons to maintain tracking and ability-grouping practices. In the 1990s, we know that tracking is both harmful and unnecessary. New grouping, curriculum, and instructional practices that are more compatible with the democratic philosophy of American society must feature in any agenda for meaningful school reform.

Negative Effects of Tracking

Despite public disappointment with the performance of American students, the contribution of daily school routines to underachievement is often dismissed as trifling. In fact, the unequal distribution of favorable learning conditions virtually institutionalizes patterns of unequal achievement among students. This imbalance allocates advantageous experiences disproportionately to those students already favored by race and class, beginning with the curriculum.

In some districts, for example, entire schools constitute a "high track" where a disproportionately white, middle-class student body has access to a curriculum that offers solid preparation for post-secondary education. At the same time, other schools in the same district may offer a mostly minority student body a comparatively remedial curriculum. In many districts, course-enrollment patterns inside individual schools replicate this pattern—with poor, African-American, Latino, and students who are recent immigrants largely absent from courses that offer access to the higher-level knowledge needed for educational success and broadened life opportunities. These students are often to be found in disproportionate numbers in the lower-level courses of the "general" or "vocational" curriculum.

At the middle level, patterns of race and class segregation and the differences in curriculum offered to various groups are obvious by the eighth grade. According to data compiled by the National Educational Longitudinal Survey of 1988 (NELS:88), African-American, Latino, Native American, and low-income eighth graders are twice as likely as white or upper-income eighth graders to be in remedial math courses. Not only do students in remedial settings receive a less demanding curriculum; their teachers are also more likely to be less experienced in the classroom. For example, researcher Lorraine McDonnell and her colleagues found that teachers in 42 percent of the remedial, vocational, and general-mathematics sections have been teaching for five years or less, compared with 19 percent of those in the pre-algebra and algebra-1 sections.

Inequalities in learning conditions extend to other aspects of school life as well. As Jonathan Kozol has documented in *Savage Inequalities: Children in America's Schools*, students who face enormous hurdles of poverty and discrimination in their personal lives also attend schools that are intellectually and physically inhospitable learning environments. In these schools, textbooks and library resources are woefully inadequate—a situation that virtually ensures that many students will not master grade-level material regardless of their effort or ability. The absence of modern learning tools such as computers further cripples achievement. In this context of "scarce resources," poor schools may be forced into allocating advantages according to their estimate of which students are "most deserving," thus institutionalizing greater opportunity for some while leaving others to manage without the necessary tools for learning.

Kozol notes that the "restructuring" efforts of the 1980s have scarcely taken hold in these impoverished schools where, in comparison with their middle-class counterparts, poor students have limited exposure to the kinds of cutting-edge classroom practices that nurture success. While schools in well-to-do districts may implement a conceptual curriculum based on inquiry, simulations, research activities, technology-assisted instruction, and authentic school-level decision making, schools in poorer districts often remain isolated from state-of-the-art improvement efforts. These disparities further situate poor schools on the remedial margins of public education.

By the same token, the antiquated practices that often characterize remedial settings further undermine achievement. One of the most harmful of these is grade retention. Although research has powerfully documented the fact that repeating a grade at any level rarely promotes achievement and frequently contributes to student disengagement and dropping out, the practice is widespread—especially for poor children. According to NELS:88, by the time American students reach the end of eighth grade, nearly one out of five has repeated a grade; however, more than one out of three students from low-income families have experienced at least one retention. Once retained, students are increasingly vulnerable to placement at a lower level or in special education. Mary Lee Smith and Lorrie Shepard in *Flunking Grades*, for example, have noted strong correlations between the use of grade retention and high rates of special education placement.

Calls for "reforms" like longer school days or greater standardization of curriculum will not have much impact on learning until harmful practices inside the schools themselves change. Reforms are needed to alter the quality of relationships, curriculum, and instruction in every classroom. Untracking, with its emphasis on enriching the intellectual and social experiences of all students, is a critical strategy for addressing the issue of quality in education.

Specific Problems with Tracking Young Adolescents

> The education of young adolescents must, of course, be an integrated venture; physical, social, emotional, and intellectual development are intertwined and interactive. To rank one dimension above the others, to try to separate them out, is to misunderstand the nature of the ten-to-fourteen-year-old.
>
> —John Lounsbury, *Middle School Journal*, 1991

Young adolescence is a unique period of development. Students from grades five through nine grow at a pace that is as rapid as that experienced from birth to age three. Their development is multifaceted and dramatic, involving not only physical maturation but also social, emotional, and intellectual growth. These changes are erratic and occur on an individual basis: for example, a pre-algebra student may also still enjoy playing with Lego or having a stuffed animal in bed with her; another who lacks confidence in basic academic skills may, nonetheless, demonstrate a sophisticated level of social awareness.

Tracking practices sharply contradict patterns of intellectual development of young adolescents. For example, the placement of students in settings that emphasize rote memorization over problem solving ignores research demonstrating that critical thinking is not inherently beyond the capacities of young adolescents. As Lounsbury and Clark have noted, most eighth graders can:

• Consider alternative solutions to problems
• Imagine consequences of a given hypothesis, and come up with reasonable answers to a variety of "What if…?" questions
• Make plans and think ahead
• Think about thinking, understand different perspectives, and consider other points of view

However, many students are rarely given the opportunity to develop these intellectual capacities. Based on their observations of eighth-grade classrooms, Lounsbury and Clark conclude that, despite rhetoric to the contrary, many activities still focus on work sheets, test taking, listening, and copying, whereas relatively little of the teaching engages students in solving problems, manipulating data, or investigating real-life situations that develop complex thinking. They note further that in these class-rooms, "students seem distanced from their own learning." Not surprisingly, then, according to NELS:88, nearly 50 percent of eighth graders report that they are bored at school half or most of the time!

The diverse patterns of early-adolescent development cry out for the kind of education that opens rather than closes doors and encourages rather than discourages intellectual and social explo-ration. Even if homogeneity were desirable, the rapid rate of adolescent development makes creating a truly homogeneous group of young people a virtual impossibility—even for one year! Recognition of early adolescence as a stage of life characterized by diverse patterns of growth underscores the benefits of hetero-geneous grouping at the middle level.

But the current state of America's young people suggests even more poignant reasons for eliminating tracking at the middle level. In 1990, the National Commission on the Role of the School and the Community in Improving Adolescent Health pro-claimed that "for the first time in the history of this country, young people are *less* healthy and *less* prepared to take their places in society than were their parents." In *CODE BLUE: Uniting for Healthier Youth,* the commission documented serious symptoms of alienation among young people related to school failure, violence, and substance abuse in the context of changing social conditions. The commission found that the lives of many adolescents were characterized by:

- Extensive poverty: one of every three urban children and one of every four children overall live in poverty
- Drastic alterations in family composition and stability
- Declining contact between young people and adults
- A deterioration of traditional neighborhoods and extended families
- Diminished parental supervision and guidance
- Increasing impact on young people of television, radio, movies, and magazines
- Continuing, and in some cases increasing, racial and ethnic hostility and discrimination, which damage self-esteem and limit the life chances of minority youth
- Inadequate housing and unsafe neighborhood environments

As *CODE BLUE* makes clear, students in the 1990s need schools that offer *more*, not less, of a sense of belonging and *more*, not less, protection from prejudice and dehumanizing experiences. Untracking is a major strategy for creating such schools.

Alternatives to Tracking: New Tools and Assumptions

Increased awareness of the harm of tracking in and of itself has not been enough to bring about change. Nor have well-publicized findings of academic and social needs provoked systemic reform. What schools have needed and what they now have are new ways of organizing curriculum and instruction so that all students can learn appropriate "grade-level" material in mixed-ability groups. New practices have demonstrated, for example, that:

- All students can benefit from the thinking-skills and enrichment activities often offered only to those labeled "gifted" and "talented."
- High expectations for everyone can be communicated through school routines and classroom techniques, which result in increased student effort and higher achievement for all.
- Cooperative learning and other innovative teaching approaches can deepen academic learning for all students while promoting self-esteem.
- Meaningful hands-on learning activities organized around themes can help students perfect basic skills and teach them to synthesize information from different sources, apply knowledge, and solve problems.
- Schools can successfully peel off the bottom levels of a grouping hierarchy—courses labeled "basic" or "general"—and expose everyone to grade-level textbooks, activities, and expectations while providing extra support for those who need it.

Educators today also know more about the nature of human intelligence itself. Although no one would be foolish enough to claim that everyone enters life with identical abilities, it is clear that intelligence is not fixed forever at birth. Human beings can *become* intelligent and can *learn* intelligent behavior; what students derive from the classroom depends to a great extent not on an "I.Q. factor" but on academic environments that equip them to use their intelligence as lifelong learners, citizens, parents, and workers. Moreover, intelligence grows as students are challenged to apply learning in settings where they interact with others who have strengths different from their own.

A Changing Economy, Demographics, and Tracking

> The modern employee must be more highly educated, better
> informed, more flexible than ever before. He or she must be,
> because what we're paying for is the ability to think, to solve
> problems, to make informed judgments, to distinguish
> between right and wrong, to discern the proper course of
> action in situations and circumstances that are necessarily
> ambiguous.
>
> —David Kearns, Xerox Corporation

The American economic and social landscape is changing.
Increasingly, decision makers are acknowledging the connection
between a healthy economy and a solid educational system.
Although an educated labor force does not in and of itself assure
economic growth, there is general agreement that the economy
of the future must be founded on a high-skill, high-wage work
force. In addition, the U.S. economy now operates as part of a
global one with business and industry acting both in competition
and cooperation with institutions from Asian and Pacific Rim
countries and a unified European Community.

More workers of the future will come from the fast-growing
population groups that today are making up a larger and larger
proportion of the school-age population—African-American,
Latino, immigrant, Asian, and Native American children.
According to many economic forecasters, by the year 2000, 85
percent of all new labor force participants will be non-white,
female, or both. Many will be called upon to perform work
oriented more toward providing services, often of a technical
nature, than toward producing goods.

These economic and demographic shifts together highlight
new directions in the reform of American education. No longer
can schools train only selected students as decision makers or
assume that those who have learned to follow directions and perform basic skills are adequately prepared for future employment.
No longer can schools conclude that most students will never be
called upon to interact with others in creating solutions to complex problems. Given rapid technological change, young people
entering the labor force now need skills that go beyond those
that prepare them for one specific job slot. They need an education that prepares them to be lifelong learners. And as the
American population becomes increasingly heterogeneous,
schools must nurture a greater appreciation of diversity.

In the future, whatever form the economy takes, high levels of
educational attainment will provide an advantage in life. At the

same time, the prospects of those with high-school diplomas or less will diminish. By implication, then, schools must assume that all students will at some time in their lives seek post-secondary education as a route to greater opportunity.

In this changing social context, public schools must assure the public that *all* students, not just "the best" ones, are prepared to take advantage of future opportunities. As the implications of changing social conditions become clear, and as more con-stituencies clamor for school accountability, tracking becomes more difficult to justify. Tracked schools that relegate those stu-dents most in need of expanded opportunity to levels that offer the least fail to meet either the needs of changing social and eco-nomic conditions or pressures for accountability.

Tracking as a Public-Policy Issue

As a country we need to realize the long-term results of tracking. Then we must commit ourselves to educate all students. Only a change in philosophy of education—away from the factory model—can bring about needed results. Our country will not survive in its present form with anything less.

—Launa Ellison, Clara Barton Open School, Minneapolis

Given the more precise understanding of the nature of human intelligence and the wider availability of alternatives to tracking that we now have, it becomes clear that tracking has less to do with ability than we have supposed. At the same time, what is apparent is that tracking has everything to do with opportunity. And the ways in which our institutions, including our public schools, structure opportunity is a matter for public discussion, debate, and policy.

Thinking about tracking raises certain fundamental questions: What constitutes an adequate education? Education for what? Education for whom? How can schools become places that offer a meaningful education to all students? These questions go to the very heart of public policy.

Since 1954, the United States has made significant strides toward opening the schoolhouse door to many children who had been excluded from educational opportunities. Public laws on both federal and state levels now affirm that everyone has a right to a free, adequate, and appropriate public-school education. But when we begin to examine the opportunities offered to our chil-dren once they enter that schoolhouse door, and when we begin to look at how these opportunities differ according to race and economic status, we begin to see that, for all our best intentions, we have not gone far enough.

In order for the promise of equal educational opportunity to be fully realized, certain steps must be taken to eliminate practices that divide students into categories of "more able" or "less able" learners and that provide unequal access to knowledge. Untracking must begin before the high-school level; when schools follow practices that deny pre-high-school students access to critical gatekeeping knowledge or fail to push them to master material necessary for success in subsequent years, they virtually bar young people from future opportunities.

Untracking requires abandoning a strategy that sorts students according to individual weakness in favor of one that groups them in terms of collective strength. It also requires a shift from nurturing the ability of some children to cultivating effort, persistence, and pride in work in all children. We must move beyond a mindset that defines good education as a scarce resource, with the "best" reserved for the most "deserving," to one that envisions a society in which good education is abundant enough for all.

Untracking necessarily provokes a reconsideration of the purposes of education. In this information age, a democratic society cannot survive with an unequal distribution of knowledge. In an era when knowledge truly is power, a redistribution of knowledge is both fair and necessary.

Ultimately, reform of tracking practices in America's schools must be sustained by the conviction that education in a democracy rests on purposes that extend beyond the goal of grooming children for their future participation in the labor market. In a democratic society, schools are moral institutions, and their purposes must include helping students to become good people. An education worthy of the name must first nurture children's full potential for participation as citizens in the human community. As schools adopt more equitable grouping practices based upon a commitment to these values, they fulfill their historical responsibility not only to help individuals improve their lots in life but also to strengthen the foundation for more just, inclusive, democratic, and productive communities.

Toward More Democratic Education for All

Most governments have been based on the denial of equal
rights; *ours* began by *affirming* those rights. *They* said, some
men are too *ignorant,* and *vicious,* to share in government.
Possibly so, said we; and, by your system, you would always
keep them ignorant and vicious. We propose to give *all*
a chance; and we expected the weak to grow stronger, the
ignorant, wiser; and all better, and happier together.

—Abraham Lincoln, 1858

This book is a celebration of the capacity of schools to make
significant changes in the most fundamental of school routines:
the grouping of students for purposes of instruction. It is an
appreciation of the principals and teachers, students, school-
board members, and other citizens who are carrying forth a
vision in which all students will learn in a heterogeneous setting.
It is a recognition of the enormous energy, creativity, resourceful-
ness, and persistence of those schools that have taken the first
steps toward dismantling tracking and ability-grouping practices, which have outlived their usefulness in our schools and
communities.

In undertaking to provide equal access to knowledge to all students, the schools in this book pursue educational goals that are
truly "homegrown" American. In light of what these schools
have accomplished, the quest for some abstract notion of "world-
class standards" becomes irrelevant. Were we to extend to all
children in America learning opportunities equal to those offered
in these schools, we would meet our own highest academic
expectations, and our classroom standards would far surpass
those anywhere else in the world. If policymakers attended to the
stories that these schools tell, they would not have to resort to
invidious comparisons with other countries to stimulate change.
The inspiration for reform lies in our own backyard.

This book is grounded on firsthand experiences with reform,
observations of effective classrooms that are heterogeneously
grouped, and visits to schools striving to help all students achieve
by providing equal access to a meaningful curriculum. The
stories of these schools form a stark contrast to tales of doom
and gloom about American schools in general and suggest that
reports of the death of public education in the United States are
truly premature. The schools in this book have taken on one of
the most serious and persistent problems in this country today—
unequal access to knowledge—and have devised solutions that
renew and invigorate learning for everyone in their classrooms.

Our study begins with an overview of the components of successful untracking in schools and districts. Subsequent chapters reexamine and explore these components in greater depth through the experiences of specific schools. These chapters also highlight innovative examples of parent involvement, reform of school culture, curriculum, instruction, assessment, and counseling, which together and separately support untracking.

PART II

Conditions
for Untracking

The starting point for reform is less important than whether the issue is powerful and inspiring enough to generate enthusiasm, reveal broader political questions, compel devoted leadership, and serve as a vehicle for community commitment.

—Robert Moses, *The Algebra Project*

Although few schools have totally abandoned grouping by ability, increasing numbers are dramatically reducing their reliance on homogeneous grouping, and many are exploring ways to provide equal access to knowledge for all students in groups that reflect a diversity of backgrounds, learning styles, and abilities. Because this process is begun at different points, the extent of untracking varies from school to school.

For example, some schools begin with as many as fifteen different levels in all subjects and reduce that number to three or four, whereas others begin with three to five groupings and narrow that number to one or at most two levels of instruction. Among untracking schools, most had initially structured each of their grades into four or more levels in reading or language arts, math, and science and into three levels or more in social studies. In the first year of change, almost all eliminated homogeneously grouped classes in social studies and science. After a few years, many virtually eliminated reading and language-arts levels, but most still offer two or three levels in math.

At a time when the term "restructuring" has come to mean different things to different people, Donald Le May, principal of Valley Junior High School in Carlsbad, California, speaks for many untracking schools when he asserts that "the elimination of tracking and by implication the categorizing of students is the only meaningful way to 'restructure' schools for success." In these schools, untracking is an ongoing process. Guided by a passion for improving student achievement and knowledge of research findings, these schools reform curriculum, instruction, and assessment to allow diverse groups of students to learn together in heterogeneous classrooms.

Untracking: An Art and a Science

As untracking schools implement reforms, they adopt techniques tailored to their own context. As Deborah Meier, principal of New York's Central Park East Secondary School, reports:

> What the "system" can do is create the structural conditions that encourage people to want to change and give them sufficient autonomy to do so, and that provide support and encouragement even when they blunder in the course of creating their interpretation of the "good school." But in the end the change must be homegrown.

Thus, the actual process of dismantling a rigid tracking system and adopting alternatives follows no particular recipe. Untracking schools recognize that changes in the school culture and involvement of parents and the community along with innovations in curriculum, instruction, assessment, and counseling are necessary to support new grouping practices. However, the pace, order, and scope of changes are not always obvious, and they vary from school to school. If untracking requires certain basic ingredients, every school works with these ingredients in different proportions, measuring each according to the taste of the school community to create a flavor uniquely its own.

Few schools, even those grounded in the deepest commitments to democratic schooling, have untracked completely. Why? Schools inhabit the real world with all its cultural norms and political realities, and a variety of "real world" constraints may slow or inhibit reform. Some of the constraints are budgetary or contractual. Others are regulatory, as is the case when state regulations stipulate that schools must offer special or separate classes for "gifted" or "ungifted" students. Still others are organizational or political.

For these reasons, the process of untracking begins at different points, engages different actors, reaches different stages within varying time periods, and strikes different compromises with the constituency groups in each school. What untracking schools do share is their willingness to move toward greater equity and excellence *despite* the constraints that they encounter, beginning at the point of least resistance.

The stories of untracking schools suggest that certain components are basic to the process of eliminating tracking. They include:

- A clear school mission articulated in terms of the belief that all students can learn and the conviction that schools must play the major role in intellectual development by ensuring equal access to knowledge

- School-based leadership with teacher and parent support for change
- A plan for change grounded in research-based practices
- Ample time for staff development
- A phase-in process supported by school organizational arrangements
- Changes in school routines to create a climate that reflects a commitment to involve all students equally in learning opportunities

These components work together in some measure to catalyze an agenda for action. The schools' own stories tell of how teachers, parents, and citizens weave these components together in ways unique to their communities.

Developing a "High Expectations" Mission

A mission statement is a powerful tool for school improvement. Properly constructed, it empowers everyone in the school to assume responsibility for the school's ultimate direction. It is, at once, a commitment, a promise, a guide for decisions, and a set of criteria by which to measure the school's progress toward its defined purposes. Increasingly, the mission statement is indispensable for effective school leadership.

—Council on Middle Level Education of the National Association of Secondary School Principals (NASSP), 1987

Untracking is not an end in itself. It is a means to an end, and that end is improved learning for everyone in a school that values the contribution of all students to a learning community. Although that mission is formulated in different ways, the common thread is the conviction that all children have the capacity to learn and that it is the schools' responsibility to develop an environment where this can take place.

At the Wellesley Middle School in Massachusetts, for example, untracking is tied to a set of core beliefs about learning that constitutes a powerful school mission. These include the following:

- All students are capable of high achievement, not just our fastest and most confident learners
- Consistent effort leads to success
- You are not supposed to understand everything the first time around
- Mistakes help one to learn

These beliefs shape the view among Wellesley staff that untracking is a route to strengthening learning for all children and a strategy of school change that has a purpose beyond itself. As principal John D'Auria says:

> If tracking would help us accomplish our goals at this school, then we would use it. But we believe in producing active learners, critical thinkers, and risk takers, and tracking our students by ability quite simply doesn't allow us to achieve our goals.

These beliefs not only form a rationale for untracking but also shape decisions about all aspects of school improvement ranging from staff development to teaching and curriculum reforms. Moreover, they are a starting point for explaining changes in student grouping, curriculum, and instruction to parents, school-board members, and new teachers. As D'Auria emphasizes:

> Heterogeneous groupings will fail without the core beliefs. It is not enough to institute a policy change on any level without a basic understanding of what you want to do, why you want to do it, and what you need to accomplish your goals.

J.T. Crawford, principal of Crete-Monee Junior High in Crete, Illinois, agrees. His school's mission embraces principles of the Effective Schools Movement, which emphasizes the conditions present in schools where all children succeed. High teacher expectations for student achievement is one of those essential conditions. "Everyone in the school has to be committed to the philosophy of high expectations, and you have to infuse every part of the school with that philosophy," Crawford insists. Crawford uses Effective Schools principles to lead regular staff discussions about annual objectives and to gauge the school's success in terms of meeting its own goals. As part of its untracking strategy, Crete-Monee focused first on closing the achievement gap between lower-testing and higher-testing students. Then, the school zeroed in on maximizing achievement among all students through professional development to support instructional changes and reduced ability grouping to strengthen the school community.

In untracking, reviewing a school's mission is a necessary step in developing consensus about the *reasons* for changing grouping, curricular, and instructional practices. A mission statement coalesces the staff around the central purpose of the school and offers a springboard for discussion about the need to change familiar and comfortable, but outmoded, practices. In the process of developing a mission statement, teachers establish a shared vision for the learning of all students which they can then use as a measuring rod for assessing the value of all school practices.

School-Based Leadership with Teacher and Parent Involvement in Change

> The principal is the captain with full authority and responsibility for the ship. But if reasonably wise and prepared for the post, he or she will make [decisions for the welfare of those on the ship] in the company and with the counsel of others.

> —John Goodlad, *A Place Called School,* 1984

Untracking cannot take place unless there is an effective partnership between the principal and teachers who are committed to change. A school's mission defines the purpose of adopting alternatives to tracking, but it is the principal-teacher partnership that sets the terms for how that mission is to be accomplished. And although at the outset it is not necessary for all teachers to support alternatives, the enthusiasm of at least some of them is essential.

School-Based Leadership

Principals in untracking schools understand that their own leadership is pivotal during a period of change. As Janet Altersitz of Desert Sky Middle School in Glendale, Arizona, warns:

> Little will happen without the principal's interest, active participation, and leadership. It will be the principal's enthusiasm and modeling that will gain the attention and respect of faculty members. Soliciting appropriate funds, reviewing test data, and keeping various publics informed are key duties for the principal.

Principals like Altersitz frequently define leadership and responsibility in terms of their role in articulating the school's mission to various constituencies and communicating research-based knowledge to teachers, parents, and school-board members— while at the same time being sensitive to alternative perspectives of all those who have a stake in the program. For example, Sue Galletti, former principal of the Islander Middle School in Mercer Island, Washington, remarks:

> I have become increasingly convinced that understanding the context within which arguments are presented (by thoroughly understanding both points of view) is more important for creating a change than being able to articulate only one point of view.

Principals in untracking schools must also be familiar with new classroom strategies for mixed-level groups so that they can help teachers develop the requisite professional skills and expertise.

As Anna Bernard, principal of Prescott Middle School in Baton Rouge, Louisiana, reports:

> The most important things a principal can do to facilitate the initial steps in untracking are to communicate the belief that eliminating ability grouping is in the best interest of the students and to help teachers make the transition. A strong, well-prepared instructional leader who knows curriculum strategies and who believes that all teachers can teach all students in their classes is crucial.

Others add that leadership in untracking schools requires certain dispositions of character. Experienced principals cite the importance of "vision and courage" as well as "persistence, patience, and willingness to risk," and they note the need for a "strong-willed, persuasive principal with a sound sense of timing." As schools adopt innovations, principals may be called on to develop and communicate strategies for school-based decision making and planning, to incorporate the concerns of dissenters into plans for change, and to diffuse tension with humor and sound judgment. "One must be both an idealist and a pragmatist to make untracking work," says Margaret Bray of Ferndale Middle School in High Point, North Carolina.

Even the most committed principals do not claim the authority to bring about change by themselves. For example, Le May emphasizes the importance of stable leadership *at all levels*, including district leaders, site administrators, and teacher leaders. He also cites the benefits of having a school-based leadership team, including the principal and teachers, in place for five or more years.

Many principals committed to reducing tracking exercise leadership by establishing conditions in their schools that enhance the likelihood of teacher success in heterogeneous classrooms. Christine Rath, former principal of Rundlett Junior High School in Concord, New Hampshire, underscores the value of organizational structures, especially common planning time for teachers. Recognizing that teachers are their most valuable assets, many principals apply for extra funding to support opportunities for professional development. To ensure that teachers communicate with one another about successful strategies, principals make scheduling arrangements that foster professional interaction and facilitate decision making on the part of teachers. In turn, these administrative supports boost the commitment of teachers to making the untracking process successful.

Teacher
Involvement
in Change

In untracking schools, supportive school leadership combines with teacher commitment to new classroom practices to effect change. This combination presupposes a certain level of teacher readiness, nurtured by the principal and supported by at least a core group of teachers. As Le May states, "Untracking is a challenging proposition. No one is going to do this if they do not truly believe that it is possible and necessary." Likewise, Bray emphasizes that "at least several *convinced* teachers and some teachers trained as 'in-house experts' on workable techniques" are the most important resources that a school needs to sustain an untracking effort.

Administrators emphasize that change is unlikely without a group of teachers who believe that they have an investment in change. Bernard reports that Prescott's teachers and administrators *together* made the decision to begin to untrack by eliminating remedial groupings in reading and math. She notes, "The decision was made based on test scores, behavior records, teachers' instructional techniques, and research findings. We took our proposal to the district's middle school director and the assistant superintendent of instruction, and it was approved."

Jake Burks, associate superintendent of Harford County Public Schools in Bel Air, Maryland, adds that involving teachers requires a school climate that both encourages risk taking and stimulates dissatisfaction with the status quo. He advises:

> You need a lot of teacher collegiality and support to make this work. It's especially important to establish a climate that allows teachers to take risks. Teachers in our school were totally safe in trying different things. We also spent a lot of time on study and inquiry. Meaningful change won't occur until the people involved experience dissonance between what we know from research and what we're doing that might be the opposite.

Teachers themselves recognize that their commitment, willingness to experiment, and involvement in planning for change are crucial to success. As teachers from the Graham and Parks School in Cambridge, Massachusetts, note:

> Untracking alone does not solve anything. It's what happens with kids after mixed-ability grouping occurs that matters. This must be put into teachers' hands—by empowering them, having them *critically* examine the current program, investigate other schools through visits or reading, and then develop their own ways.

Among the first challenges that teachers and principals face is how to reorganize classroom practices to realize their goals.

Teachers must be involved in reviewing research, designing grouping alternatives, selecting or developing appropriate curricula, learning new instructional approaches, and communicating with parents. For many teachers, these are new roles that require focused opportunities for development of new skills.

Parent Involvement in Change

Parents can be powerful allies in the process of untracking. They can also be powerful opponents. Parents of children who have been placed in "special" programs are especially sensitive to changes in grouping. Parents of students with disabilities are often wary of changes that they fear will overwhelm their children or result in less attention being paid to individual learning needs. Likewise, parents of students labeled "gifted" may fear that changes will result in fewer challenges or undermine their children's chances to excel.

In many schools, the adoption of alternatives to tracking has entailed educating parents about relevant research and alternative approaches to curriculum and instruction. Educators must persuade parents that untracking strengthens the student body as a whole, so that every child ends up mastering complex material. Principals and teachers may be called on to demonstrate that students have more to gain from learning together than from learning apart in separate, labeled programs. Moreover, once untracking begins, schools must endeavor to sustain parents' support.

In many communities where educators seek to implement heterogeneous grouping, the most vocal parents opposed to change are often those who expect their children to enter selective programs for "gifted and talented" students. These parents may be both politically powerful in the community and sophisticated in their ability to counter arguments in favor of heterogeneous grouping. They can be led to reconsider their opposition to change if they come to understand that inclusive schooling offers all students an education that is sometimes reserved only for those students labeled "gifted."

Galletti tells this story:

> Our school is in a district where test scores are significantly higher than other districts in the state. Our parents are all college educated, and they were very committed to sorting kids into gifted programs. When our school made the commitment to more inclusive programs, some of our parents were sophisticated enough to counter all our arguments with their own about why certain children needed to be separated into gifted classrooms. At the time, we had about ten percent of our students in gifted classes, and we used a variety of

measures to put them there. Based on the California Test of Basic Skills (CTBS), we required students to have an I.Q. score of 130, and we used this marker plus achievement scores on sub-tests to arrive at a total score for identifying "gifted" students.

We had lots of parent meetings, but this did not work effectively to convince parents to abandon the program. Finally, we called in a group of thirty parents who were most vocal against eliminating separate gifted programs. We met in the library, and we gave them the sixth-grade test data that we use to select students for the gifted classes for 250 real live kids. Their task was to identify 26 students for the gifted program. The parents quickly realized that 55 of these students had an I.Q. of 130 or above, but one student had an I.Q. of 150 but would *not* qualify because of his achievement scores and another had an I.Q. of 129 but *did* qualify once achievement scores were included. When the parents realized that they couldn't make decisions, they began to ask to expand the gifted program. I explained that even with an expanded program, I knew how some of the students would rank, and that many of the parents in the room had children who would not quality.

At that point, the whole tenor in the room changed, and I saw lots of non-verbal reaction. We then began one hour of serious conversation, and those parents walked out of that meeting understanding that what they needed was a "gifted" program for 100 per cent of the kids. At the time, that meant a "Humanities" program with integrated instruction, cooperative learning, and a focus on thinking skills. The parents decided they would go to the school board with this idea, and I thought the community was going to massacre us. But they didn't. They lauded us and the proposal as the only way to go! We still identify "top" kids by I.Q., but it's used purely to make sure that we spread those students around into different working groups. And the parents are very happy with what we have done.

Other successful strategies to win support of skeptical parents for untracking include offering opportunities to learn about alternatives and to discuss changes with the teachers who will be implementing the new curriculum. For example:

- At Crete-Monee, when several parents who opposed changes in grouping practices and instructional approaches wrote "To the Editor" letters and spoke out at parent meetings, school staff invited them to join professional development sessions in cooperative learning. Crawford explains, "Lots of parents worry that cooperative learning is replacing regular instruction. They need to watch it to see that this is something we do to improve and augment instruction. They need to know it doesn't replace direct teaching of specific subject material like fractions."

- At the Jericho Middle School in Jericho, New York, principal Anna Hunderfund assured parents concerned about the elimination of the school's pull-out "gifted-and-talented" program that nothing would be taken away from their children. She explained that changes in the nine-period day simply allowed *all* students to experience the enrichment curriculum formerly offered to only a few.

- At the Wellesley Middle School, John D'Auria worked to build parent support for untracking through monthly "coffee evenings" at the houses of parents where he could present research findings about tracking and discuss the school's core beliefs that were developing among the faculty. D'Auria explained the school's core beliefs and described hurdles to their implementation: society's belief, shared by children, that intelligence is synonymous with speed, and a fear of improvising and venturing opinions on the part of children concerned with not getting the right answer. He asks how many parents have heard themselves or others say "He seems to do this effortlessly," as if to discount hard work, or "My brother is the smart one. I had to work hard for my grades," as if to imply that working hard at something is a sign of limited intelligence.

Ultimately, an openness to negotiation and a willingness to proceed slowly can nurture trust between parents and school staff and win support for untracking. However, even the most carefully thought-out process may not reduce all resistance. In some communities, discussions with parents may continue over months or years. As Ann Foley and Nanna Brantigan of College Place Middle School in Lynnwood, Washington, say, "The hardest factor is to integrate the 'challenge' students so that you have true integration. [But] without this component, a school is still tracking." Schools that have been successful say "Keep trying!"

Professional Development and Support

Heterogeneous grouping is more difficult for most teachers; here is a real educational dilemma and a reason why teachers and administrators resist practices that they are told are better for their students.... Teachers must be helped to develop instructional strategies which work and which do not require major new sacrifices of energy and time; making teachers feel guilty will not achieve the changes in classroom practice which research and exemplary practice suggest so strongly.

—Paul George, "Tracking and Ability Grouping:
Which Way for the Middle School?" 1988

Perhaps more than any other ingredient, staff development for teachers is essential to the success of untracking. In fact, when asked what they might do differently if they were to begin again, many principals emphasize "More staff development!" Susan Masck of Tucson's Sierra Middle School is one who advises, "Prepare teachers to accept more responsibility, then delegate it." Others stress the need to provide teachers directly with more exposure to classroom techniques that are effective with hetero-geneous groups, either through special seminars or by asking skilled teachers to serve as resources for in-service meetings.

Professional development in untracking schools takes three major forms:

- Staff development in skills needed to plan for whole-school change and strengthen organizational communication to promote risk taking and ongoing planning
- Training in effective classroom instructional strategies for working with diverse students
- Teacher development related to implementing specific curricula new to the school and its teachers

Within this framework, staff development may include strength-ening teachers' skills in participatory planning and team building; reviewing methods for communicating high expecta-tions to all students; developing skills in mastery learning and cooperative learning; implementing "high content" curriculum; and designing curriculum-embedded assessment strategies.

Above and beyond specific efforts, teachers and principals alike recognize the importance of establishing a safe professional climate that allows teachers to flounder as they try new approaches. Teacher Roene Comack of Harding Middle School in Cedar Rapids, Iowa, encourages, "Jump in! Even mistakes are better for kids than what's now happening." Such boldness means that principals must let teachers know that they need not be afraid of failing at first, and staff development is key to creating a climate that encourages teacher openness to experimentation. As Pep Jewell, principal of Helena Middle School in Helena, Montana, remarks:

> In-service is an investment in the experienced professional. A professional growth strand as part of the evaluation process gives teachers permission to take the risk to be less than perfect in trying something new. Student- and teacher-teaming during the process gives support.

Educational leaders Chris Lim and Ann Hiyakumoro, principal and project director, respectively, of Willard Junior High School in Berkeley, California, summarize the importance of reforming school structures to support teachers. They cite the needs for "wiping out teacher isolation in the school building" and for additional support for teachers "in every way possible, including extra preparation periods, paid curriculum-development time, paid staff-development time, good materials, and tutors for students."

Over time, in many untracking middle-grades schools, staff development may become less a one-shot event than an accepted part of the school culture that treats teachers as professionals who must keep up with current issues in their field. Thus, principals regularly circulate articles from professional publications to their staff. Some schools like the Louis Armstrong Middle School in New York City hold regular but informal brown-bag teacher lunches to discuss provocative articles, and at the Middle School of the Kennebunks in Maine, principal Sandra Caldwell sponsors a regular "Reveille," a voluntary 5:00 A.M. opportunity for teachers to discuss the implications of recent educational research for classroom practice.

In untracking schools, staff development is often intensive, especially in the early stages, and may include study groups, summer institutes, all-day trainings, staff retreats, visits to other schools, conferences, modeling, coaching, and consultations. For example:

- At the Bartlett School, in Lowell, Massachusetts, a "change facilitator" funded with money from the state's dropout-prevention program has worked part-time to arrange for teacher visits to other schools using heterogeneous grouping, identify innovative programs, and help teachers assess whether such programs could be incorporated into Bartlett.

- At the Rutland, Vermont, Middle School, all staff participated in a focused series of paid professional workshops designed to meet Rutland's own goals of heterogeneous grouping school-wide by 1993 as well as state goals related to the education of all children, including students with disabilities, in the same classroom. In addition, teachers attended the University of Vermont Middle Level Summer Institute where they worked on grade-level plans for implementation of heterogeneous grouping and integration to complement the district policy of phasing in mixed-ability grouping over three years.

- At Prescott Middle School, in Baton Rouge, Louisiana, where grouping changes focused on reading and math, many departmental meetings included professional development. In addition, full faculty meetings helped all teachers improve their instructional techniques in cooperative learning, peer tutoring, and in-class flexible grouping. Despite limited time, the school continues to use weekly team meetings and monthly departmental meetings to share ideas, resources, and professional research. Discussions frequently focus on implementing the expectation that all teachers will plan at least two different instructional strategies each period with an emphasis on "hands on" learning.

- At the Wellesley Middle School, a tradition of parents' lobbying for placement of their children into the classrooms of specific teachers had contributed to teacher beliefs that they were capable of teaching only certain kinds of children. Thus, staff development first focused on developing teachers' commitment to and capacity for teaching all students. During weekly meetings before and after school, staff became familiar with research on tracking, expectations and motivation theory, and cooperative learning; and teachers had the chance to try out new techniques and approaches that they could use during the change process. Underlying this strategy was the understanding that if risk taking was a trait that the school wanted to encourage in students, the climate in the school needed to reflect that trait, and teachers had to take risks themselves as part of their own learning about working with different groups of students.

Changing the Paradigm: First Steps in Staff Development for Untracking Schools

Untracking requires many changes in schools, beginning with certain assumptions that educators, parents, and students hold about schooling. For this reason, staff development for untracking often involves teachers in a reexamination of values and priorities concerning education. For example:

• Some principals have used "The Business of Paradigms" and "The Power of Vision," videotapes distributed by ChartHouse International Learning Corporation, to help staff understand how deeply rooted assumptions can get in the way of exploiting new opportunities. The tapes begin with the questions "Why is it so difficult to anticipate the future?" and "Why should we take the time to think about the future?" As Brad Neal, president of ChartHouse, explains, "The films help people challenge fundamental beliefs in a safe environment. By giving everyone a common foundation for discussion, you come to understand why you resist new ideas and how you can move beyond routine ways of thinking."

• The Coalition of Essential Schools encourages dialogue about "essential questions" among school staff engaged in change. By exploring these questions in extensive small-group conversations, teachers develop fundamental principles that will shape their school's reform process. Essential discussion questions include: "What do we want students to know and be able to do when they leave our school?" "If schools were to foster the attributes, skills, and habits that characterize the people whom staff admire, what kinds of practices and structures would they have to set up?" "What is the most powerful learning experience that you have ever had?" "Where in the school is such learning already going on?" "What are the conditions that allow that to happen?" and "What keeps it from happening throughout the school?" "Which of the Nine Common [Coalition of Essential Schools] Principles would be easiest and hardest to adopt in the school?" and "If you were to put the most difficult principle into practice, what would you need to do so, and from whom do you need those things?" When responses from small groups are merged, they point to core principles that guide school change.

- The Massachusetts Department of Education helps schools begin discussions about tracking with a set of questions designed to guide educators through a retrospective of their own schooling, focusing on the assumptions and consequences of grouping in the schools of their childhood. As teachers think back to the experiences, remembering themselves among their classmates, group leaders facilitate reconsideration of their own memories of sorting, labeling, and placement and the effects on teachers' own learning and aspirations. Group leaders ask questions such as "Do you remember how you learned which of your classmates were considered 'smart' and which were considered 'slow?'" "What do you remember about any role that standardized testing or other selection mechanisms may have played in grouping or determining access to knowledge among your schoolmates?" "Who in your schooling had information about special programs, course offerings, and further educational opportunities, and how was this information distributed?" and "What is the one opportunity that you feel you missed in your own schooling?" First in pairs and later in a group discussion centered on these questions, teachers come to understand the prevalence of tracking in American education; examine assumptions about intelligence; identify the impact on achievement, self-esteem, and equal-educational opportunity; and debate the purpose of schools in a democratic society.

- When asked to present "awareness workshops" about tracking for school faculty, Paul George of the University of Florida distributes a true-false quiz entitled "What's the Truth About Tracking and Ability Grouping...Really?" His list of questions requires teachers to assess their own understanding of tracking and to separate common misconceptions about the benefits of tracking from findings that have dramatically demonstrated its harmful effects on student achievement, self-esteem, aspirations, and school and classroom climate.

Each of these approaches works to raise awareness of the ways in which basic assumptions about education can either foster or inhibit change. These approaches can unleash teachers' emotional energy for change and shake loose entrenched ways of thinking about schooling, clearing the way for a more open vision of educational purposes and structures.

Principals at untracking middle schools are ever on the lookout for materials that will stimulate teachers' growth as professionals. At Louis Armstrong, for example, principal Mary Ellen Levin says that the Association for Supervision and Curriculum Development (ASCD) videotapes on cooperative learning helped orient her staff to this new method of instruction for heterogeneous groups. The school has supplemented all-staff viewing of the videotapes with further training in cooperative learning designed for specific subject areas. Through their partnership with Queens College, Louis Armstrong teachers receive support in implementing new curricula and instruction while, at the same time, offering students enrolled in preprofessional programs on-site internships with experienced teachers.

In addition, many schools send groups of teachers to conferences or summer institutes. For example, the Association of Illinois Middle-Level Schools (AIMS) encourages schools to send teams of teachers and administrators—financially supported by their school boards, community service groups, or corporate sponsors—to their Summer Institutes. It is understood that team members will serve as a resource for change when they return to their schools. Likewise, the New England League of Middle Schools (NELMS) and other affiliates of the National Middle School Association (NMSA) sponsor both school-year and summer institutes on heterogeneous grouping.

Planning for Change

The essential ingredient for schools that produce intelligent adults is the presence of a community of people exercising their intelligence on a daily basis, coming up with ideas for change and then having the freedom to act on the conclusions they reach. Nothing less than that will work (although more than that is also needed).

—Deborah Meier, principal, Central Park East Secondary School, New York City, in *The Nation*, 23 September 1991

Successful untracking depends on planning for change, a process that builds upon teacher commitment to heterogeneous grouping. Planning for alternatives to tracking requires putting aside time for a representative group of teachers to work with administrators to discuss new routines, schedules, teaching approaches, curricula, and relationships. Planning in these groups may take place schoolwide, in each grade or department, or in a "house" or teacher team within the larger school.

If successful planning for untracking begins with broad agreement about the school's mission, it continues by involving all participants—teachers, parents, and administrators—in thinking about what they expect all students leaving their school to know and be able to do. School staff also review data regularly to determine how close they are to realizing their goals. Over time, the comparison of "where we are" with "where we want to be" becomes a habit among all members of the school community.

In planning for change, participants are especially attuned to recent findings in the field of educational research. Says Sierra Middle School's Masek, "We set out to adopt the practices known to benefit our students. Heterogeneous grouping was one of those." As teachers learn to apply research to school practices, they become accustomed to inquiry. Sandra Caldwell, principal of the Middle School of the Kennebunks, Maine, for instance, reports, "We question practically everything. We ask whether our practices align with research, and when we find gaps, we work team by team to figure out action plans to close them."

In short, untracking schools follow a research-based, data-driven, problem-solving planning process that is not a one-shot event but becomes a norm of school culture. This process, which Leslie Hergert, Janet Phlegar, and Marla Pérez-Sellés describe in *Kindle the Spark: An Action Guide for Schools Committed to the Success of Every Child* as "rolling planning," involves developing a vision, gathering data, setting targets, and finally taking another look at the vision. This process parallels a variety of "outcomes-based" planning models, including the well-known "Outcomes-Driven Developmental Model" (ODDM) developed in Johnson City, New York, which some schools have adopted as a key planning tool. In their emphasis not only on the importance of using the best research available to make all decisions, but also on the expectation that all students can learn, these planning approaches are particularly useful for untracking. Brenda Lyons, Director of Secondary Education and Communications for Edmond Public Schools in Oklahoma, explains:

> The entire philosophy and teaching techniques associated with outcome-based education are extensive and detailed. However, the main idea is that all students can succeed when given enough time. If a mastery learning model is followed with correctives given for students who do not master the material and enrichment provided for those who do, then students of all levels can be taught in the same classroom. As a result, tracking can be eliminated.

Some schools begin their planning process with a "consciousness raising" period, during which principals flood staff with data and teachers read research articles related to tracking and its alternatives. During this time, teachers visit heterogeneous classrooms in other schools to understand the benefits and challenges of mixed-level grouping. Groups of teachers may also research specific grouping and curricular changes, make decisions about new directions, and plan staff development to ensure that these changes are effective.

Whatever the model, the process of untracking takes place over several years, sometimes spanning a five-to-eight-year time period. Christine Rath describes a six-year transition to heterogeneous grouping at Rundlett Junior High in Concord, New Hampshire, emphasizing, "I consider we are still at the beginning stages!" Like Rundlett, many schools are guided by a multiyear plan for change that, although not written in stone, provides the necessary steady course toward implementing new practices.

Although some schools that initiated grouping changes in the early or mid-1980s have taken up to eight years to untrack, principals of these schools emphasize that in the 1990s it need not take so long. "We now have much better evidence documenting the harm of tracking," says Janet Altersitz, whose school dismantled more than thirty instructional levels during a seven-year period and, in the process, became one of Arizona's exemplary educational programs. She adds, "Given what we know from research and the resources now available to develop alternative approaches to curriculum and instruction, schools should be able to make great gains in three years."

A Phase-in Change Process

> You have to understand that different people have different comfort levels. We don't expect everyone to do everything at the same time. We have always, with everything, piloted with teachers who felt comfortable. We have never made major changes overnight, but we need to allow people who are ready to go, to go ahead, piloting, starting small.
>
> —Sandra Caldwell, principal, Middle School
> of the Kennebunks, Maine

Very few untracking schools do introduce schoolwide change overnight. Although these schools accept change as a norm, they proceed systematically, introducing in stages heterogeneous grouping, new curricula, and greater diversity in instructional techniques. They follow no formula. Typically, however, changes are implemented one grade, department, cluster, or team at a time—first in science, social studies, and language arts, then in math.

Often the number of instructional levels in all disciplines is first reduced by folding the lower levels into the middle ones. Many schools also make beginning changes on a trial basis—sometimes, as in the case of the Chestnut Street Junior High in Springfield, Massachusetts, by persuading the teachers' union to endorse a "test run" of new practices. Whatever approach the schools may follow, their plans remain flexible and open to change as necessary.

The process of phasing in alternatives may depend on several factors: the complexity of existing tracking practices; the degree of teachers' investment in change; the availability of resources and support to develop alternatives; and extenuating circumstances. For example, the plan for improving education at Crete-Monee begins with the elimination of two low levels of math during a two-year period to prepare for offering pre-algebra to all by the fourth year, and it ends after six years with heterogeneous grouping in all English and language-arts courses. Due to a planned move from one school building to another, the adoption of heterogeneous grouping in all language-arts courses has been delayed; but, says the principal, "We've already bought the new textbooks, so everyone will be reading the same green book, and we'll be doing away with labels on report cards, so our high school won't be automatically placing any students into a predictable level."

Peeling off the bottom tracks sometimes results in an unexpected benefit: freeing teachers who have worked exclusively with lower-scoring students in remedial, compensatory, or special education classes to work in heterogeneous classrooms—either on their own or paired with other teachers. For example, as untracking proceeded in Wellesley, once teachers were no longer needed for "Level 3" classes because students were succeeding in heterogeneous classes at "Level 2," the school could use the "extra" teachers to co-teach heterogeneous grade-level classrooms, with remedial or special education teachers matched with "regular Level 2" teachers. Although students in these classes had to master more complex material than they had been accustomed to, they also had the resource of an extra teacher to support them.

A Phased-in Plan for Heterogeneous Grouping at Rundlett Junior High: 1985–1991

It took Rundlett Junior High School six years to move from homogeneous to heterogeneous grouping in all seventh- and eighth-grade subjects other than math, which still maintains some leveling. Christine Rath describes how the school introduced changes in program organization and instruction:

1985–1986: Replacement of Level 3 classes with small-group Study Skills offered to all students. Study Skills allows students having difficulty to receive reteaching, reinforcement, and remediation from their regular cluster teachers while others are offered enrichment activities.

1986–1987: Introduction of block scheduling in grade seven with built-in common planning time that allows teachers to make their own decisions about flexible student groupings and plan for heterogeneous grouping in science and social studies.

1987–1988: Introduction of heterogeneous language workshop classes in grade eight. Teams construct heterogeneous science and social-studies classes. Cluster teams had the option of placing students flexibly in temporary groupings after pretests in September.

1988–1989: Continued block scheduling, grouping, and regrouping of students in grade-seven clusters. Clusters decided on heterogeneous social-studies, science, and language-arts classes. Clarification of philosophy and goals of heterogeneous grouping with concerned parents. Increased staff training for new instructional methods such as cooperative learning.

1989–1990: Reorganized special education services; increased in-class professional and paraprofessional support for students with special needs. (This increased both the heterogeneity of students in classes and the amount of adult support, which provided opportunities for flexible subgroupings and small-group instruction within class.) Grade-eight teachers elected to begin the following year with more heterogeneous groups for instruction. In grade nine, the citizenship course was reviewed and revised to meet the needs of a broader range of students.

1990–1991: Implementation of heterogeneous groupings in English, Language Workshop, social studies, and science in grade eight, with three groups remaining in math. Administration hand-scheduled grade-eight students to achieve groupings in all areas and to minimize scheduling problems so that teams could concentrate on instructional, not organizational, work. Specialists and aides joined cluster teachers for in-class and out-of-class support for lower-performing students. Higher-performing students were challenged to do additional work, such as challenge problems in math, independent projects in English and history, in-depth reading in science, and expanded research in all subject areas. Language-arts centered on common themes, using different novels depending on students' interests. Cooperative learning and peer tutoring took place. Discussions began with grade-nine faculty about possibilities for more heterogeneous groupings. Increase in reassigning students in Level-3 courses to Level-2 courses in ninth grade.

1991–1992: Implementation of two levels only in math with all students taking at least pre-algebra. Ongoing changes in instruction included continued development of cooperative learning, colloquium, independent projects, laboratory approaches, writing process, and peer tutoring. Clarification of course outcomes and expectations for *all* students continued. Continued implementation of in-class support for all three grades.

Throughout this process, Rath encouraged teachers to try mixed-ability groups within an organizational structure that allowed teachers to control instruction. As teachers experimented with changes, they shared success stories with one another. Physical-education and unified-arts teachers who had experienced success with heterogeneous groups offered advice, and the librarian offered support with research-based projects.

Little by little staff noted a variety of real benefits: more students described as "high achieving"; "average" and "slower" students working harder with less resistance and absenteeism; higher numbers of students electing algebra and foreign languages; a significant drop in suspensions; and increasing participation in extracurricular activities. Rath reiterates. "Let teachers try small steps. Then spread the good news!"

Adjustment of General School Routines

> I think all programs like Catching Kids Being Great are bull
> because only the popular preps are caught being good because
> the teachers only want to find them. Us losers have feelings, too!
>
> —Middle school student, in Lee McDonough,
>   *Middle School Journal,* November 1991

Untracking schools do not rely solely on changes in technique or
even on community support for success. Many look beyond the
classroom to challenge norms and assumptions that shape the
culture of the school. Committed to nurturing the growth of all
students within a democratic school community, these schools:

- Review and revise school routines that separate students from
  one another, communicate reduced expectations, limit access
  to knowledge, or undermine a sense of belonging, particularly
  among students who vary from "the average."
- Work to eliminate any routines that label students or suggest
  that some deserve more opportunities than others because
  they have more potential for development.
- Unfreeze the structures that exclude certain students from
  opportunities for learning and personal development.

In short, untracking schools are wary of rules or routines that iso-
late groups of students from one another and result in lower-
quality curriculum, instruction, and resources—or lower expectations, not simply in the classroom, but in all aspects of school life.

*Alternatives
to Grade
Retention:
Extra Support*

Untracking schools are uniformly commited to providing all students with the support—both academic and emotional—that
they need to succeed in school. But, almost without exception,
these schools have rejected "pull-out" approaches, whether
under the guise of compensatory or special education, for students who need extra help. Instead, they make that help available
in regular classes, rearrange schedules to allow additional time
for students who need assistance, or introduce formal teacher-
advisory programs. For example:

- At the Holyoke Magnet Middle School, teachers offer students
  a lunchtime "Math Club" where they can eat with their
  teachers while discussing problems that they might be having
  with their academic work. Teacher Marsha Bailey says,
  "Everyone has the same invitation, so there's no labeling or
  stigma. I tell students, 'The definition of a fine and admirable
  student is one who takes the initiative, who reaches out for
  what he or she needs and wants. That's what grown-ups do.'"

- At Honolulu's Castle High School, ninth graders are grouped heterogeneously in all subjects, with those who need extra help slotted into homogeneous small groups during one of two "electives" periods or enrolled in a double period in particular subjects.

- At Louis Armstrong Middle School, any student who needs extra help is invited to come voluntarily to a before-school tutoring program where teachers are available to offer support. And although school officially begins at 8:40, the library is open for extra help starting at 8:00 A.M.

- At Lassiter Middle School in Louisville, Kentucky a "no-fail" policy provides an additional week at the end of the school year in which students who must complete work required for promotion can get extra help.

- At Louisville's Iroquois Middle School, the "Clean-up Crew" permits students who are overage for grade to sign contracts allowing them to complete two grades in one year in exchange for extra work and effort.

- At the Prescott Middle School, students in danger of failing meet on a regular basis with school counselors, their parents, and their teachers to develop learning plans for strengthening study routines and habits and building personal confidence.

- At Valley Junior High School, individual students who are experiencing academic difficulty are monitored closely and provided tutorials with extra support services coordinated through a Student Study Team (SST). Levels of student failure have declined drama-tically, and by 1990 only one student was retained in grade while fewer than 2.5 percent of all grades issued were "F"s.

Strengthening a Caring School Climate

In the belief that differences are sources of learning, untracking schools work hard using classroom-based guidance and teacher-advisory programs to reduce the separation of student groups and to create a caring community.

For example, at Crete-Monee Junior High, the "Community of Friends" program is a key strategy to "develop and promote friendship, trust, safety, and school identity (a 'we' feeling)" and orient students to the school's expectation that they will act toward one another with mutual respect." Compiled by Crete-Monee guidance counselors Ronald Allen and Deborah Hart, the school's "Building a Community of Friends" catalog includes concrete activities for teachers to use during the first three weeks of school to help students get to know one another, cooperate on joint tasks, assume responsibility, and negotiate conflict. Role-playing, paired discussions, and circle games are designed to evoke laughter, stimulate thought, and clarify perspectives so that students can appreciate rather than put down differences. With the help of Allen and Hart, teachers become increasingly more comfortable using the exercises, and the school schedules entire days around the activities to allow students to experience the program in a meaningful sequence.

The "Community of Friends" program at Crete-Monee, where significant racial and class differences characterize the student body, has helped establish a positive climate in which diversity is honored and enjoyed. School staff also call on the program to prevent problems during high-anxiety periods of the year. For example, staff report that tension often arises during gift-giving holiday periods when some students anticipate expensive presents and vacations while others are uncertain about whether their parents can even afford a holiday meal. At those times, say Allen and Hart, "We pull out 'Community of Friends,' and everyone feels relieved."

Many untracking schools further a norm of caring through regular, formal teacher-advisory meetings between a small group of students and a teacher, an administrator, or other adult in the building to discuss topics of importance to students. These heterogeneous groups reduce barriers among students and forge common bonds of support across differences. The practice also puts students in immediate, consistent contact with adults who come to know them and their families over a period of time, thus paving the way for group projects in the community.

Expanding Social Learning Opportunities

Recognizing that knowledge is acquired through a variety of social experiences, many untracking schools adopt practices to expand opportunities for students to make friends beyond their conventional social group and to build a sense of community. In these schools, student activities are considered an essential aspect of learning, *not* privileges for only a select few who qualify for them through grades or other criteria. Not surprisingly, then, many schools report that student participation in after-school programs greatly increases with untracking.

In a changing society that values responsibility and teamwork, student activities can become an alternative source of knowledge, experience, and education for life. Whether in the form of service clubs, interest groups, or athletics, they expand opportunities for interaction among diverse groups of students and further reinforce the value of effort and responsibility regardless of ability. Broad encouragement to participate in such activities, with students grouped according to shared interests rather than ability or age and with admission without qualification, become important means of enhancing untracking and building a school community. For example:

- Principal Cecil Floyd of the McCullough Middle School in Dallas, Texas, reports that the elimination of a selective group of cheerleaders in favor of a pep squad open to all eighth-grade girls makes for greater participation and stronger school spirit.

- At the Jericho, New York Middle School all students, including those with disabilities, who want to play varsity sports or participate in cheerleading activities can sign a contract to attend practice and share "play time" equally with their teammates. Likewise, if the school play has fewer parts than students who want to act in it, several productions are staged to allow everyone interested to participate. Students with acting roles in one production also work backstage in other plays. Finally, at graduation, says principal Anna Hunderfund, "No children parade across the stage at the expense of others." Instead, all students receive a certificate of recognition noting specific areas of achievement and the contribution that each has made to the school.

- At the Wellesley Middle School, staff concerned about the social exclusion of certain children during lunchtime proposed assigned tables to foster new and different friendships among a greater mix of students. Unexpectedly, this also enhanced relationships between students and teachers who found that they could more easily get to know individual children if they were predictably in the same seats.

Fair Distribution of Scarce Resources

A number of untracking schools work at changing aspects of school life to ensure that the same high-achieving students are not repeatedly favored with the benefits of limited resources, tangible and intangible. For example:

- At the Shutesbury School in Massachusetts, teacher Ron Berger reports that sixth graders themselves decide how "scarce resources" such as donated tickets to special events will be equitably distributed.

- Some schools make sure that all students share in the glory when the school is acknowledged publicly. Students are selected by lottery to accompany staff to ceremonies at which the school is slated to receive an award. When Crete-Monee won a national recognition award, the school closed for the afternoon and threw a party for students, staff, and parents as a way of communicating that "the students really accomplished this."

In these schools, free tickets to the symphony, field trips to museums or a local television station, opportunities to work with mentors from local industries or universities, and other enrichment experiences are not treated as rewards that recognize the achievement of only a few. Rather they are considered learning experiences in their own right and subject to fair distribution so that all students can benefit.

Establishing a Policy Context for Untracking

Untracking begins first and foremost at the school level. When schools do not have the resources or clout to "go it alone," however, a district- or state-level policy can reinforce progress, provide a cushion of support against resistance, and otherwise establish a broader climate for change. Although a paper policy is not enough, a formal message in the form of a policy advisory, position statement, or implementation guidelines from key decision-makers can create a climate that increases the likelihood of change.

Although many untracking schools do receive support from their district offices and school boards, many also successfully adopt new grouping, instruction, and curricula without affirmation from district leadership. For some, the lack of a supportive policy presents a formidable obstacle to reform. When the district does not share responsibility for change, schools can claim their own success, but they also risk bearing the entire burden in the event of failure. Absence of supportive policy can further perpetuate the misconception that *only* extraordinary principals and teachers working on their own can make schools change.

On the other hand, supportive policy coupled with technical assistance can make change possible for many more schools. Adopting alternatives to tracking often involves reversing long-established practices that may favor powerful parents or teachers. Because new practices can upset the apple cart of tradition or convenience, policies that reward risk taking with concrete support and technical assistance offer change-minded educators and parents the extra incentive that they need to begin to eliminate tracking.

District Policy   Generally, the most useful support comes from the office of the district superintendent in the form of overall leadership, encouragement for risk taking, and identification of sources for support and technical assistance. At the district level, systemwide policy can provide direction for schools beginning to explore alternatives to tracking; it can also work to endorse initial steps for change taken at the school level. Moreover, in the process of developing policy, district-level staff can work with school-board members to develop an expectation for change that includes community leaders as well as educators at individual schools.

In Burlington, Vermont, for example, Monica Nelson, director of curriculum, reports that the curriculum committee of the Burlington School Board spent one full year reviewing research on tracking and discussing the pros and cons of student grouping practices. This process proceeded in tandem with change at the school site; indeed, teachers at one middle school had been engaged in their own discussions about tracking which paralleled those at the school-board level. Following from this dialogue, the school board adopted the curriculum committee's "Grouping Motion" in March 1991. An important aspect of this motion allows the two middle schools in Burlington to develop their own individualized plans for untracking over a three-year period—a policy that takes into account differences in school readiness for change.

Other notable features of Burlington's Grouping Motion include:

- A direction to both the board itself and the superintendent to include discussion of alternatives to ability grouping in their three-year goals
- A direction to the district's curriculum director to explore and apply for grants and other financial support for alternatives to the current ability-grouping system
- The expectation that each of the district's schools will, within nine months, submit an initial plan of action to address alternatives to ability grouping, including indicators of achievement for each portion of the plan, with the goal of implementing alternatives to the current system by fall 1994
- A direction to the board's Finance Committee to include expanded staff development in its yearly budget-evaluation criteria for three years

Implementation of this policy will result in the district's allotting federal Title II money for travel expenses and fees for teachers who want to attend workshops and conferences beyond the contractually agreed-upon course work. Moreover, as part of an evaluation/self-evaluation process, all teachers will include in a statement of their professional goals a description of steps they will take to prepare for teaching heterogeneous classes. A teachers' contract provision entitling them to one paid three-credit graduate course every year facilitates this policy.

The policy also established that heterogeneous grouping will be implemented within a three-year time frame, a goal that principals must account for in their school plans. As Nelson explains, "I told the curriculum committee, 'A small but vocal group will always think this is the pits. If they're going to retire in seven years, they'll say you can do it in eight. If you really want anything to happen, you need to set a date.'" This time line backed by technical assistance conveys a seriousness of purpose about districtwide accountability and school-level decision making concerning implementation.

District policy in Milwaukee, Wisconsin also provides schools embarking on an untracking process with the support of a coherent citywide vision for broad curricular and instructional change. Efforts to address problems of tracking in Milwaukee Public Schools include:

- Equity 2000, a project, in cooperation with the College Board, that trains secondary math teachers, beginning in eighth grade, to provide all students with the skills that they need to succeed in algebra in the ninth grade and in successive courses in the math sequence
- Attention to racial bias and equity in selection for the Gifted and Talented Program
- Whole and flexible group instruction in reading
- Increased integrated learning opportunities for special education students
- Curriculum innovations and use of schoolwide approaches in the Chapter 1 program
- Staff development in the Teacher Expectations and Student Achievement (TESA) program and multicultural awareness
- Integration of higher-order academic learning into vocational courses
- Reconsideration of policies that mandate separate tracks for students who have not passed standardized tests for language and mathematics competence

As the plan notes, "In dismantling tracking, three areas need to be addressed simultaneously: a) policies and structures; b) beliefs and values; and c) practices." The plan encourages discussion with parents and teachers at each school, and the administration commits itself to ongoing reform of tracking in the district. In this policy context, schools can make no mistake that untracking is Milwaukee's strategy of choice for school improvement.

State-Level Policy

State-level policy statements are also crucial for creating momentum for untracking across a state. Three state-level policies from Massachusetts, California, and New York provide examples of how state officials can promote change through leveraging discretionary funding, nurturing networks of changing schools to share resources, and expanding available technical assistance by training educators to train others in innovative practices for heterogeneous classrooms.

Massachusetts

In Massachusetts, the Board of Education's 1990 policy advisory, *Structuring Schools for Student Success: A Focus on Ability Grouping,* has given a push to untracking and has set the stage for local school reform in its recommendation that "schools consider eliminating the use of widespread ability grouping and tracking practices, and implement alternatives." The body of the advisory is devoted to setting out guidelines for school-based assessment and planning; grouping of students; curriculum and instruction; staff development; and student and family support. Finally, the advisory outlines examples of schools and districts making a transition to heterogeneous grouping.

But paper policies are not enough. The most important feature of the Massachusetts policy is the state's commitment to direct concrete resources to schools, especially those in high-poverty districts, that adopt heterogeneous grouping. Dan French, director of the department's Bureau of Student Development and Health and administrator of the state's discretionary dropout prevention and remedial grants, asserts:

> We *do* know that heterogeneous grouping has more positive impact on student achievement than homogeneous grouping. Since we want to tie our funding to educational approaches that work, we direct our resources to schools that are working to adopt good practice. In awarding both dropout and remedial grants, we've included heterogeneous grouping of students as one of our required objectives.

In addition to using discretionary dollars to stimulate desirable practice, state support also includes on-site technical assistance and professional-development opportunities to schools adopting heterogeneous grouping. The department sponsors statewide conferences and regional seminars on pivotal issues, including tracking and grade retention, and pairs schools working on grouping issues with others who may be "a little further along" in untracking. Massachusetts officials report that the state advisory and additional resources have together fostered changes in grouping practices in rural and urban schools alike. "Many districts need incentives to try something new, especially if it's controversial," French insists. "A state policy promoting heterogeneous grouping can supply a necessary safety net for districts willing to take the risk, but linking resources to change is what really boosts the credibility of the effort."

California

In California, a broad initiative directed at reforming the state's middle-level schools provides the context for untracking. In 1987, *Caught in the Middle*, a report published by the California Department of Education, included recommendations for substantial reduction of tracking and the advice that no student should be tracked in grades six, seven, and eight according to ethnicity, gender, general ability, primary language, or handicap. With other recommendations related to curriculum, instructional practice, academic counseling, "at-risk" students, and staff development, the report also established a vehicle for transforming the reform agenda into practice: a partnership involving local school districts, institutions of higher education, and the California Department of Education to develop 100 state-of-the-art middle schools that would catalyze reform throughout the state.

In response, the Office of Middle Grades Support Services at the California Department of Education swung into action. First the department invited all middle-level schools to participate in regional networks, each comprising ten "membership" schools and a lead or "foundation" school. Joining a network required an "uncommon commitment" to creating a cadre of state-of-the-art schools in California. In other words, schools would receive no extra money for their participation in the partnership.

Despite the lack of financial support, several hundred schools responded, and 115 joined the regional networks for the first three-year cycle. Within each network, schools reviewed the findings of *Caught in the Middle*. Then they selected from the recommendations the reforms that they would pursue in their individual schools with the support of their network—a process that reinforced principles of local control and mutual collaboration for school improvement.

From the beginning, issues of untracking and equal opportunity were paramount among networks. Through monthly meetings of principals at rotated sites, visits to "sister schools," newsletters, directories, telecommunications networks, and collaborative staff-development days, schools shared strategies for realizing the goals of heterogeneous grouping and curriculum reform. In addition, a summer symposium on "Equal Access" highlighted workshops on expanding the access of low-income and ethnic-minority students to the highest and most valuable curricula in the middle grades. Although at the outset the partnership had no extra funding to distribute to schools, by 1989 the initiative raised enough foundation money to provide each network with funds for regional conferences on such topics as "Equal Access Is Possible" and "Equal Access to a Common Core Curriculum." Despite limited subsequent funding, an additional 111 schools have declared their own "uncommon commitment" to a second round of networking for middle-level reform.

Donald Le May of Valley Junior High School commends the partnership and his regional network for supporting his own school's plan for untracking. "The partnership gave me the courage to speak out," he explains. "It put me in contact with others who were thinking along similar lines. It gave me leverage to be able to say to skeptics in my district that we were not alone."

New York

As in California, the state department of education in New York has chosen to include guidelines for untracking within a broader policy statement, *Regents' Policy Statement on Middle-Level Education and Schools with Middle-Level Grades,* which advises, "Schools enrolling middle-level students should...use student grouping strategies that maintain heterogeneous classes but group for specific purposes and for brief periods." The New York policy is designed to develop a self-sustaining, locally based support system to help educators untrack their own schools. This support system rests on six interdependent components in a comprehensive strategy that recognizes that primary responsibility for reform lies with the principal and the school. These components include:

1. A public position that tracking in the middle grades is a harmful educational practice
2. Public educational forums to disseminate information on the impact and effects of tracking in the middle grades
3. A cadre of experienced middle-level practitioners who can train other middle-level educators to teach heterogeneous classrooms effectively
4. Support for local schools' efforts to untrack, especially through procedures allowing them to get a variance from regulations that are obstacles to untracking

5. Identification of untracking middle schools that can serve
   as models for other schools interested in changing grouping
   practices
6. Documentation of the results of untracking in New York's
   middle-level schools

Like Massachusetts and California, New York has coupled
formal policy with significant technical assistance to schools that
adopt cutting-edge middle-grades practices, including heterogeneous grouping. For example, David Payton, Director of Middle
Level Education for the state, has designed a series of "turnkey
training" workshops to spread the word about grouping innovations among educators. These workshops build on the knowledge and skills that support heterogeneous grouping, including
information about current theories about human intelligence,
levels of critical thinking, and cooperative learning. Through collaboration with the National Resource Center on Middle Grades
Education, training programs have reached key New York educators who in turn provide in-service programs for their colleagues. The state's manual of resources and teaching modules is
an additional resource to prepare teachers for mixed-ability
classrooms. This approach builds a foundation for the gradual
but steady movement toward untracking in New York schools.

Policies from Massachusetts, California, New York, and others
from states like Nevada and Maryland highlight the potential of
states to assume leadership in defining the conditions that bring
about high achievement among young adolescents. Research-
based, equity-oriented state policy communicates to practitioners research findings about tracking. It also establishes a
climate to encourage risk taking in local districts and schools
that choose to venture into innovative grouping, curricular, and
instructional changes.

School Reform of the 1980s: An Accelerated Middle School as a Setting for Untracking

We ask [school staff] to look carefully at their school to ask
if this is the school that they would choose for their own
offspring. If it is not good enough for their own children,
it is not yet good enough for any child.

—Henry Levin, director, Accelerated Schools Project

Concerns about public education that emerged in the 1980s fostered a variety of reform movements that have begun to bear

fruit in the 1990s. Although none of these explicitly recommended untracking, their principles inform a change process that invites untracking in part because of the comprehensive nature of the reforms that each proposes.

In untracking schools, staff often begin a change process within the context of the lessons of the middle-school movement. Many have deepened their insights from this movement with perspectives gleaned from the school-reform strategies of the 1980s including the Effective Schools Movement, the Coalition of Essential Schools, the Partnership for School Renewal, the Padeia Proposal, and the Montessori Movement—all of which are wholly compatible with untracking. One example from the Accelerated Schools Project illustrates in detail how untracking may proceed within the context of a major school-reform movement.

The Accelerated Schools Project is one comprehensive approach to school change that is hospitable to untracking. As staff member Wendy Hopfenberg explains, accelerated schools enroll large numbers of students who risk school failure because of a mismatch between the resources and experiences that they are exposed to at home and the expectations that they encounter at school. Accelerated schools provide an enriched, challenging environment rather than a remedial one in order to bring all students into the educational mainstream.

The Accelerated Schools Project is both a *way of thinking* about academic acceleration for all students and a *concrete process* for achieving it. Three central directions guide all actions:

* Create a *unity of purpose* that reflects the school's commitment to making all students academically successful.
* *Empower* teachers, administrators, other staff, parents, students, and community to make decisions while *taking responsibility* for implementing the decisions and for the outcomes of these decisions.
* *Build on the strengths* of all members of the school community.

These three principles come alive within a school as teachers review curriculum, instruction, and organization as complete, interdependent components of their accelerated school, with each one building on and influencing the other two. Underlying the principles and the three components of learning are values of equity, participation, communication, community, reflection, experimentation, entrepreneurial risk taking, and trust.

Project schools do not follow a prescribed checklist for change. They do use a systematic, all-inclusive process of change to encompass all students within the accelerated program. The school begins by "taking stock" of itself to describe its current status. From there, a vision is formed of the kind of education that should be offered. School staff then select specific priorities or challenge areas by looking at the differences between where the school is and where it wants to be. Task forces, called cadres, study each challenge area. The cadres are critical components of the governance structure that provides real power to the staff, students, and parents.

As schools become accelerated schools, the cadres use an "inquiry process" to focus thoroughly on the problem areas, brainstorm and synthesize solutions, develop an action plan, pilot-test the new program, evaluate their effectiveness, and reassess priorities. The cadres bring the results to the steering committee which, in turn, incorporates the decisions into the total school community, known as the School-as-a-Whole.

Before adopting the accelerated-schools philosophy as a guide for change, the Burnett Accelerated Middle School in the San Jose, California, Unified School District was heavily tracked, especially in language arts, social studies, and mathematics. As Burnett began to embrace the accelerated-schools philosophy, a number of forces affecting grouping practices came into play. Initially these included taking stock of the school's current situation, creating a school vision, and reexamining curriculum and instruction in light of research by staff members and committees. Later, as teachers experimented with heterogeneous grouping within their classes, individual staff members became major forces for change. Finally, state and local budget cuts, which resulted in the loss of several positions and the repositioning of remaining staff members, may, ironically, have facilitated untracking by reducing the resources available for remedial classes and forcing the staff to focus on defining the skills and knowledge that they expected all students to master. These disparate forces, rather than a clear set of guidelines, contributed to the complex road to untracking.

Taking Stock and Creating a Vision

As an initial step on its path to acceleration, school staff took stock of their school's overall performance and found extreme differences in student course placement by ethnicity. Although the school had taken tentative steps to place more minority students in higher-level courses, teachers learned that these students tended to be disproportionately represented in the lowest classes while white students were disproportionately represented in the highest classes. Alerted to this pattern, the entire school community created a new vision, underpinned by the belief that all students had a right to a challenging educational program.

After defining their vision, Burnett teachers examined the gaps between where the school was and where they wanted it to be, then created several cadres to address the challenge areas. As the cadres studied these areas, it became clear to both the Curriculum Cadre and the Instruction Cadre that the concept of untracking had to be addressed. Accordingly, the Curriculum Cadre began taking steps to change the curriculum to provide for equal access and more untracking, and the Instruction Cadre sought out new teaching methods that would facilitate the move to heterogeneous grouping.

Staff on all cadres took current research into account in their planning. The accelerated-schools governance structure provided a community-wide forum for discussion of untracking. As the year progressed, teacher aides and other staff members, as well as teachers and administrators, began to emphasize approaches that built on the strengths of all students.

Teacher Experimentation

Beyond the "formal" accelerated-school process, individual members of the school community were forces for change in their own right. Individual teachers and staff members started to realize that existing tracking practices were incompatible with the ideas of accelerating all students. Teacher Connie Posner began experimenting on her own with untracking in her English as a Second Language (ESL) classes. Instead of creating low, medium, and high groups, Posner worked with the administration and mixed the three groups. She found that all the students progressed more rapidly and were able to enter regular classes more quickly.

Likewise, the accelerated-schools project was the stimulus for teacher Kris Estrada's shift to "making things more exciting" for all students and for herself. No longer were test scores and student records the basis for assigning different curriculum activities to different students. Instead, all students were given challenging, relevant, and empowering projects. For example, Estrada asked the eighth-grade classes to do a writing project in which *they* evaluated their assignments at the school. Students from all "levels" responded that group projects and active learning in real-life situations were the most powerful learning experiences of all.

Still another teacher, Steve Novotny, realized that he was giving the students in his "lower" classes less exciting opportunities and experiences in the computer lab than he was offering "higher" classes. Novotny decided to see what would happen if all the students got to do the "fun, challenging" projects in programming and robotics. He was thrilled with the positive response from everyone as he observed first-hand the results of the project's goal of building on students' strengths.

Plans for the
Future

In preparing the year's schedule at Burnett, the administration in conjunction with the Curriculum Cadre and the School-as-a-Whole realized that tracking was not compatible with their vision and goal of equal educational opportunity for all students. As a result, plans for future years included integrating language-arts and social-studies classes to offer everyone equal access to integrated, accelerated learning. Math teachers also worked together to revise their program to ensure that all students have success in algebra before they complete the eighth grade. Burnett sixth graders are now enrolled in heterogeneous accelerated math classes, while all seventh graders take pre-algebra, and eighth graders take algebra 1.

The path to untracking is a complex one. At Burnett, this path gains rationale, strength, and momentum from the philosophy and framework of the Accelerated Schools Project. And within this framework for school reform, Burnett staff have surprised themselves with the speed and success of their charted course.

Is It Worth It?
Documenting Untracking Results

> I've never worked so hard being creative, but I'm also convinced that I'm teaching better while I'm saying less. Kids really do learn without a data dump from us. I also know the students better because I can participate in the class instead of lead it. We teachers are still in charge of organizing, planning, and scheduling, but the kids are a part of every class.
>
> —Roene Comack, teacher, Harding Middle School,
>   Cedar Rapids, Iowa

Untracking is not a trouble-free undertaking, but staff and students in schools where the process has begun tell us that it is worth the effort. Schools report that achievement is up for the "low" and "average" students, while undiminished and sometimes improved for the "high" students. They report that discipline improves dramatically, including the behavior of special education students. And they report noticeable improvements in the school climate and teacher morale.

In the interest of accountability, some schools have taken careful steps to document the effects of their untracking efforts on student grades, test scores, and course placement as well as attendance, discipline, and graduation data. These data are useful both for planning further change and for demonstrating to parents, the community, and teachers themselves the ways in which heterogeneous grouping has affected student performance. Several approaches have been taken to generate this information.

One approach is to compare students in mixed-level teams with those who are grouped in homogeneous classes. For example, at Castle High School in Hawaii heterogeneous clusters of students were compared with matched groups of students to assess differences in outcomes. After one year, the school found that:

- Only 7 percent of the students in the heterogeneous core team had ten or more absences per quarter compared with 23 percent in the control group.
- Thirty-three percent of the students in the heterogeneously grouped team were rated "exemplary" in terms of academic performance compared with 18 percent in the control group; 34 percent were rated "below standard" compared with 56 percent in the control group.
- Discipline referrals to the principal have been "greatly reduced" in the heterogeneously grouped team, with teachers reporting that discipline "is not the time- and energy-consuming process it was in the past."

A second approach to assessing the impact of heterogeneous grouping is to compare the achievement of entire grades or groups of students from one year to the next. Two untracking schools in Massachusetts adopted this method.

At the Wayland Middle School in Massachusetts, principal Richard Schaye and the school's teachers persuaded their town's school board that they would try heterogeneous grouping on an experimental basis conditioned on evidence that mixed-ability classes did not harm student achievement. In that school, staff invited teachers from two neighboring suburban districts to act as outside assessors of student performance before and after implementation of heterogeneous grouping in English classes. The observers were to compare composition papers written by unnamed Wayland seventh graders in heterogeneously grouped classes with papers written by unnamed advanced-level seventh graders of the year before, when leveling was in effect. These objective assessors found that the quality of the compositions done the second year was equal to or higher than those of the previous year, convincing the school board of the value of mixed-ability grouping.

Similarly, staff at the Wellesley Middle School determined to document the impact of grouping changes to ensure that student achievement would not suffer from heterogeneous grouping.

Principal John D'Auria describes how his school assessed the impact of heterogeneous grouping on student academic performance in the sixth and seventh grades:

> When the school began to explore the idea of heterogeneous groups, the school decided to group some classes heterogeneously, while some continued to be grouped homogeneously. At the end of the year, an evaluation was done to monitor the success of the subjects that were being taught to heterogeneous groups. At that point, the school discovered that students who would fall into a "Level 3" category based on testing results had virtually disappeared and that students who were in the "low" group in homogeneously grouped classes were achieving "average" levels when they were in untracked classes.

This focus on results has since been extended to the higher grades, and as the school moves into heterogeneous grouping in the eighth grade, Wellesley superintendent Karla Deletis describes plans to study its effects:

> We're going to subject what we do in our school to rigorous examination. Specifically, during the final year of homogeneous grouping in eighth grade language arts, the Wellesley Middle School will ask all "top level" students to write papers. At the end of the first year of heterogeneous grouping, all eighth graders will be asked to do the same assignment which will be scored holistically for writing and thinking. If the proportion of "5"s is equally distributed, there's no loss. But over time, a larger proportion of "3"s, "4"s, and "5"s should come from heterogeneous groups.

Deletis concludes:

> We want to derive all the benefits we can and minimize any potential losses. Our goal is to move all our kids into the highest levels in the high school. This strategy holds a lot of promise and some risk, but I don't know how to close the gaps in achievement otherwise.

Teacher and Student Responses to Untracking

If alternatives to tracking are to be sustained over time, it is essential for both teachers, who are on the front lines of change, and students, the ultimate customers of schooling, to experience satisfaction and success. The experience of untracking suggests that teachers are most likely to endorse heterogeneous grouping when they see concrete results that make them feel more effective as teachers. For example, Anna Bernard reports that since untracking occurred at Prescott, "student behavior is much better! There is a more positive climate for teachers and students, and students seem to care more about their academic success." She concludes:

> Because we do not have gifted classes and because our students are at the lower end of the economic ladder, we have had almost no resistance to this change. It has been a *positive* change for teachers and students: No more slow classes, better behavior, better teacher morale, more variety in our instructional program, easier scheduling—and we are improving our test scores, slowly, but surely.

Whereas those teachers who initiate grouping reforms may plunge in on the basis of research and their own beliefs about the nature of learning, others clearly adopt a "wait and see" posture. But these teachers, too, are often won over in time. For example, at Louis Armstrong, Mary Ellen Levin says, "When we opened, many of our teachers, veterans of the junior high schools in New York City, wanted homogeneous grouping. At this point, *no one* would hear of it. Even diehards are converted."

Such changes are not lost on students, who welcome the new opportunities for learning that come with heterogeneous grouping. In untracking schools, students comment on expanded opportunities for success that accompany new grouping arrangements. For example:

> *Now they don't put us in different groups. We get lots of work, but it's better because if we need help, we work in groups, and you get a lot more accomplished.*

> *I think you learn more because you get to talk the problems over with your friends.*

> *I felt smarter when I got moved up. They teach me more here. People pitch in, they help, they don't just push you off.*

> *I have a person who is helping me with my term paper. We work together. I never thought I could do one.*

*I admire people who have to work harder and longer than I do
for the same project. Now I know that it isn't just brains.*

Students also remark on the ways in which their heterogeneously grouped, sometimes multilingual, classes boost their
self-esteem, sense of membership in the school, and commitment to their classmates:

*The teachers are fair. The students are nice. They don't make fun
of you or anything. We are just all the same.*

*I make more friends. I feel that I'm part of a group; I'm not
left out.*

*The class was exciting. Different people [were] helping each
other. I felt like part of a group. We knew each other a lot, and
now we continue to help each other.*

The good thing about this school is that we're all together here.

*Kids made fun of you [in my old school.] Here we really learn
how to talk things out.*

*I like school this year. I feel 'in.' Having everyone all mixed up in
classes makes me feel part of the whole group, not just with my
own few friends.*

Ultimately, the greatest rewards for teachers in untracking
schools come from the changes in students' achievement, sense
of self-worth, and commitment to the school community.
Reports Sue Galletti:

What I've *stopped* seeing is very talented, bright children
feeling they're not worth a bit of salt because they haven't
made it into an elitist program for students labeled "gifted."
I'm seeing all kids realize there are lots of kids who can
contribute to learning even when what they contribute
is different.

PART III

Strategies and Tools for Reform

Whatever you can do, or dream you can,
Begin it.
Boldness has genius, power, and magic in it.

—Goethe

Untracking is an art as much as a science. School staff who seek to release their students from the rigid labels, categories, and routines that undermine learning in tracked schools are challenging entrenched practices. They begin by taking a hard look at outmoded assumptions that stand in the way of success for all students. Often they must tread with caution as far as vested interests are concerned. They must act wisely and thoughtfully because they have few models from which to learn. They must build trust and confidence among other staff, parents, and students so that they will be able to weather any mistakes. They must have finely tuned judgment about the nature and timing of changes that staff, students, and parents can accept.

Although the process of untracking is not painless, the results are worth the effort. The stories of different schools do not signal any one right way to go about reducing and eliminating tracking in the middle grades. They do suggest, however, that a purposeful, thoughtful approach to change can bring about reforms in grouping, instruction, curricula, and school organization. The chapters that follow will document specific examples of successful steps taken to untrack schools across the country.

1 · Involving Parents and the Community

Communicating with Parents: Promoting Understanding of Untracking

First of all, I'm in favor of mixed-ability grouping. But my concern is that we can do it only if we hold down class size, which we can do next year. But what about the year after? If we have to increase class size, will that make this move unrealistic?

I hope with this program we try to get as much academic excellence as we can. What consideration was given to opening up algebra to all students but keeping an accelerated group? The assumptions I've heard are not realistic. You're asking the teachers to bite off an awful lot, and the kids at both ends of the spectrum may be hurt.

It is a winter night in New England, and the large lecture hall at the Wellesley Middle School is filled with parents of the school's seventh-grade students. Armed with the kinds of questions that parents typically ask when they are worried that change may threaten the well-being of their children, these parents have come out tonight because the school's teachers have told principal John D'Auria that they are ready to try heterogeneous grouping in the eighth grade. In response, D'Auria has figured out a plan that will allow the school to pilot this approach in the coming year. Average class size will be reduced from twenty-nine to twenty-one, and the sharing of the school's teachers with the high school will be eliminated.

Because this class size cannot be guaranteed in subsequent years, D'Auria and superintendent Karla Deletis have decided to move more quickly than usual. Although they have received preliminary approval from the school board, they have had time to tell only those parents most active in the school's PTO of the change. As a result, many parents are suspicious that something is being put over on them; some even plan to protest at the next school committee meeting.

Prior to the meeting, D'Auria has sent a letter to all parents describing the proposed changes. The letter outlines the school's plan to adopt a core science, English, and social-studies curriculum for all eighth-grade students along with heterogeneous grouping that mirrors arrangements already in place in the sixth and seventh grades. The letter also describes the school's proposal to continue offering three eighth-grade math levels; a "Level 3" pre-algebra course; a "Level 2" transitional algebra course based on the University of Chicago Mathematics Project's textbook series, which focuses on probability, statistics, and geometry; and a traditional algebra course offered as an accelerated course. In the letter, D'Auria also notes:

> The staff is eagerly anticipating these changes in curriculum and grouping format. We think these revisions will benefit *all* our students—from our most confident to our least confident learners. I view these recommendations as outgrowths of our core value work and our experiences in developing ways to challenge every student in heterogeneous settings.... We have seen considerable success in these settings. We have examined the research.... We have looked to our middle school neighbors.... This evidence encourages us to offer all our eighth-grade students the rich curricular experiences that once were available to only a few.... Our judgment is reflective of the needs of middle school–age students.

Parents have come here tonight for further discussion of this letter and the four agenda items that D'Auria flashes on the overhead projector at the outset:

1. Exact nature of changes
2. Context for these changes
3. Gain for students
4. How we plan to assess the outcomes of these curricular and instructional modifications

Parents listen carefully as D'Auria reviews the school's core objectives and values related to teacher expectations and student effort. He lists the new skills that teachers have developed in preparation for heterogeneous grouping—cooperative learning, mastery learning, and the use of instructional technology. He describes how students have risen to higher expectations and how, as a result, teachers have recommended fewer students for "Level 3" courses, obviating the need to offer such courses. He concludes, "We think these changes will bring our goals off the pages and into the daily lives of all our students."

> *My daughters are very confident and fast talkers, and I love the attitude of the teachers here. But I'm still concerned about teachers' being able to handle a wide range of differences and build self-esteem among students who are not so good at organizing their work. Won't this affect the quality of classroom atmosphere?*

> *I have very serious concerns. I have trouble with a teacher teaching something and gearing it to all students.... After all, you can learn cooperation and respect in extracurricular activities. This came too fast....*

The parents have legitimate questions, many best answered by the teachers who chair each department: Linda Smith, social studies; Peggy Mongiello, English; and Bill Atherton, science and math. In turn, Smith, Mongiello, and Atherton provide an overview of the curriculum and describe the enthusiasm of their colleagues for heterogeneous grouping and a more interesting curriculum for all. Teachers in the audience nod when Smith observes that heterogeneous grouping and curricular changes in the earlier grades have resulted in better instruction. "Students do better in school when they're invested in their work and in inherently challenging assignments," she concludes. Mongiello adds, to more nodding, "Good teaching is based on a situation that challenges all students."

What do challenging assignments for students of diverse abilities look like? The teachers provide examples:

- In English: Students studying the autobiographical form in literature and experimenting with different writing styles read Roald Dahl's *Boy* and are then asked to write their own autobiography in a similar anecdotal form, covering any experiences that they choose. Given no limits, one "Level 1" student wrote seven pages; one "Level 2" student submitted thirty-five pages.

- In social studies: Using nothing but information gleaned from a variety of maps, students research habitats of Africa. With assignments requiring them to work out scale, distance, and travel time, students analyze and synthesize information, develop hypotheses about climate, terrain, and ethnic groups, and ultimately write postcards to their friends and family about their "trips."

- In science: According to Atherton, "What is different is the routine you get youngsters into. Every kid will be at a lab station, working with a partner. I work all year on making myself superfluous while kids learn to form questions and solve problems. Sometimes I surprise them and drop an old eyeball preserved in formaldehyde in their beakers. They have to figure out what it is. These are not special things. All kids can do it!"

Teachers all emphasize that parents' concerns are those that any educator would share, whether for the least or the most confident students. They explain that they take into account the needs of slower learners, not by watering down the curriculum, but by preparing students for assignments, structuring assignments clearly, and applying mastery concepts for skills so that those who do not achieve 80 percent mastery are rechecked until they do. They note also that they consciously provide gifted students with extra opportunities to excel through independent assignments and contracts for honors work.

I came here really negative. Now I'm only indifferent. I'm concerned we're diluting the education of our top students. I think you're sacrificing the most motivated for the good of the rest of the class. How do you take the kids and give everyone a sense of achievement without diluting the achievement of the "high" kids? It seems to me that the more kids compete with each other, the harder they'll work.

I'm beginning to understand why I have a problem with this. If you carry the logic to its extreme, if average kids can benefit from a more challenging curriculum than they're getting now, why can't the "high" kids benefit from a curriculum that's harder for them?

What gains do Wellesley staff envision for all students? D'Auria wants everyone to understand that improvement is significant at all levels, and he projects the anticipated gains for "Level 1" students onto the screen:

1. Students will learn more varied and diverse problem-solving strategies: At the Wellesley Middle School, staff work on helping all students think about alternative solutions to many problems.

2. What students learn will be more lasting: When students explain their answers and point of view to others, they integrate their learning in a more lasting way. Learning theory demonstrates that students retain ten times more information from a discussion-group format than from a lecture.

3. Students will be supported in greater risk taking: In a tracked setting, "high" students frequently come to believe that asking questions is a sign of stupidity and fear that their placement in the top group has been a mistake or that if they show uncertainty, they will be removed from their group.

4. Students will have more opportunity to unlearn some self-limiting beliefs such as "If I can't learn it quickly, then I'm not good at it"; "If I can't learn it quickly, then it's not worth doing"; and "Being smart means being able to learn many ideas quickly and lots of facts." These are not beliefs that will help one in life. We want students to know that achievement derives more from consistent effort than anything else.

5. Students will learn greater acceptance and appreciation for others: we want students who can identify, describe, and view the world from the perspective of others.

Reviewing gains for students at other levels, D'Auria presents similar advantages such as the benefits derived from exposure to curriculum that is rich and challenging, developing different and diverse ways of thinking, and the opportunity to unlearn self-limiting beliefs. Noting that in tracked schools "children in the middle can sometimes feel a little lost," he acknowledges concerns of parents of average learners. By encouraging risk taking among *all* students, he points out, greater confidence and more adventurous learning has emerged most dramatically in mixed-ability groups.

> *Even after all this discussion, I can't help but think there's benefit to homogeneous grouping in certain settings and certain times. I know I benefited from both. Is there some way to make sure that students have the benefits of working in homogeneous grouping from time to time?*

> *What I'm concerned about is that with this new heterogeneous grouping in grade eight, kids won't be prepared for the levels they encounter in high school. What I want to know is whether elimination of levels at grade eight will make the transition to high school more difficult.*

The questions continue—all of them reasonable, all reflecting the kinds of concerns that most parents have for their children. The superintendent, who has been in the audience, assures parents that the proposed plan does not reflect a "hidden agenda" to eliminate levels at the high school. Classroom teachers, specialists, and counselors in the audience further respond:

Yes, we can regroup kids in smaller groups when that's
appropriate, and we can give kids extra-credit assignments.

In fact, there's enormous variability in every class, even
ones you think are homogeneous. You can't really rank
children on a continuum in every skill at every level. The more
we use different alternatives, the more we can accommodate
the variability.

We will always be calling on the guidance counselor to
help out. It will be her job to make sure our high school staff
is clear about the tasks at the different high-school levels.
Then our students can decide how much they want to stretch.
When they leave our school, they will know they have been
successful learners. Their choice will have to do with their own
interests. But for eleven-, twelve-, and thirteen-year-olds, we'd
like to be sure that options are not foreclosed for them.

It is 11:00. John D'Auria concludes:

We have a challenge in front of us to make sure we provide
intellectual challenges for all kids. A core curriculum means
teachers can develop the best of the strategies that will bring
out the best in kids—the best cooperative learning activities,
the best assignments. We need the support of parents, and we
need to hear from parents about what's working and what's
not so we can better and better match what we do to what
your child needs; so we can challenge kids appropriately, but
not confuse coverage for depth; so they can learn ideas,
concepts, substance.

The meeting is over. After a two-hour presentation and an hour
and a half of questions and discussion, a few parents still feel
unsure; even the best answers have not taken away all their
misgivings. But most seem satisfied; everyone is better informed;
and the support is so substantial that although the discussion
continues at the subsequent school-board meeting, the proposals
pass community review and are approved for implementation
the fall.

Gaining Parent Support for Untracking

> You have to give parents the guarantee that their child is not going to be harmed. Parents ask, "Can you be sure my child is not going to be worse off?" I can say "She won't be worse off, and we hope she will be better off."
>
> —Janet Pearson, teacher, Kammerer Middle School, Louisville, Kentucky

As schools embark on the process of untracking, all parents want to know how grouping changes are going to affect their children. Parents of students with disabilities need to know that someone has been thinking about how newly designed grouping arrangements will promote success for their children without overwhelming them. Parents of academically confident children need to know that heterogeneous classes do not result in "dumbed down" curriculum or instruction geared to "the middle." Parents of "average" children need to know that their children will not be lost in classrooms that allocate most of the teachers' attention to students at the extreme ends of the learning spectrum.

Not too long ago, grouping practices at Kammerer Middle School in Louisville, Kentucky, strictly mirrored district policy: advanced placement was determined by standardized testing across the district; placement in honors and comprehensive classes was determined at the school level. Given the force of habit and tradition, it had never occurred to many teachers or parents that alternatives to this approach existed.

However, not everyone at the school level was entirely comfortable with tracking, particularly when it seemed to result in in-school segregation. As Kammerer's language-arts teacher Claudia Runge reports:

> Many of us were concerned that our "comprehensive" classes were racially identifiable. We had concerns about labeling. With ability grouping in the elementary grades, by the time the kids got to us, they weren't doing the work they should have been doing. We were getting kids who had a pretty low self-concept, and we weren't doing anything to help that.

At Kammerer, teachers and parents never set out *intentionally* to adopt alternatives to tracking. Rather, untracking—and parent participation in that process—evolved as an outgrowth of the school's overall policy of parent involvement. In 1986, principal Nancy Weber had convened a Parent Roundtable simply as a way for teachers and parents to meet to talk about the needs of middle-grades youngsters. Meeting monthly with two or three school staff, the Parent Roundtable provided a forum for reacting to various articles and reports, including the Carnegie Commission's *Turning Points,* about young adolescents and middle schools.

Tracking *per se* was never on the agenda, explains Runge. But, she says, "If you read a lot of middle-school material, you're bound to come across the topic. It popped up in everything we read. After two years of the Roundtable, tracking became an issue. We just kept coming back to it."

By early 1989, teachers on one of the school's two sixth-grade teams were eager to pilot the academic integration of students from all levels. At the same time, as a result of the Parent Roundtable, school staff had developed a positive relationship with a small core group of influential parents who, says Runge, "didn't necessarily support the idea of untracking but were at least familiar with the material." And so, in August 1989, Weber sent a letter to all parents describing how the school's process for academic integration would be implemented to reflect current recommendations for improving middle schools, including the elimination of tracking.

Even with such preparation, the introduction of academic integration at Kammerer did not move forward without a hitch. In fact, says Janet Pearson, sixth-grade team leader, "*We* were convinced that in order for all students to achieve at the highest levels we needed heterogeneous classes. But we misread our constituency. In the minds of our parents, this was an experimental program." Even a special orientation meeting designed to present information to in-coming sixth-grade parents did not fully allay fears. Pearson relates, "I began to realize that unless we had one-to-one meetings with parents to tell them about our intentions, they were not going to listen. Over the next four weeks, I personally spent hours and hours on the telephone and in personal conferences with tearful parents. Many wanted to do this, but it was an agonizing decision for them when they feared they were removing their child from the 'protected surroundings' of the track."

During that first year, the pilot sixth-grade team combined one regular, one honors, and two advanced-placement classes, maintaining this ability-grouping proportion both in each science and social-studies class as a whole and within small in-class groups in those subjects. Although students were randomly mixed for allied-arts and physical-education classes, in math and language arts the team continued to offer separate AP classes to conform with district policy.

This approach paid off. That first year, according to Pearson, "While some parents requested the transfer of their children to the second sixth-grade team that had retained tracking, most stayed with us." Throughout that year, teachers continued to make themselves available for questions and provided progress reports to parents through a team newsletter distributed every four to five weeks.

Tracking continued to be the focus of discussion at Parent Roundtable meetings where teachers reported on the progress of new approaches, entertained questions, and were able to assure parents that:

> Instruction is directed to the highest level, encouraging expression of a variety of perspectives among students....
> Discipline problems are definitely reduced in all groups on all levels, and...previously lower-performing students have new role models, and find they can compete.

By April 1990, parents and teachers meeting together at the Roundtable reflected positively on the year's progress, reporting in the group's minutes that "this discussion group itself is amazing in that teachers, parents, and administrators are discussing alternatives in schools. This could not have been predicted a few years ago." As Pearson notes, "The Roundtable at first was a place for open, philosophical discussions. Once we jumped into the change, the Roundtable was a vehicle to help implement our plans."

Teachers at Kammerer took the lessons of parent involvement seriously as they moved to advance their program. Prior to the second year of integration, staff set up spring meetings at each of the feeder elementary schools to explain the program to parents. Again, not all parents were persuaded of the wisdom of heterogeneous grouping, and when some registered complaints with the central administration, school staff adapted their approach by offering the choice of a heterogeneously grouped team or a tracked team in both the sixth and seventh grades. Staff and parents also planned for an initial orientation for parents, additional Roundtable discussions about tracking, and a continuation of the parent newsletter with regular reports on the progress of academic integration. Pearson says, "This time we knew we were not going to drop a bomb. We knew what parents were looking for."

The efforts worked. Of the 120 sixth-grade students moving on to seventh grade, parents of all but one chose to continue on the "blended" team, and the team had to draw up a waiting list. By the start of the third year, 104 of the 116 student places on the heterogeneously grouped team in the sixth grade had been spoken for by the initial sign-up deadline, and the heterogeneous teams in the upper grades had waiting lists of students from all levels—including one whose parent had been an early and vocal

opponent of the pilot program. This high level of parent enthusiasm, Pearson emphasizes, comes from being open to working
with parents at every step of the process. "We're not trying to put
anything over on anyone. No one feels coerced," she says.

Guidelines for Involving Parents in the Untracking Process

Principals aren't trained to be politicians, yet this is a political
issue. I learned you need to be politically savvy.

—Sue Galletti, principal, Islander Middle School,
Mercer Island, Washington

The experiences of schools where untracking has been successful
offer suggested guidelines for involving parents in the untracking
process:

• Be aware that parents need to be involved in the change
  process. Even though you have a plan that you are certain is
  a good one, don't hesitate to talk it over with everyone who is
  going to be affected, in large groups if necessary, but especially
  in small groups and in individual parent conferences.

• In communicating with parents, be sure that you can
  articulate the expected outcomes of innovative grouping
  practices in terms of benefits to all children. Understand that
  the word *restructuring* without further elaboration can imply
  undirected experimentation, and that few parents will
  willingly allow their children to be guinea pigs in such
  an experiment.

• Be prepared for the possibility that not all parents will endorse
  proposed alternatives to tracking. If, even after extended
  discussions, some parents continue to object, school staff
  may decide that, as teacher Claudia Runge says, "You just
  have to take the plunge." In such situations, phasing in heterogeneous grouping and monitoring outcomes may help resolve
  concerns of parents who are likely to complain to district
  decision makers.

• Be sure to maintain a high level of instruction for all students.
  Explain changes in terms of how you have strengthened
  curriculum and instruction for all students. Assure parents
  that children will not be experiencing a "watered-down"
  curriculum—with the "same old basal readers" simply adopted
  in mixed-ability classes—by providing them with specific
  examples of individualized assignments that enrich learning.

- Don't abandon efforts to communicate with parents after the initial stages of implementation. Keep parents informed through regular progress reports, newsletters, meetings, and formal and informal evaluations. Involve them in staff development related to new curriculum. Let parents know about academic successes and changes in discipline and student attitudes.

Above all, successful parent involvement in untracking requires a sincere and ongoing invitation to parents to raise questions and make suggestions—with school staff sharing research findings, information about state-of-the-art classroom practices, the developmental needs of students, and learning theory to create a consensus about the school's responsibility to all students. As Kammerer parents and teachers noted after their first year, "Teachers and parents must believe that all students can learn well and base action on this." A successful partnership between parents and schools engaged in untracking can flourish on the strength of this belief.

Preparing for Tough Questions: What Do You Say When...?

> The change process is anxiety-producing. This anxiety surfaces in numerous ways: questions are raised, resistance is generated, unrelated issues surface, and rumors abound. Recognizing that each of these will occur is the first step in addressing them.
>
> —Ron Williamson and J. Howard Johnson,
> *Planning for Success: Successful Implementation of Middle Level Reorganization*, 1991

Like many institutions, untracking schools have constituencies that resist change, including parents. These schools have learned some lessons from their experience of listening and responding to teachers, parents, and community constituencies who would prefer to leave traditional grouping practices untouched. Educators in these schools advise being prepared with research findings and examples from experience when addressing concerns of skeptics. Here are some responses to some tough questions:

"It seems to me that mixing groups of students together is going to hold back the learning of the smarter students."

Of the hundreds of research studies conducted on heterogeneous groups, the vast majority conclude that high-achieving students do not lose ground in diverse-ability classes. In almost every case, classroom environment is found to be far more important than student enrollment. When curriculum and instruction are engaging, students of all levels benefit, including the most confident learners.

These findings apply even to the "top" 3 percent of students. In a recent study Robert Slavin and Robert Stevens of Johns Hopkins University compared student progress in heterogeneous classes that were using the Cooperative Integrated Reading and Composition (CIRC) curriculum with that in homogeneously grouped classes. Students rated among the top 33 percent, 10 percent, and 3 to 5 percent were examined. The result was that, in fact, the reading and writing performance of the heterogeneously grouped students surpassed that of the homogeneously grouped ones at all levels.

Educators emphasize that attention be paid to these findings. As Jake Burks of Maryland's Harford County Public School District, reminds parents:

> We need to make educational decisions based on the best knowledge available; we have to have research inform everything we do. I want *all* parents to say, "Meet my child's needs." That's their job. But in our job, we're not in the business of educating one group of students. As professionals we're responsible for educating everyone, and there are things that we must not do. That's a moral and professional issue.

Teachers' own experiences also contradict the notion that more confident learners are held back in heterogeneous classes. As teacher Suzy Ronfeldt of the Albany Unified School District in California explained to Nancy Kreinberg and Harriet Nathan in *Teachers' Voices, Teachers' Wisdom:*

> During our first untracked year when we also did more cooperative learning, some parents felt their children were just helping others to learn. They felt their children might be losing out, and they missed being able to say "My Sally is in the top math group."
>
> I had to talk about several of the positive aspects of untracked classrooms. First of all, when a child has to explain her thinking and reasoning so another child understands it, she clarifies her thoughts and really learns what she is trying to teach. Second, you begin to realize that each child has his

or her own way of conceptualizing. Third, if you are able to put yourself in the other person's shoes and see how he thinks and interprets, your own understanding is enriched.

In a classroom that honors children's thinking and problem solving, tracking is too narrowing. How do you track children as they try to figure out which is longer—the length of the fifth-grade hall or the height of the school building? As my class worked in groups of four on this problem one of them had posed, they arrived at a rich variety of strategies.

One group used the large outside blocks on the building to figure the height. Another group used string tied to a piece of tanbark and threw it from one roof level to another to measure the height. Another group got hold of the blueprints for the building. Still another group measured the two levels of stairs using each step to figure some of the building height. Another group simply went outside and held their hands as blinders on each side of their head then sighted in on the length of the hall, turned their heads and sighted in on the height of the building. The last group took down the architects's drawing from the office wall and measured the length and height from that. Do you label one of these strategies as the "gifted" approach or are they all "gifted" approaches?

In Albany, I have not had questions about tracking from the parents in the last three years. They seem to feel their children are being challenged.

"Won't 'slower' students feel overwhelmed by their 'smarter' counterparts in heterogeneous classes?"

Children with learning disabilities or others who benefit from different kinds of explanations may derive the most noticeable benefits from heterogeneous grouping. Exposed to grade-level curriculum, instruction that conveys high expectations for their learning, and concrete support, these students make significant gains that can narrow achievement gaps between their performance and the accomplishments of the more confident learners. Self-esteem also improves as students experience access to learning in heterogeneous groups that have no stigma attached to them.

According to Darcy Yearley, Director of Guidance and Student Support Services at the Wellesley Middle School:

One of the most important lessons we've come to learn is that good instruction in regular classes is good for kids with learning disabilities. After we began integrating special education students in heterogeneous classes, we had only

one "D" the first term and two "D"s the second term. In only
two cases did children achieve less than satisfactory.

Remember, for these kids, school has always been a risk.
These are the kids who always have to say, "I don't get it."
We've been exhilarated by the tenacity these students have
shown in going after knowledge now that they have the
chance.

We've also realized that the major reasons special education
students don't achieve has more to do with the failures of
adults than of students. We've been able to make heterogeneous grouping work for these kids as well as other kids
because we've improved our communication between regular
education and special education teachers, and we've improved
our communication between school and home.

**"I've read all the research documenting the harms of
tracking, but I'm still not sure whether it's tracking
itself that harms students or the inferior teaching and
curriculum offered in the low track. Couldn't we just
work harder to make the lower tracks better?"**

Principal John D'Auria of Wellesley Middle School has this to
say:

If we want students to learn only facts and information,
perhaps upgrading the lower tracks will be adequate. But if
we want all students to become intellectual risk-takers and
learn the skills necessary for lifelong learning, heterogeneous
grouping is superior to homogeneous grouping no matter
how good each track is.

Let's look at a question from a standardized I.Q. test as an
example. Here's an analogy: "A book is to an empty bookcase
as what? Take your pick from four alternative answers—
Three eggs is to a basket? A carton of eggs is to a refrigerator?
An egg is to a rooster? An egg is to a frying pan? Only one of
these answers is considered "right."

If we track our students, we will end up with all the students
who choose the "right" answer to questions like these in
one class called the "high" class. But several of the "wrong"
answers could be very good answers depending on how you
think about them. We want all our students to learn as many
varied and diverse strategies for solving problems as they
can, and we think that the way to do this is to expose them
to different ways of thinking so that they learn that there
is more than one way to process information and create
new knowledge.

Many of our classes spend time thinking about thinking. They consider questions such as "If thinking were like Lincoln Logs, what would thinking be like?" and "If thinking were like Tinker Toys, what would thinking be like?" The answers come slowly to questions like these, and often the kids who get the ball rolling are the kids who are willing to take risks and who don't have the experience of worrying that a "wrong" answer will knock them out of the top group.

Students interacting with a diverse group of peers learn to develop equally diverse ways of communicating ideas. Students who learn that everyone has something to contribute to understanding a problem develop skills in asking for help when they need it. Students working on assignments which require contributions from all students learn that effort often matters as much as ability. In short, heterogeneous groups offer students valuable learning experiences which tracked settings cannot provide no matter how good they may be.

Promoting Parent Knowledge about Tracking

Entrance to school brings with it forms and releases and assessments... and somehow the results of my tests got confused with those of another student.... I was placed in the vocational track, a euphemism for the bottom level. Neither I nor my parents realized what this meant. We had no sense that business math, typing, and English-Level D were dead ends. The current spate of reports on the schools criticizes parents for not involving themselves in the education of their children. But how would someone like Tommy Rose, with his two years of Italian schooling, know what to ask? And what sort of pressure could an exhausted waitress apply? The error went undetected, and I remained in the vocational track for two years.

—Mike Rose, *Lives on the Boundary: The Struggles and Achievements of America's Underprepared, 1989*

If, in principle, *all* parents need to be informed about school grouping practices, too often only a few of them are familiar with unspoken norms that *seem* unremarkable but may have enormous impact on the future of their children. For example, many parents believe that math 8 is the only eighth-grade math course, whereas in reality it may be the lowest track in a particular school's math sequence. Other parents may not realize that enrollment in certain "gatekeeping" courses, such as pre-algebra and algebra in the middle grades, predetermines later access to enrollment in higher-level courses at the high-school level.

When sociologist Elizabeth Useem reviewed district and school placement policies and interviewed parents of seventh graders about their children's course placement in math, she discovered that access to "high" levels of math in the middle grades varies considerably from district to district. In some districts fewer than 15 percent of eighth graders are placed in algebra, compared with 50 percent in others, with more highly educated parents favoring enrollments in advanced math.

Useem also found that patterns of enrollment vary with the degree of school tolerance for parent involvement, and that schools use a variety of policies to discourage parents who seek to enroll their children in higher-level math courses. In particular, in districts with the lowest enrollments in "gatekeeping" courses, Useem found that:

- Many schools do not give parents all the information that they need about course sequences and their implications to enable them to make wise choices.
- Some schools tell parents that enrollment in the "high" curriculum will "mess up" a student's schedule, particularly if, after trying the course, a student decides to drop down a level.
- Course-planning materials for parents and students often use language discouraging enrollment at the high level. Courses are described as "fast paced and rigorous" or for students who are "mathematically talented" or have "exceptional ability," rather than simply "able" or "interested."
- Standardized test scores are often used as a rigid "cut-off" mechanism. When standardized tests are not the sole criterion for course selection, local tests are used to persuade parents that their children are not qualified for high-level groupings in *that* district.
- Parents are discouraged from pushing for "overrides" of school-placement decisions by requiring school conferences with teachers or requesting that parents sign waivers according to which they assume full responsibility for any future failure of their children in accelerated courses.

The ability of parents to be involved in decisions about course assignment depends largely on the school's belief in the capacity of all students to learn. Moreover, parents' access to decision making varies dramatically according to social status. For example, when there *is* parental involvement in course-placement decisions, parents of African-American and Latino students are involved only half as often as those of white students.

As the National Urban League and the Educational Testing Service found in surveys of thousands of parents in six cities, parents do believe that the level at which a student is placed

Information for Parents and Citizens about Tracking

All parents need and have the right to the facts about tracking in their schools. Educators can go a long way toward providing this information by making clear both the formal and informal mechanisms that underlie tracking arrangements in each school. In *Making the Best of Schools: A Handbook for Parents, Teachers, and Policymakers,* Jeannie Oakes and Martin Lipton make suggestions about general information that parents should have in order to establish a common ground for discussion with schools about tracking. They recommend that schools make public:

- The scope of the tracking policy, whether determined by the district or defined within the school

- How decisions are made about track placement

- How teachers are assigned to classrooms

- The number of classes in which subjects and grades are tracked

- All curriculum choices available in each subject

- The kinds of material in each curriculum

- The number of children moving from low tracks onto higher levels each year

- The percentage of students enrolled in each track by race and grade compared with those percentages overall

- Expectations for the future of students in each curriculum

Answers to these questions can be gathered through interviews, observations, questionnaires, or an analysis of school records. Sometimes the process of asking such questions can in itself begin a positive dialogue; at other times, the process may reveal strong fears of and resistance to change. But the sharing of such information is a critical step toward defining and addressing the problem of educational inequity resulting from tracking.

makes a difference in learning, especially in math, and many expressed a desire to be involved in placement decisions. Like the low-income parents in Elizabeth Useem's study, however, few urban parents know that there is any choice of math available to eighth graders, even when they are aware of the existence of different course levels, ranging from "basic" through "honors." Moreover, few parents, outside of some whose children attend magnet schools, know how schools decide which students will be placed in gatekeeping eighth-grade math courses; and although some believe that schools can be responsive "if you push the issue," generally they observe that schools make their decisions first, leaving parents to review those decisions after the fact.

The Challenge for Parents: Asking the "Right Questions"

> Low-income parents are constantly discovering—through the experience of their children—the fault lines in public education, but how does their knowledge inform both research and practice? How can we link what parents know at critical junctures to what researchers name as the problem? What might happen if researchers and educators could learn more about the benchmarks along the path toward educational failure as observed by parents and if parents could name the manifestations of the problems the experts use to predict the same outcome?
>
> —Dan Rothstein, The Right Question Project

Whereas upper-income parents frequently understand the implications of a placement decision and also have the skills to negotiate about a situation that may be detrimental to their children, low-income parents may not have these advantages. Some parents, for example, may not know the "right questions" to ask or feel confident about asking any questions at all, even when they intuitively understand that their children's future is at stake. The Right Question Project works with low-income parents in urban school districts to develop and create strategies for engaging them in decision-making processes that affect their children.

Through a series of community-based workshops, the project endeavors to translate the formal parlance of educators such as "tracking" and "academic placement" into a language that helps parents "name" the matter at hand in their own terms. After having attended the workshops they can say to themselves, "That's pretty clear why that's an important issue for my kid"

and "Now I have some ideas about what I can do about it."
Rothstein, project director, describes how a workshop on
tracking focuses on the impact of grouping on children:

> We give each participant two sheets of paper stapled together.
> On the first page we write: "What Your Child Should Learn:
> The Curriculum for All the District's Schoolchildren."
> Underneath is a drawing (an original by a six-year-old) of a
> boy and a girl sharing a book, standing under a smiling sun.
>
> On the second page we write: "The full curriculum is 100
> pages long." On half of the papers we hand out a second page
> that reads: "Your child will be taught the full 100 pages." The
> other half of the papers state: "Your child will be taught only
> the first 50 pages."
>
> We then ask parents what they received. (We ask for
> volunteers because if some parents cannot read, they will also
> be able to participate fully.) When the parents who received a
> curriculum that states that their child will be taught only the
> first 50 pages hear that others are being taught the full 100
> pages, they ask:
>
>> Why is my child only being taught 50 pages?
>> What does it mean that he's only taught 50?
>> Who made that decision?
>> When was it made?
>> Why is this important?
>> If I want to know, is this something I have a right to know?
>> Am I supposed to be involved? Can I be?
>
> On a few of the papers we put down some grades in English
> and math. The grades were all "A"s. We ask what kinds of
> questions the parents have about the grades. Here are some:
>
>> What does the "A" mean?
>> Does it mean the same for the 100- and 50-page
>>   curriculum?
>> Do they tell us somehow on the report card which
>>   curriculum it belongs to?
>
> We then ask them to reflect on the significance of the grades.
> One father said: "If I didn't know that there are different
> programs, then I'd be happy if my son brought home "A"s.
> But I'd be pretty upset if I knew there was a 25-page
> curriculum, a 50-page curriculum, and a 100-page curriculum."

Parents' newfound awareness of the consequences of placement
decisions and differential curriculum for their children leads to
further questions. Frequently African-American, Latino, and low-
income parents may begin to wonder about the likelihood of

their children being assigned to the "low" classes, and decide to take action to change that placement. Understanding the implications of tracking can also become the basis for parent-initiated review of systemwide placement practices and collective action for change.

Community-Based Pressure for Untracking

> Reformers who emphasize "quality," and who mean by it higher expectations for all, will be tolerated only to the point where they can find a willing audience; beyond that point they will be resisted.
>
> —Arthur G. Powell, Eleanor Farrar, and David K. Cohen, *The Shopping Mall High School,* 1985

Resistance to change is not the exclusive province of parents. In fact, in some districts, expanded consciousness about tracking is leading to the formation of citizen groups seeking to challenge grouping practices in schools where educators themselves resist untracking. Sometimes these groups are composed of parents alone. Sometimes they are made up of parents in coalition with teachers and other citizens with a common concern about improving the quality of education for all students. These groups can be a powerful force for untracking.

Building a Constituency for Change Through Information-Gathering and Education

Parent advocacy for particular placements traditionally benefits individual students, but parents collaborating together may challenge tracking practices for an entire school or district. In fact, educators who support change may have no stronger allies than parents and citizens knowledgeable about the extent and harm of tracking. Community-education efforts that raise the level of public awareness about grouping practices can create a positive context for change.

In Albany, New York, the Albany Citizens for Education (ACE) has developed a context within which alternatives to tracking can be discussed openly. Founded in the throes of an electoral campaign designed to endorse a set of independent, nonmachine candidates for the Albany School Board, ACE is made up of parents and citizens intent on improving education for all students in that urban district. Over several years, citizens have succeeded in electing a reform-minded majority to the school board. At the same time, with more openness on the board, ACE members have worked closely with board committees, including one mandated to develop a Strategic Plan for Albany Public Schools.

Included in that plan, approved by the board in 1990, is a recommendation that the tracking system at every level in Albany schools be replaced or modified.

ACE's early information-gathering efforts that led to this recommendation raised key questions pertaining to districtwide grouping practices. In a letter to the superintendent, ACE began its research by asking for data on students placed in the district's "academically talented" classrooms, background on procedures used for selecting students for these classes, and information about curriculum differences between that program and "regular" classrooms. After a long waiting period, district staff responded with information that enabled ACE to clarify district tracking policies for parents.

With the district's tracking policies finally available in writing, ACE moved forward to make placement policies more widely known through public forums and school-board meetings. But ACE members also wanted to put out the message that alternatives to tracking could improve schooling across the board and that all children could benefit from curriculum and instruction currently offered to only the most able students. Therefore, during the school year 1990–91, ACE joined with the Urban League of the Albany Area, the Albany NAACP, and the City School District of Albany itself to sponsor a Saturday conference "to promote a long-term, broad-based effort to enrich, diversify, and strengthen education in Albany."

Despite cold winter weather, approximately two hundred people joined ACE and its partners at the all-day conference. The theme "Tapping Every Talent: Expanding Achievement Opportunities for All Students" conveyed the belief that education must and could be improved in heterogeneous settings. Reinforcing the theme that *all* students have gifts and talents to be developed, workshops highlighted research on tracking, effective instructional strategies, and successful programs. In addition, a local attorney offered a workshop called "Advocating for Your Child in a Tracked System," which focused on the kinds of decisions used to place children in academic tracks and techniques for obtaining standardized test scores. With the energy level still high at the end of the day, participants convened in the school cafeteria to collect recommendations from each workshop. Several participants advocated specific programs. Others, with heightened awareness of the variety of alternatives available, expressed a sense of urgency about pressing for more general tracking reforms.

ACE has begun to see some results from these efforts. In 1991, the district moved to reduce the number of tracks from four to three and adopted a transitional math curriculum to replace the practice of introducing algebra to a selected group of "high" students in seventh grade. While public debate continued at Albany School Board meetings, the School Department formed several committees including parents, teachers, and administrators to research alternative approaches. After several months of meetings and investigation, including field trips to other communities, committee members became excited about "Project Opportunity"—a promising model that they observed in Ithaca, New York, which encompassed both curriculum enrichment in heterogeneous classes and built-in opportunities for strengthening teachers' skills. Although change will begin in the elementary grades, parents will not stop there. As Joan Ekengren, a parent member of ACE, reports, "We just have to keep persevering and hammering away at the issue, it seems. We hope that people will realize we're not going to drop this. It's too important!"

Challenging Resegregation in Tracked Schools

A desegregated school system does not necessarily provide equal education for everyone. In Selma, Alabama, the resegregation of the schools through a tracking system has become the focus of parent and citizen pressure mobilized through a citizen organization called the Best Educational Support Team (BEST). BEST works to address inequities in a district where materials and facilities in predominantly African-American elementary schools are demonstrably inferior to those of white schools and where, in the high school in 1988, only 3 percent of the African-American students were enrolled in the highest track, known as Level 1.

Since its inception, BEST has worked to reform the tracking system and its effect of resegregating African-American and white students into virtually separate within-school systems. Assignment to tracks was based solely on teacher recommendation without clear criteria for making selections. Thus it was possible for African-American students who were as capable as whites to be excluded from such Level 1 courses as algebra 1, biology 1, or computer sciences—and the future opportunities inherent in them.

BEST's arguments against tracking, bolstered by data demonstrating its discriminatory effects, resulted in changes in criteria for placement in Level 1, with grade-point averages and test scores replacing teacher recommendations. This change alone boosted the enrollment of African-Americans in the highest track to 10 percent. However, protests by white parents also followed, and in December 1989, the school board's white majority voted not to renew the contract of Selma's African-American superintendent, Dr. Norward Roussell. As BEST member Rose Sanders said, "Only when [Dr. Roussell] moved to get rid of the tracking system, did they move to get rid of him."

Since that time, citizen boycotts and student sit-ins have marked Selma's community protests. Both white and African-American students increasingly realize the impact of tracking on their lives. As student Malika Sanders, a member of Students Marching Against Racial Tracking (SMART), the students' counterpart to BEST, told *Rethinking Schools:*

> I think a lot of Level 1 students are beginning to understand that everyone should get a chance to take Level 1 courses. In Level 2 and 3 they don't give you college preparatory courses, they just give you the basics.... The Level system has leveled the confidence of the students. But it's not true that they can't do the work. I've taken some Level 1 courses, and I can tell you that they are not that hard. Everyone should have a choice whether they want to take these courses or not.

In addition, BEST members have taken to the road to speak out against tracking at community forums across the country. As BEST member Connie Tucker says, "The powers that be think we will get tired, but folks are not willing to let this die."

Community "Consciousness-Raising" for Citizens and Educators

At the eastern end of Long Island, New York, the National Association for the Advancement of Colored People (NAACP) has a long history of concern about the educational achievement of African-American students in the schools of the region. In 1990, some branch members started to wonder: "Has public education, 'the great equalizer' in the words of Horace Mann, become the great tranquilizer instead?" "To keep things quiet, are troublesome students shunted to separate classrooms or even buildings under the guise of special education?" "Are some students on the low-ability track, the one that rarely leads to college, put there simply because they are members of minorities?"

To explore these issues, the group's Education Committee sought information through a series of letters and freedom-of-information requests about what kinds of programs the students that they represented were experiencing. What they learned was disturbing. As similar inquiries have revealed, African-Americans at East End schools were overrepresented in special education and underrepresented in high-level honors classes. Given this pattern, it is not surprising that almost half of the white graduates went to four-year colleges, whereas only 16 percent of the African-Americans did so.

With these data in hand, the organization initiated a series of informational meetings to raise awareness about unequal educational opportunity and discuss remedies. First, they invited York College education professor James C. Hall, Jr., to speak to branch members, teachers, and parents about the benefits of mixing children of disparate abilities and backgrounds in classrooms at all levels. Second, the committee prodded the Suffolk County Chief School Administrators Association and the local Board of Cooperative Educational Services (BOCES) into cosponsoring an afternoon "awareness" conference for educators to expand understanding of both research related to tracking and alternatives.

Along with an official from New York State's Department of Education and several Long Island school principals, the panel of speakers included Dr. Dominic Annacone, former superintendent of the Sag Harbor School District. Dr. Annacone described how Pierson High School's planning process had included "at least ten meetings" with parents to discuss concerns that curriculum would be "watered down" for the most confident students and that special education students would be in "over their heads." These concerns, he explained, were addressed over and over in packed meetings prior to the opening of the new school year. But once parents had seen changes for themselves, they were enthusiastic. Two months into the school year, Dr. Annacone reported, only four parents turned out for a review meeting.

Community-School Partnerships for School Reform

In California, The Achievement Council, an organization dedicated to increasing academic achievement among Latino, African-American, and low-income students of all ethnic groups, is demonstrating how community-based organizations can work effectively with schools to forge a vision of schoolwide improvement dedicated to closing the achievement gap between these students and other young people. Part of that vision is the untracking of curriculum in order to open college-preparatory opportunities to underrepresented students. Another goal is to change conditions that reinforce patterns of low student achievement, including categorical programs that sort students into separate groups with different curricular and instructional approaches.

The council's framework for change begins with an analysis of the *culture* of each school—the values, attitudes, and norms that influence behavior, relationships, and expectations. In assessing school culture, the council follows key principles that shape each of its projects: the principles that 1) "all students deserve a rigorous core curriculum, rich in concepts and ideas, drawing on the best sources to stimulate both analysis and awareness of the underpinnings of world culture"; and 2) that "all students benefit from heterogeneous groups for most learning activities." The Achievement Council also acts on the belief that educators, students, and parents together form a community of interest for school improvement, with school staff exercising professional responsibilities to translate the vision into a cooperative action plan. These core beliefs are critical to guiding the council's projects for improving student achievement for the state's most vulnerable students.

There are four central elements in the Achievement Council's strategy to implement change in low-performing schools: 1) expanding the accountability system and improving professional performance; 2) implementing a rigorous curriculum for all students; 3) developing staff-development and school-improvement programs in low-performing schools; and 4) undertaking an aggressive statewide initiative to address low student achievement. This four-pronged strategy generates such activities as a statewide Principals' Institute, which is designed to identify effective approaches to school improvement while pairing principals who have been successful in turning around their schools with others who want assistance to develop a blueprint for change. A Guidance Counselors' Infusion Model has also been fashioned to support counselors as change agents in their schools so that the number of students who enter college-level courses may be increased, the college pipeline may be opened early in a student's career, and teacher expectations may be modified.

Other activities of the council involve promotion of a challenging curriculum for all students, especially in mathematics; an emerging parent involvement project; and a concerted effort to link the needs of staff in urban schools with resources to nurture and sustain school-based reform and professional growth. Working with low-performing schools in Los Angeles and San Francisco, the council's ultimate objective is to enlarge the pool of college-eligible Latino and African-American students by strengthening their preparation for and access to college preparatory courses.

Ultimately, says Jean Adenika of The Achievement Council, real school reform requires providing access to educational opportunities that are equal to those offered in the "best" schools. By fostering school-community partnerships for change, The Achievement Council develops institutional efforts that go beyond those of individual guidance counselors, teachers, or community groups to contribute valuable community-based support and resources for school changes, including untracking, to close achievement gaps schoolwide.

National Citizens' Organizations

Citizens' groups and student-advocacy organizations increasingly realize that tracking undermines the achievement of most students. Organizations such as the National Coalition of Advocates for Students, Quality Education for Minorities Project, and the Hispanic Policy Development Project have taken strong positions against tracking. In addition, as attention to the issue of tracking intensifies, citizens' organizations outside of traditional educational circles have also become involved. These include the National Coalition of Education Activists, a multiracial organization of parents, teachers, and citizens working for fundamental school reform including high-quality heterogeneous classes; Schools Are for Everyone, a national coalition of families, consumers, and advocates united in the belief that "all children learn best in heterogeneous classrooms where individual differences are celebrated"; and Rethinking Schools, a working group of teachers and citizens, which publishes a bimonthly newspaper concerned with issues of democracy and equity in education, including tracking and multiculturalism. Each of these organizations promotes educational materials and events to support a growing network of activist teachers, citizens, and parents seeking alternatives to tracking.

Parents, Teachers, and the Community: Together Is Better

Untracking proceeds more smoothly when everyone affected is informed and involved. In some communities, it is parents who first raise doubts about the compatibility of tracking with the goal of excellent education for all students. Parent concerns provoke educators to explore their own capacity for change, examine their beliefs about the nature of intelligence, assess their preparation for working with academically integrated classrooms, and launch "catch-up" efforts to learn about effective teaching approaches for heterogeneous classes.

In other school districts, principals and teachers are eager to adopt innovative approaches for heterogeneous classrooms, whereas parents are the ones who worry that losses of the "safer" traditional classrooms will outweigh promised gains or that the end of tracking will result in fewer supports or challenges for their children. In these communities, parents first need information about the nature of proposed changes to increase their willingness to work with school staff and strengthen their confidence that a school-parent partnership represents an honest alliance to support the learning of all children.

2 · *Expecting the Best*

Determination + Discipline + Hard Work = Success

—Formula placed next to the clock in the classroom of Jaime Escalante, teacher, Garfield High School, Los Angeles

Studies of schooling consistently find that differences in teacher expectations for student learning vary dramatically according to group label and placement, which in turn justify those expectations. Students from whom more is expected produce more; students from whom less is expected produce less, even when this result is not intended. Typically, distribution of grades reflects a bell-shaped curve with only a finite number of students achieving at high levels. Students in the highest tracks are most likely to receive "A"s; those in the lowest tracks frequently receive "D"s or failing grades.

Not surprisingly, the skewing of success in this way alters the climate of classrooms and entire schools. For example, researchers Jeannie Oakes and Martin Lipton tell of a high school that, after adding an "honors" calculus class to its math program, found that student performance declined overall. With the establishment of a "top track," students and teachers alike came to assume that *only* students ranked at the top could achieve at the highest levels, and all involved expected less than before of those in the regular class. In this way, tracking institutionalizes the perception of intelligence as a fixed characteristic that some students have "more" of, while others have "less."

Untracking schools reject both the unequal distribution of high expectations for student performance and the inevitability of a bell-shaped curve of achievement. Rather, common to almost all untracking schools is the expectation that nearly all students can and will learn at the highest levels, coupled with a schoolwide commitment to create learning environments necessary to help students *become* smart.

Teacher Expectations and Untracking: The Vital Link

The most pervasive, institutionalized, and entrenched forms of differential educational treatment for low-income and nonwhite children appear in regular classrooms, as part of the daily routine and mundane transactions between students and teachers.

—Richard deLone, *Small Futures*

Classroom observations conducted by researchers such as Thomas L. Good and Jere E. Brophy have revealed that teachers, like anyone, are subject to unconscious biases that surface in the unequal distribution of attention to high- and low-performing students. In practice, despite teachers' best intentions, those students whom teachers perceive as being most able to achieve often receive teachers' most positive attention, whereas those regarded as "low achievers" are least likely to receive the kind of teacher intervention that aids in learning. For example, Good and Brophy have found that:

- Teacher interaction with "low achievers" is less motivating and less supportive than interaction with "high achievers"
- Teachers may ask "high achievers" three to four times more questions than they ask "low achievers"
- Teachers tend to give "high achievers" more time to respond to questions than they give "low achievers"
- When "high achievers" do have difficulty, teachers tend to probe, give clues, or rephrase questions more frequently than with "low achievers"

Observing eighty-nine middle-level math classrooms to understand differences in interaction between teachers and students from one ability level to another, Ruth B. Eckstrom and Ana Maria Villegas also found that academically oriented teacher-student interactions were significantly more frequent in classes labeled "high ability" than in those designated "low ability." In low-level classes, teachers spent more time giving behavior-oriented comments, which were usually critical in nature. More-over, in classrooms at all levels, minority students received five criticisms for every critical remark made to a white student and six behaviorally oriented comments for every one made to a white student.

Differences in subtle interchanges between teachers and students constitute an often invisible form of prejudice—what author Richard deLone has called "discrimination by expectation." When teachers unconsciously communicate with students in disparate ways, the children placed in low-level courses quickly learn that they are not required to focus on academics. Furthermore, with the virtual assurance that they will not be called on, or that they will receive attention from their teachers more for disciplinary than academic reasons, many lose motivation for learning. Ironically, the resulting differences in student engagement often become further grounds for student sorting and grouping.

Communicating High Expectations

> If we had even an iota of belief in our children, we'd keep teaching them until they learn. How dare we give up on them?
>
> —Lorene Cary, writer

The belief that all students can learn at high levels and the conviction that teachers play the most significant role in that learning are put into operation first in the classroom. In classrooms where these beliefs prevail, staff do not point to poverty, family needs, or inherent ability as insurmountable hurdles to learning. They *do* ask themselves, "What do I have to do better to help my students learn?" and then adopt practices that communicate to students that they are expected to put forth their best effort in everything that they do.

What constitutes "high expectations" in middle-level schools? These are as variable and diverse as teaching itself; and as teachers put research findings into practice, expectations become real in all kinds of ways—ranging from the physical organization of the classroom to academic assignments and disciplinary strategies. For example:

In a combined seventh and eighth-grade social-studies class:

The subject is Ireland. Teacher Kathy Greeley takes green chalk and draws a big circle representing Ireland on the blackboard. She asks how many of the students have some Irish heritage and what they know about Ireland, listing student responses on the board. She then asks what the most common language for the Irish is and if anyone knows why it is English. As she acknowledges different children, she asks them to identify their respective backgrounds and the major language in their country of origin. Moving to a large world map on which purple yarn links their city in the United States to the countries of each student's heritage, she points them out: Haiti, the Dominican Republic, Ethiopia, Yugoslavia, Ireland, and others.

Greeley then introduces a taped song about Irish immigration, passing out a sheet with the words on it and giving some brief background information. As she plays the music, the students listen carefully, reading the verses and sometimes humming to the refrain. When the song ends, Greeley reviews each stanza asking: "Who's speaking?" "How do you know?" "Whom is John sending money to?" "Why?" "How does this song make you feel?" One student says that the song reminds him of his father, who died the previous year, and he feels sad.

Greeley links the son's story and student reactions to Irish history. Describing measures that denied the Irish the right to vote, carry a gun, or use their native language in their own country, she asks students why they think such rules existed and if they are aware of similar laws in the modern world. The children respond with information about Turks in Greece and indigenous groups in Central America, and one student describes the status of Jews in Hitler's Germany.

When the students' information is wrong, Greeley responds, "Not a bad theory, but not correct" or "Try again, but think about it in these terms...." She probes, posing such questions as "Why do you think that...?" "What do you infer from...?" "Can you give other examples of...?" "How do you think they felt when...?" or "How does that compare with the situation today?" She calls on those with their hands raised, but she also asks the children who have not raised their hands to answer particular questions. As she walks among the desks, lightly touching the students' shoulders and suggesting points that deserve special attention, Greeley makes a special attempt to engage children who appear to be restless or are talking out of turn.

Lessons can communicate high expectations if they:

- Build on and validate students' prior knowledge and experience
- Help students construct their own knowledge
- Communicate information in a variety of ways
- Engage in dialogue that evokes more than one-word answers
- Require thinking skills such as comparing, contrasting, and applying knowledge
- Incorporate students' own cultural backgrounds into learning
- Involve students through a variety of activities that engage different kinds of intelligence
- Involve all students whether or not they volunteer answers or comments

During the first week of a double-period seventh-grade class:

Miss Elizabeth holds the small Nerf football as the class sits quietly in a circle. "Izzy," she says, handing the ball to the boy on her right. Izzy takes the ball and yells "Tashem!" at the boy across from him and tosses him the football. Tashem makes an effort to get the ball back across the circle, establishing eye contact with Charles and calling his name, but the ball slips past Charles's hand and falls toward the floor. The group groans collectively, but the ball falls into Marcee's lap without touching the ground. They are saved.

After the football makes a complete journey through the group without touching the floor, the ball starts its course again, following the same path. This time, however, students pass a tennis ball right after the Nerf ball. As long as neither ball touches the ground, the group juggle is a success. As the group succeeds in passing the balls around successfully in the allowed twenty minutes, another ball is added. The first time, the group collectively juggles the balls just once. But only a few weeks later, the students manage to help one another pass three balls around the circuit. Their goal is ten; by then, it is likely that all students will understand that each of them is equally valued and needed in the classroom.

A teacher communicates high expectations for students by:

- Introducing activities in which every individual becomes invested in the group effort
- Communicating that making mistakes is part of learning and that practice and concentration promote improvement

- Creating an environment of mutual trust and cooperation among students and between students and the teacher
- Arranging seating in such a way that no student is "invisible" to the teacher or others

In a sixth-grade language-arts classroom:

Julia Young's classroom wall sports the following reminder:

"Finished Early? What Can You Do?"

1. Write anagrams of your vocabulary words
2. Select an interesting book to read
3. Write a different ending for your story
4. Write an original story using ten vocabulary words
5. Read a classmate's reading journal

Permanent classroom "decorations" can convey high expectations so that:

- Students understand that learning continues beyond the completion of a classroom assignment and that "extra" time is still learning time
- Students work in an environment that stresses their responsibility for their own learning
- Teachers are relieved of the necessity of repeating directions related to assignments, allowing them to remain engaged in coaching or dialogue with students

In a seventh-grade language-arts class in a two-way bilingual school:

According to teacher María Campanario, "The way to build expectations is that you don't assume ability level. What you assume is that every child wants to learn." On her feet every minute, she moves around the room in a review of essay-writing skills:

> CAMPANARIO: "I've never seen a paragraph in my life. You're the teacher. Tell me how I can tell a paragraph."
> ZAIDA: "By the punctuation."
> CAMPANARIO: "By the punctuation. Does it have sentences?"
> ZAIDA: "Yes."
> CAMPANARIO: "Is there anything else you can tell me, teacher?" *(Zaida hesitates; Campanario waits.)* "Okay. Let me give you an example." *(Without reading it, Campanario holds up a piece of paper with a paragraph written on it.)* "Explain it to me. Describe the paragraph form. *(Silence)* How about the first

line? Is it in the same place?"

ZAIDA: "No. It's indented."

CAMPANARIO: "Indented! A paragraph is indented. All the way?
Every time?"

ZAIDA: "Only at the beginning. Just at the first line."

CAMPANARIO: "Well, I've never written a paragraph before.
How do I know when I'm finished?"

MEGAN: "Well, when you write five sentences…"

CAMPANARIO: "Oh, so five sentences is a paragraph?"

ARTIE: "NO!"

YOHEL: "A paragraph can be five or six or seven sentences as
long as it talks about one topic."

CAMPANARIO: "So each paragraph has one topic. I'm not too
good with vocabulary. Can you define a topic for me?"

ISAAC: "It's about the same thing."

CAMPANARIO: "You mean if I say that my dog likes to chew
slippers and pee on the bed, I'm talking about the same
thing?"

ISAAC: "You cut it into sections so one paragraph talks about
the dog peeing on the bed."

MEGAN: "Each paragraph talks about a single thing."

CAMPANARIO: (*To everyone*) "So I can become a great paragraph
writer?"

CLASS: "YES!"

A teacher can communicate high expectations by:

- Allowing students plenty of time to answer questions
- Giving hints and working with students if the answer does not
  come quickly
- Creating a student-teacher partnership in the uncovering
  of knowledge
- Putting students in the role of teacher

In a middle-grades math classroom:

The bulletin board beside Joanne Hatem's front desk is titled
"Careers." True to its name, it conveys information about a variety
of work opportunities, including job requirements and salaries.
Alongside this information is a cartoon in which a female student
addresses a male student: "I'm going to be a famous doctor when
I grow up. Would you like to be my nurse?" On another bulletin
board entitled "Weekly News," one student's name is posted as
"Student of the Week"; a note congratulates the basketball team;
and a third item welcomes a new student to class. In the back of
the room, students' models of nineteenth-century textile mills are
on display.

A classroom environment can communicate high expectations by:

- Letting students know that their schoolwork is preparing them for life, not just the next grade
- Providing images and information that encourage students to stretch their aspirations to include the possibility of a wide range of future options
- Distributing legitimate recognition to as many students as possible in as many ways as possible
- Assigning projects that require extended effort
- Providing examples of high-quality work as models of what is expected from the class

In a combined seventh-and-eighth-grade homeroom:

At the end of a day that began with a gathering where four students were recognized for helping to create a better learning environment in the classroom, teacher Kathy Greeley congratulates Domingo and asks, "Do you understand why you were chosen for that award?" When Domingo says only "I think so," Greeley cites specific examples of some important and challenging questions that he had asked in class without having denigrated other students in the process. "But Simon does that, too," Domingo says. Greeley agrees but replies, "The way you handled that subject, especially when some of the others were still confused about the story, was very helpful to everyone."

Praise from teachers can reinforce high expectations when:

- Praise informs students about the value of their accomplishments and orients them toward a better appreciation of their thinking and problem-solving abilities
- Praise focuses on the specifics of the accomplishment
- Praise is authentic and leaves students convinced that the teacher has given thoughtful consideration to performance and means what she says

In an eighth-grade multidisciplinary cluster, all students who sign up for the Discovery Academy also sign a contract designed by teacher Barbara Ernst-Digennaro and ready to go home to parents the first day of school:

DISCOVERY ACADEMY CONTRACT (1989–90)

I hereby agree to support my child's learning by:

- Assuring prompt and regular attendance
- Providing regular time and space for my child to do homework
- Reading, discussing, signing, and returning my child's weekly evaluation
- Attending a midyear conference

I also give permission for my child to accompany the class on all Discovery Academy trips.

    Parent signature:_____

I hereby agree to:

- Come to school promptly and be prepared
- Follow school and class rules
- Do all homework and class assignments
- Pay for extra activities when required

    Student signature:_____

A classroom can create high expectations through:

- A set of explicit guidelines that emphasize the school, parents, and students working together as a team
- Parental involvement in monitoring and supporting their children's work
- Provisions for keeping parents informed of student progress through regular and frequent reports, not just at report-card time
- Regular face-to-face meetings between teachers and parents

In the hallways and principal's office...

Two students race through a corridor engaged in usual twelve-year-old horseplay. The principal calls them by name and smiles. "Come on into my office for a minute."

The two run in and take seats in a group of chairs placed at a distance from the principal's desk. After a brief exchange of words about running in the halls, the principal asks, "Why do you think I stopped you?"

"Because we were going to trip..."

"Naw, because we were wrecking the quiet up there and the classes had started."

The principal confirms the answers and then proceeds to talk about other interests of the students.

"Are you still interested in the leadership group?"

"Yes, when will it start?"

"We'll figure that out soon. We need to get more students involved. Stop by later and let me know if you have any ideas for doing that."

The students leave, assuring the principal that they will not race to class. Their teachers will note their tardy arrival in classes, which have started without the reminder of loud, institutional bells, and a second conversation will reinforce the students' commitment to improving their behavior.

In situations calling for disciplinary action, adults can reinforce high expectations by:

- Using every occasion to encourage students to discover their own responsibility to respect others
- Treating disciplinary discussions as serious enough to warrant privacy and confidentiality
- Building on a potentially alienating situation to engage and reconnect students with positive school experiences by soliciting their suggestions for improving school life

Schools that create a climate of high expectations begin with the most intimate of interactions between the adults and children in the school. These interactions, as they accumulate, form a necessary foundation for untracking and underscore the most fundamental values of the untracking process: that all students regardless of economic or social background can master worthwhile academic and social challenges, and that it is the job of public schools to foster that mastery. The further challenge for untracking schools is to make high expectations the norm of the classroom and extend them throughout the school.

High Expectations and Whole-School Reform

The principle of high expectations is an enduring tenet of many school-reform efforts, including, for example, the Effective Schools Movement. In like manner, the belief that school climate should reflect the value of "unanxious expectation" ("I won't threaten you, but I expect much of you") is one of the nine common principles guiding the Coalition of Essential Schools.

Yet despite recognition that high expectations are essential for student success, this ingredient is frequently lacking in the lives of young adolescents—particularly in urban schools. For this reason, the Program for Disadvantaged Youth of the Edna McConnell Clark Foundation has put forward seven expected outcomes that should be attained in the middle grades:

1. Disadvantaged youth will gain the active involvement and support of their families in their educational development.
2. Disadvantaged youth will receive at least forty hours of competent, individual guidance each school year, designed to advance their educational development.
3. Disadvantaged youth will remain in school and successfully complete the required curriculum on time.
4. Disadvantaged youth will (a) take and successfully complete courses beyond those in the required curriculum, or (b) move from an ability group or curriculum track serving lower-achieving students to one serving higher-achieving students.
5. Disadvantaged youth will score above the fiftieth percentile on the comprehension section of a nationally normed, standardized reading test when taking the test for the first time.
6. Disadvantaged youth will participate in one or more high-quality courses or programs that increase their understanding of post-secondary career and education options, and of the relationship of those options to curricular choices in grades nine through twelve.
7. Disadvantaged youth will (a) enter the tenth grade with a written plan either to prepare for employment after high school or to pursue post-secondary education, and (b) will be helped by the school to enroll in curricula which will enable the students to carry out the plan.

These expectations set a standard for raising the educational expectations of all students in middle-level schools in any community. Equally important, they challenge those schools to shape every aspect of schooling so that their students can leave the intermediate level with a strong foundation for future success.

Making High Expectations a Norm

If you treat a person as he is, he will stay as he is; but if you treat him as if he were what he ought to be, he will become what he ought to be and could be.

—Sign displayed in the Teacher Planning Area, Sierra Middle School, Tucson, Arizona, 1991

As Ronald Edmonds wrote of improving schools in his studies of effective schools, "The school as a total environment has the capacity to depress or elevate individual teachers' capacity for effective or ineffective teaching." As important as individual teacher beliefs and interactions are to improving achievement, then, teachers themselves are more likely to maintain high expectations for student performance when their school as a whole reflects a commitment to developing student achievement and affirming the school as a community of learners. Communicating this norm of high expectations to all students is as important an aspect of untracking as the technical changes in curriculum and instruction.

In untracking schools, the schoolwide norm of high expectations grows out of a definition of students as citizens of the school community. Within this philosophical framework, every aspect of school life assists students in undertaking increasing levels of responsibility—not because responsibility is a privilege for a few but because it is a necessary part of educating everyone for life. While opportunities to contribute to school life bond students to the school community, additional routines emphasize the partnership of students and teachers in the learning process—with effort and opportunities for second chances recognized and encouraged as means to improved achievement. At the same time, in the spirit of an inclusive community that values every student's contribution, school staff consider ways in which they can eliminate labels that communicate a hierarchy of achievement.

Reinforcing School Citizenship Roles

Schools first build a norm of high expectations into regular routines by involving students in decisions that affect their lives. Settings in which students can practice citizenship skills offer opportunities for all students to have their opinions taken seriously and acted upon. Building these opportunities into school routines emphasizes that schools are institutions where students, no matter what their background, are expected to learn skills that prepare them for responsible adulthood in a democratic society.

At the Graham and Parks School, it is 9:00 on a Thursday morning in late October, and ninety seventh and eighth graders are arranging their chairs in a semi circle in preparation for the weekly "Community Meeting" with their teachers. On the front blackboard is the agenda in Spanish and English: 1) Student Council—Introduction and Issues; 2) Awards; 3) Black Student Union; 4) Other Items. One of the teachers opens the meeting, and the students settle down to discuss issues that they want raised at the next student council meeting.

One boy suggests that the school needs a longer recess, and others quickly support his comments. Another explains, "Recess seems too short, you know, because we aren't allowed to leave the classroom until we're all quiet, and sometimes this takes a few minutes." He says, "I don't understand why we have to be quiet just to leave the classroom for recess. I mean, isn't that what recess is all about—being able to talk with your friends?" Another student proposes a five-minute break between classes to allow time to go to the washroom without risking being late for the next class.

At this point, the teacher who is designated "Timekeeper" reminds students that they have time for only a few more suggestions if they are going to finish their agenda; she suggests that they write down any items that they would like to have addressed at the meeting on the agenda sheet posted in the hallway. Another teacher notes jokingly that in order to accommodate a longer recess and five minutes between classes, they might have to extend the school day by forty-five minutes. This suggestion proves that no one is asleep: the room is quickly abuzz as students reject the idea. The remaining few issues are suggested and commented on: field trips, initiating after-school sports, team and school spirit, and finally, "Let's have just one dance this year but make it a good one." All suggestions go on the list.

"Awards" is the next agenda topic. This is the time when teachers acknowledge a student from each class who merits special recognition. In turn, the teachers come to the front of the room and call a boy or girl forward for a photograph and citation. Acknowledgedgment is given for a variety of reasons:

1) most remarkable turnaround since the last quiz; 2) highest mark on an exam; 3) helping to create a challenging environment within the classroom; and 4) working hard and asking questions when information is not clear. Several students express surprise at being selected, but they come forward graciously while their classmates applaud.

In the previous year, Community Meeting had initiated a Black Student Union, and today one of the teachers wants to hear from the students whether they want to continue the union this year. She requests any interested students to contact her. This suggestion opens up a wide-ranging discussion. When the union began the previous year, it was an activity for black students only. Later, after much airing of beliefs that the union was splitting the school into groups, the attendance rules changed to include members of all races. Now these concerns are revived, and students begin speaking out of turn with their own interpretations about what happened the previous year. It takes a moment for teachers, then students, raising their hands high, to bring the group back to order. Carefully, one of the African-American teachers explains that the purpose of the Black Student Union was to help any interested student learn about black culture.

As the meeting ends, the boys and girls who have been recognized for their accomplishments are again acknowledged. Students are also reminded that they can write any ideas for the student council's agenda on the sheet in the hallway.

The Graham and Parks School is not alone among untracking schools in communicating the expectation that young adolescents can play responsible roles in the operation of the school. For example:

- At the Bartlett School, students are formally and anonymously asked for comments about their classroom teachers and assignments, and teachers use these comments as guides to reshape teaching and curriculum. In addition, students elected by their classmates participate in the "Principal's Cabinet."

- At the Wellesley Middle School, each lunchroom table is provided with a broom and dustpan, and a different student is responsible for cleaning up under the table each day. "Some people would never believe that young adolescent kids would pick up their own crumbs," says the school principal, "but they do."

- At Crete-Monee Junior High, during the first week of school, teachers orient all incoming students to "Pit-Stop Survival Skills," through an activity designed to help students assume more responsibility for organizing their day and be more punctual and better prepared for their classes. Using a floor plan of the school building, students draw pathways between their locker and their classrooms and anticipate such situations as the best time to return to their locker, use the washroom, or visit friends.

- At Crete-Monee, students can choose an elective on a par with band, chorus, or home economics to work as office aides for the principal, assistant principal, or guidance office. Students of all ability levels, including those with disabilities, answer the school telephone, deliver messages, make copies of classroom materials for teachers, or otherwise help in the daily tasks of running Crete-Monee.

- At the Middle School of the Kennebunks, students volunteer to help prepare breakfast and lunch, provide tours, and conduct workshops to describe school activities for guests attending the school's regular open house for visitors.

- At the Holyoke Magnet Middle School, students participate in the school's "town council," the decision-making body composed of teachers, parents, and students from the school community.

- At the end of each week at the Graham and Parks School, three students in each seventh- and eighth-grade class rotate clean-up duty, not as a punishment but as part of an understanding that their efforts contribute to the smooth functioning of the school. As all the children prepare to leave, the three designated for the week go to work with no prompting from their teacher: one student cleans the blackboard, another sweeps, while a third picks up chairs and stacks them on the desks.

- At the Louis Armstrong Middle School students volunteer as peer mediators to resolve disputes among themselves. As one sixth-grader said, "Peer mediation keeps small problems from turning into big ones. It helps to keep the peace around the school a lot more." Likewise, at the Graham and Parks School, seventh and eighth graders are all trained as peer mediators and are called upon to resolve conflicts between individual students, among groups of students, and between students and school staff, including the principal.

In these schools, students' opinions about and contributions to the running of the school are valued while opportunities to participate in "grown-up" roles are not considered privileges for a few but open to all.

Valuing Effort and Offering Second Chances

Untracking schools put their belief that all students can learn into operation through practices that communicate the value of effort and couple "second chances" for success with concrete resources to promote achievement. In addition, untracking schools build recognition of best efforts into school routines so that all students are acknowledged for trying hard. For example:

- At Jericho Middle School grades include "A," "B," "C," and "I," indicating "Improvement is needed." Students continue to work until they complete assignments at at least a "C" level. There are no "D"s or "F"s.

- At Crete-Monee Junior High, any student can sign a quarterly "Crete-Monee Improvement Company Academic Improvement Contract" to win a place on the honor roll. Students agree to get a passing grade in each class, bring up grades a minimum of one letter in two classes without letting any other grades slip, avoid missing more than three days of school, and spend a stipulated amount of time on homework nightly. A homework center staffed by the school's teachers supports students in meeting their contract by providing extra help until 5:30 in the afternoon. Moreover, "Academic Improvement Contracts" require a parent's signature commitment to homework supervision each night.

- At Valley Junior High School and others a "High Achievement Instructional Model" includes teachers' analysis of students' examinations in order to pinpoint skills that need to be worked on. After review, students are retested and can claim the higher grade as their final one.

- In many schools, every single student is "adopted" by an adult in the school each year to receive simple forms of "special attention"—a watchful eye and an encouraging word daily—regardless of how "deserving" he or she may be.

- At Jericho Middle School, the "Catch a Rising Star" program rewards achievement in twelve different areas including academic progress, personal growth, and task commitment. *Every day,* teachers send out postcards addressed to parents of different children whom they have "caught" making improvements, complimenting students for specific gains. Over the year, Jericho's teachers send out over 3,000 postcards to parents of their 450 students, with no student excluded. Photographs of students are taken on a random basis and placed on a rotated display in the entryway showcase. In the belief that young adolescents appreciate private accolades, parents are invited to come to school to be recognized quietly by the school's principal.

- At the Graham and Parks School, lists of students whose achievement is worthy of note are presented in ways that give different ones the chance to be listed first—reversed alphabetically, for example, or randomly scrambled. All adults in the school join in a recognition program, including school custodians who make early-morning announcements to commend specific classroom groups for their order and clean-up jobs.

Approaches like these illustrate ways in which untracking schools make recognition of student achievement and effort so much a part of everyday school life that no student is invisible or "at risk" of falling through the cracks. With the expectation that every child will be acknowledged for his or her contribution, any suggestion that some are more "deserving" than others is discouraged and the concept of a community to which everyone can contribute is reinforced.

What's in a Name? The Power of Public Labels

One of the tracking practices that acts powerfully to undermine student self-esteem and sense of belonging to a community of learners is the labeling of entire classes by level of instruction. For example, Wellesley Middle School math teacher Judy O'Rourke had equal expectations for the preparation and quality of the homework of her "high" and "low" students. It turned out, however, that a change in the official label of her course—from "low" to "pre-algebra"—motivated her students as much as anything that she did in the classroom. She writes:

Over the past couple of months in my math 8 class, we've made the transition from basic math to pre-algebra. As we performed operations using integers and rational numbers, I often encouraged and prodded them. I would say something to the effect that we were no longer a math 8 class but had truly turned the corner. We were now a pre-algebra class. We can do this work and we'll leave here in June confident and ready to do well in algebra 1.

The students turned this around one day and asked me why our course wasn't *called* pre-algebra. We discussed it, agreed that all of us would think about it, and we discussed it again at their request on more than one occasion. They finally asked me to see what I could do about it.

After discussion with the special education teacher, Mrs. Whitman, Mr. Atherton, math department chairperson, and Mr. D'Auria, our principal, they agreed with the request, and the change was made. (Thank goodness for flexible administrators and the flexibility inherent in eighth grade.)

I must confess I used this change as a "carrot" for several weeks before I told the students that the change had officially been made. My announcement coincided with the introduction of more "abstract" work which leads into solving equations algebraically.

The students were thrilled with the change. It definitely increased their confidence, and I was seeing smiles and self-satisfaction—"Oh, I got it!"—from students who were still somewhat resistant, negative about their work, and expecting to do poorly. I think they were also pleased that they were important enough for four adults to spend time discussing them, their performance, and, therefore, a course name change that symbolized our belief that "they can do it!"

Typically the concept of "high expectations" has focused on the interaction between students and teachers in classrooms. In untracking schools, however, this concept extends beyond the walls of the classroom so that it affects the entire atmosphere of the school. By building a climate of high expectations throughout the school community, schools lay the foundation for equal citizenship for every student, free of public labeling, where all are encouraged to make their best effort to realize the highest standards of individual achievement and to contribute to the well-being of others.

Untracking and Ethnic Diversity: Creating a High Expectations Culture in Ethnically Diverse Schools

Across the country, growing racial and ethnic diversity underscore the necessity of untracking as part of a broader strategy to promote integration and develop schools as communities where students of different social backgrounds learn together. In communities undergoing intense change, planning and school-development strategies are essential at both district and local levels. The most successful of these strategies focus on developing a culture of high expectations for all students at the district and school level.

District-Level Planning in Desegregating School Districts

Nancy Peck, associate director of the Southeastern Desegregation Assistance Center in Miami, has worked with many school districts that implement new grouping practices as part of a desegregation plan. In her work with superintendents and school boards in districts where tracking has reinforced race stereotypes and bolstered in-school segregation of students, she urges adoption of a multistep strategy for a districtwide climate of high expectations:

1. **Prepare a positive climate for change.**
   - Enact proactive leadership from the top down. The superintendent and the school board must play leading roles and set a positive tone by promoting healthy public dialogue on the subject of grouping procedures and their effects upon student learning.
   - Disseminate information on the positive effects of alternative grouping procedures and high expectations of students to all involved personnel.
   - Invite a knowledgeable consultant to speak and work with principals to allay fears and prepare them to provide effective leadership for their schools.
   - Encourage dialogue between interested teachers and parents by hosting meetings to discuss issues and concerns.
   - Demonstrate to parents that *all* children will benefit by citing examples of successful implementation in other school systems.

2. Form a task force to discuss issues and plan for a smooth transition, including central office staff, two to four principals, two to five teachers, parents, and a community liaison.
   • Study the alternatives to ability grouping and weigh advantages of each for the school system. Consider a plan that provides for gradual change.
   • Identify models of other school systems that have implemented alternative grouping procedures with successful outcomes.
   • Examine structures and policies of the entire school system. Assess the changes that will be needed to support new grouping procedures including changes in scheduling patterns, testing policies, staff development, structures for shared decision-making, instructional materials, extracurricular activities, Chapter 1 programs, and exceptional/special education.

3. Ensure that sufficient time is provided to plan for all necessary changes that will facilitate first-year success.

4. Create a realistic time line. Full implementation usually takes more than one school year!

5. Provide intensive staff development for principals to give them the necessary information and skills to become positive change agents in their schools. Teach principals strategies for flexible management so that they, with their teachers, can make decisions regarding implementation that reflect the consensus of the needs of their school.

Peck's steps for implementing heterogeneous grouping at the district level parallel the process described by untracking schools. Like schools, untracking districts must model policies of inclusiveness that encourage the best effort of every actor in the school system.

Creating "High
Expectations"
Routines at the
School Level

*A parent of one of your students dies. He expresses a desire
for you to come to the funeral, but the religion is not familiar
to you....*

*Several immigrant parents write to you stating that they do not
want their daughters participating in physical education....*

*Several twelve-year-old girls in your class are seeking permission
through their parents to travel to their home country for two or
three months to have their marriages arranged....*

*Several teachers on your staff appear to be uncomfortable with
the multicultural mix of the students, express the belief that these
students are being "catered to," and raise questions about the
rights of "real" Americans....*

Nowadays, schools have increasing numbers of students who are
newcomers to America or who speak a language at home that is
not English. These children may be isolated from the life of their
peers and sometimes experience their education as a separate
track unto itself within the school building. In such schools,
untracking takes on special challenges.

It is not language alone that isolates students from one another.
Customs, religion, and value systems also present differences
that schools with large numbers of students who are newcomers
to North America must accommodate. In these situations,
untracking requires a reexamination of all school routines that
relegate newcomers to low-status positions in the educational
process; the presence of non-native students must be viewed as
an asset rather than a liability. Furthermore, means must be
found to reduce the isolation felt by these children by creating a
climate of multiculturalism in every classroom and throughout
the school.

With 650 students of 77 different nationalities, Valley Park
Middle School in Toronto, Ontario, faces daily challenges in not
only accommodating different heritages but also in *honoring*
diversity. Schools like Valley Park must alter school routines to
transform the academic community into, in the words of Valley
Park's vice principal Susan Hiraishi, a "global village." To do this,
Valley Park staff and others suggest:

- Refrain from referring to students as Asian or Hispanic;
  refer to their specific country of origin—Cambodia, Vietnam,
  Guatemala, El Salvador, the Dominican Republic, Haiti, the
  Philippines. Emphasize that each country has its unique
  culture that defines itself beyond a common language. For
  example, Mexico, Puerto Rico, El Salvador, and Peru have very
  different histories and cultures despite the fact that Spanish is
  spoken in all of them.

- Display world maps that feature the Eastern Hemisphere in the center or show the world from the perspective of the Southern Hemisphere. In classrooms, pinpoint students' places of birth on the map and connect each country by yarn to your city.

- Translate school signs into all the birth languages of your students—welcome signs, office signs, bathroom signs, cafeteria signs. Encourage English-language students to learn the translations.

- Promote the three *R*'s—Responsibility, Reason, and Respect—among students and staff. Make it clear that inside the building everyone will be safe from violence or name-calling, and initiate peer-mediation and conflict-resolution programs to work out student disputes.

- Be flexible in application of school rules, such as dress codes requiring girls to wear uniforms that bare arms and legs or include trousers or shorts, that might violate students' religion.

- Meet with the director of the school meals program to consider how to make lunches more in tune with the dietary restrictions of students. Respect some cultures' prohibition against eating pork or beef, for example, or provide alternative selections for children from ethnic groups that are prone to lactose intolerance.

- Welcome students' speaking their own language. Explain directly to the English-speaking children the value of knowing two languages and the benefit of using a language spoken at home as a prerequisite for learning a new language; reassure the English-speaking students that the newcomers are not talking about them when they speak their own language.

- Use your school as a site for community-based self-help groups, immigration counseling, adult literacy, or English programs for adults from your students' communities so that newcomers recognize the school as a resource for the whole family.

- Bring community-based organizations into the school to work on professional development for all school staff on various aspects of different cultures, including perspectives on family-school involvement and child rearing.

- Don't count on a one-shot staff-development event to get staff up to speed on multiculturalism. Help staff become sophisticated about cultural diversity through regular staff newsletters and circulation of pertinent articles.

- Be sure that at least one adult in the school speaks the birth language of all students. If this is temporarily impossible, be sure to identify several people who can be called upon to communicate with parents in the event of an emergency.

- Reach out to parents in a personal way. The Hispanic Policy Development Project has found that simple efforts like contacting parents through a handwritten note on personal notepaper are far more effective than writing to them on school stationery. And bear in mind that meetings held in neighborhood settings frequently draw more parents than those held at the school site.

- Refrain from assuming that just because parents do not speak English they cannot be helpful to their children. One important study in London, for example, found that children could be assigned to read at home to their parents and, even when grown-ups' understanding of English was not extensive, academic gains were dramatic.

- Implement Big Brother, Big Sister, or Welcome Wagon approaches for newcomers by pairing experienced students with those entering your school at mid-year.

- Develop thematic curriculum units on immigration; ask students to interview family members or friends in pairs so that similarities in the immigration experience can be identified. Invite parents to talk to the class about their own immigration experiences. Design interdisciplinary units that emphasize common themes across cultures—family relationships, housing designs, or adolescence.

- Develop pen-pal relationships with schools or classrooms in other countries or between bilingual and monolingual classes. Research the countries and regions where the sister schools are located. Begin stamp or postcard collections from letters received, and display the collection for the whole school.

- Offer bilingual students the chance to take literature courses in their birth languages for foreign-language course credit.

- Ask students in your bilingual or ESL classes to write stories, poetry, "foto novelas," or newsletters for use in the foreign-language courses taken by monolingual English-speaking students.

- Make tutoring bilingual or ESL students in the lower grades a requirement for monolingual English-dominant students enrolled in foreign-language courses.

These actions take into account the fact that different cultures are sources of enrichment and learning for all students. Viewed together, they can infuse the school climate with the message that everyone can contribute to building a multicultural learning community.

Professional Development to Raise Teacher Expectations

> This heterogeneous grouping is a good thing. The only flaw is that the teachers have to really accept it. You've got to take it to heart. You have to really believe that everyone is equal.
>
> —Joshua Poole, student, Pioneer Valley Regional School, Northfield, Mass.

In untracking middle-grade schools, every teacher, counselor, and staff member must put the principle of high expectations into practice in every aspect of school life, from the classroom to the most taken-for-granted school routines. It is essential that staff consistently act on the belief that all students have the capacity to master the skills and knowledge that will open doors to further opportunity. Real commitment to high expectations means that teachers say not only "You can do it!" but also "And I'm going to show you how!" Moreover, in untracking schools, principals must go to great lengths to support teachers as they adopt these attitudes of "friendly firmness" and acquire the skills to communicate high expectations to all students.

Sharpening awareness of research that focuses on teacher expectations and achievement is a first step in helping teachers learn specific techniques of communicating high expectations to all students. Sometimes this results in confronting outmoded responses to students, especially those who are perceived as low achieving. It may also result in greater self-reflection by teachers about how their own behavior may contribute to variations in achievement among different students.

Addressing
Teacher Belief
Systems

Lip service to high expectations is not enough. As Poole says, "You've got to take it to heart." This means that school staff must examine both their beliefs about achievement and the ways in which they put those beliefs into practice. Over and over again, research on effective schools confirms that students succeed in a climate of high expectations founded on two major beliefs: 1) that all students can learn and 2) that it is the responsibility of schools to see that they do learn.

Recent research on teacher beliefs at the middle level has taken this correlation one step further. At the University of Southern Maine, researchers David Silvernail and Joseph Capelluti have found that teachers who prefer heterogeneous grouping are also likely to assume responsibility for the learning of all their students and, in the process, reexamine their own teaching practices when students are failing rather than pinning the blame on social circumstances or native ability. In contrast, teachers who prefer homogeneous grouping are more likely to attribute failure to student ability. Silvernail and Capelluti conclude that staff development to facilitate the transition to heterogeneous grouping must address teacher belief systems even *before* teachers receive training in innovative instructional strategies. They emphasize:

> All effective educational practices are based on sound
> theoretical constructs. To skip the process of examining
> teacher beliefs is to guarantee that the new practices will
> not be understood or fully implemented as intended. Schools
> will not appreciably improve unless teachers believe in the
> practices they are required to perform.

Based on their findings, Silvernail and Capelluti suggest that a first step in school reform is an assessment of teachers' beliefs using a questionnaire that asks them to attribute student success or failure to a variety of factors falling either within or outside of teachers' control. This tool can trigger an "awareness" discussion; it can also be used to develop a profile of the range of beliefs among all teachers within a school. This assessment process followed by an open discussion about the findings raises the chances for bringing about a lasting and effective transition to heterogeneous grouping.

*Teacher
Expectations
and Student
Achievement
(TESA)*

"It's only human," says Chuck Weed, staff developer for the Teacher Expectations and Student Achievement (TESA) program in the county-based Board of Cooperative Educational Services in Latham, New York. "You're a teacher, and you've got some kids who come into class unprepared day after day. They're chewing gum when they're not supposed to; they never have a pencil. And somehow their behavior contributes to your *perception* that they're low achievers. What happens? You start to do things that communicate to those kids that you think they *are* low achievers. Then you're in trouble."

Originally known as "Equal Opportunity in the Classroom," TESA is grounded in research on the importance to academic progress of teacher-student interactions. Developed by educators Mary Martin and Sam Kerman, TESA raises teachers' awareness of their own responses to students whom they have defined as "high achievers" and "low achievers." Says Weed, "What goes on in TESA is that we're not about changing kids, we're changing ourselves through revealing ourselves. It's risky, but there's a real payoff when you see all your students improve academically."

TESA's director Kerman emphasizes that the major objective of TESA is to accelerate academic gain of students perceived to be the "low achievers" in any classroom, including those in highly selective universities where professors may perceive students as "high genius," "average genius," and "low genius." However, TESA may be most useful in schools where great social diversity tends to make teachers especially vulnerable to subjective judgments of ability. Some metropolitan districts, including Indiana's Decatur Township, have found this staff-development program to be critical during the early years of desegregation.

TESA's emphasis on voluntary participation is a key factor in engaging teachers' commitment and reducing the threat of change. Over the course of five three-hour sessions held one month apart, teachers review research and examine their practice in three "strands": questioning of students; providing feedback to students; and communicating personal regard for students. They discuss the impact of appropriate teacher-student interactions within each strand, including such techniques as affirming or correcting performance, giving praise, listening, delving, and higher-level questioning.

Fundamental to the program is one consistent rule of thumb applicable to each area: "If you're using any one technique, take a look at *how* you're doing it, and do it as much for the students you perceive as 'low-achievers' as for those you perceive as 'high achievers.'" For example, TESA helps teachers learn that for any one time that they call on a "perceived high" student, they owe a question to a "perceived low" student; likewise, teachers owe the same amount of "wait time" to the "perceived lows" as to the "perceived highs." Weed emphasizes that this principle of "equitable distribution of response opportunities" is "the most potent" of all TESA's techniques in its impact on student behavior."

In terms of teacher behavior, the most powerful learning takes place, not in TESA seminars, but in four follow-up observations during which participants use release time to monitor one another's equitable use of behavior that communicates high expectations to all students. These peer observations involving the simple counting of interventions for "perceived highs" and "perceived lows" are truly designed to be *observations*, not evaluations, to provide clear feedback to teachers as they practice new behavior in their classrooms. Weed reports, "After the first observation, which can be threatening, the observations are *the* most valued and liked aspect of the program."

TESA's observation schedule recognizes that teachers' behavior cannot be modified overnight. As Weed notes, "It takes about three weeks to break a habit, and it takes kids about three weeks to get used to new teaching." Once they have adopted new and more equitable ways of interacting with students, however, teachers schooled in TESA report that they maintain the program's techniques many years after the training. Weed, for one, has no doubts that the gains are worth taking risks and waiting for. "It's the most important work I've done in twenty years in education," he says. And as one participant in the program in Indiana's Decatur Township saw it, "TESA is the cornerstone that led to, and fits into, all staff development programs in the school system."

The Efficacy Institute

In tracked schools where teachers and students work with the unspoken assumptions that ability is distributed according to a bell curve, it may be easy to discount the value of effort in the process of learning. In the beginning, then, untracking may seem difficult not only because expectations about fixed human intelligence can present hurdles to change but also because students themselves may have come to accept their former teachers' definition of their potential. When students have internalized a negative assessment of their potential, they will need to *un*learn these assumptions in favor of more self-affirming perspectives. Recognizing this, some districts have found that professional development focused on expectations coupled with joint student-staff discussions about motivation and effort can contribute to enhancing the commitment of both teachers and students to academic success.

The Efficacy Institute is a not-for-profit organization with a focus on providing educational consulting services in the areas of student development and motivation to urban school districts. Efficacy's work rests on the belief that underachievement results from the *interaction* between children and their environment, including low expectations about the potential of minority students to learn and the practice of ability grouping. Designed to help teachers, students, parents, and community volunteers put into practice the saying "All children can learn," activities enable children and adults alike to value intellectual development, to understand obstacles to development, and to learn to manage these obstacles.

"Consciousness is power," says Dr. Jeffrey Howard, founder and president of the Efficacy Institute. For this reason, exposing students to the Efficacy Process of Development can complement untracking by addressing explicitly the sometimes unspoken belief of minority students that "A's are white grades." Does this approach work? Many teachers and parents think so, including those at the Wayland, Massachusetts, Middle School. There eighteen out of forty minority students made the honor roll for the first time after they had attended a single Efficacy retreat where they discussed internalized myths of inferiority and learned alternative ways of looking at achievement.

The Efficacy Institute also offers programs for teachers, parents, and community volunteers designed to change school and community norms related to expectations about achievement.

The message "Smart is not something you are; smart is something you *get*" is basic to all Efficacy projects and materials. For example, a curriculum for middle-level students uses realistic stories about a group of urban adolescents to introduce the idea that they can become intelligent through effort and to give them concrete ways of understanding that what matters most in achieving is effort, not ability.

Changing the Focus from Ability to Effort

> His natural gift for the keyboard may not have been the
> equal of Vladimir Horowitz's or Arthur Rubenstein's, but
> no one worked harder at becoming a better pianist than
> Serkin did, and his students recall how he would speak of
> certain technical problems in terms of the number of years
> it would take to solve them.... There was always an element
> of struggle in Serkin's playing that made the element of
> conquest all the more exciting and exalting.
>
> —Richard Dyer, music critic, writing on the death
> of Rudolf Serkin, *Boston Globe,* 10 May 1991

Making heterogeneity work requires including all students in a
school culture that communicates expectations that everyone
will master the skills and knowledge that have until now been
considered the domain of the most confident learners. Whereas
tracked schools rely on practices that compare students to one
another, and in the process lower expectations for all but those at
the top, untracking schools assume that nearly everyone can
achieve at high levels, thereby raising expectations for all. What
counts most is the effort and motivation that both teachers and
students bring to every task.

Most important, it is not left to individual teachers to communicate high expectations of effort. In untracking schools, the
norm of high expectations is *institutionalized* in the choices that
each school makes about school routines. That norm is further
put into practice in the school's grouping arrangements, curriculum, instruction, and access to experiences that will raise
students' aspirations for their future.

3 · Organizing and Grouping for Diversity

I felt good when I was with my [elementary] class, but when
they went and separated us, that changed us. That changed...
the way we thought about each other and turned us into
enemies towards each other—because they said I was dumb
and they were smart.

—Junior-high-school student,
U.S. News & World Report, 3 July 1989

Guided by a set of beliefs about the intellectual potential of their
students, new grouping arrangements in untracking schools
reflect both a commitment to providing equal access to knowledge and the view that diversity is itself a resource for learning.
In many schools, the organizational mechanism that makes
these new groupings possible is the interdisciplinary team.
Within the team, heterogeneous grouping takes various forms—
including flexible grouping, grouping for multiple intelligences,
controlled heterogeneity, integration of "regular" students and
students with disabilities, nonstigmatizing approaches for
Chapter 1 students and students whose first language is not
English, and multiage grouping. Although student demographics
vary from school to school, the common denominator of innovative grouping arrangements is the belief that learning in heterogeneous groups enriches learning for all.

Teaming Is Fundamental

One person can make a difference; a team can make a miracle.

—Susan Masek, principal,
  Sierra Middle School, Tucson, Arizona

Is there a key organizational strategy for promoting mixed-ability grouping? A variety of schools say *yes*. That strategy is teaming: the dividing of students into smaller clusters within a school and assigning to each cluster a team of teachers who work in collaboration to plan, organize, and implement the education of their students. Teams typically include core-curriculum teachers joined by special education teachers and, when possible, specialists. The more personalized interdisciplinary composition of the teams works to identify and address ongoing student needs, promote reflective practice on the part of teachers, and build a sense of community among both students and teachers. As *Turning Points*, the 1989 report from the Carnegie Commission on Adolescent Development, stated, "Teaming provides an environment conducive to learning by reducing the stress of anonymity and isolation on students."

Teams can meet daily in a common planning period, and thus add consistency and continuity to their teaching. At these sessions teachers can discuss the learning needs of specific students who are not fully engaged in school. By setting common expectations, norms, and rules, teachers can send a consistent message about discipline, homework, and accountability. Teams can also work in partnership with community-based organizations and parents to mobilize extra help or support services for students who need them.

Teachers who work in teams are also more likely to raise to the level of discussion, and then of solution seeking, problems related to school programs, including tracking. In fact, in many educators' view, effectively operating teams are a prerequisite for tackling the untracking process. For example, Arthur King and Thomas Stone of the University of Hawaii's College of Education tell how team organization at Castle High School, a large rural/suburban high school near Honolulu, has set the stage for heterogeneous grouping in the ninth and tenth grades:

Castle High School has had five tracks of ability groups for many years. The vast majority of secondary teachers have taught only homogeneously grouped classes. Further, the senior, experienced teachers have usually been assigned to superior sections and the older students. Because of the tendency for the more unsuccessful students to drop out of school before the upper years, the teachers' experience with successful teaching of the full range of students has been limited.

However, many teachers and other educators never felt good about the type of education students in the lower tracks received, nor about the tracking system itself. The practice was tough to change. It was traditional, and each teacher's practices were intertwined with patterns involving the entire school—teacher assignments, student assignments, scheduling practices, text materials, and every other factor in the school's program and practices....

In the Castle High School project, the teacher team proved to be the key that released the set of interlocking features that had been the impediments to change. During the first year in the team experience, the traditional curriculum was followed, although more sophisticated teaching approaches, especially cooperative learning techniques, were adopted and cultivated through in-service workshops. In planning for the second year, the teachers adopted a common curriculum with little segregation in mathematics, science, English, and social studies.

The core teams agreed to "mainstream" previously segregated handicapped students. Hence, one special education teacher was assigned to each core team. They were called "resource teachers" to avoid the limiting label of "special education," since they helped all students needing assistance, while still closely monitoring and assisting the special students. One evidence of the success of the system is that observers have been unable to identify the special education students in the mainstreamed classes....

Teachers on teams can focus their energies for staff development. When they became interested in heterogeneous grouping, they obtained information and training in one strategy that has proven effective with mixed-ability grouping, cooperative learning.... They found that when they all employed that same instructional strategy, the students learned to cooperate in groups more quickly.... They also found that they had an immediate support system for learning new strategies.

The use of teams to promote heterogeneous grouping has been so successful in Castle High's ninth grade that in 1991–92 the school year opened with seven heterogeneously grouped teams, including all the ninth- and tenth-grade students. Every student takes algebra 1 in ninth and geometry in tenth grade. A second period of algebra with extra teaching and support is offered for approximately one-fifth of the ninth graders to keep them in pace with their class.

The existence of teaming in and of itself does not guarantee heterogeneous grouping. In fact, in some middle schools, the team itself may become a track. However, a heterogeneously grouped team organization *can* facilitate the introduction of alternatives to tracking, allowing a variety of grouping arrangements to develop in response to the makeup of individual teams.

In their work with teams at Castle High School, King and Stone observe that teachers working in small groups increasingly become risk takers. They are also convinced that "when a team gets a vision and a plan, teachers feel empowered; together they find a way to make that vision into a reality." Moreover, the team structure enables teachers to experiment with new grouping practices team by team as they feel ready to do so. As "pilot teams" introduce new grouping practices, others can then learn from their experience.

Variations on Heterogeneous Grouping Practices

If we are not in competition with each other—if we are not threatened by our differences or busy trying to rank them— then our differences become our resources. I'm not like you, and I don't want to be like you, because then I wouldn't have anyone around me who could tell me anything I didn't know, show me anything I couldn't see. I want you because you are different. We're not the best daisy vs. the worst daisy. We're a bouquet.

—Poster in an Illinois middle school teachers' room

Student groupings need not be limited to two alternatives—total homogeneity or total heterogeneity. In fact, grouping practices in untracking schools reflect a variety as great as the diversity of their student enrollment. In turn, these variations lead to adoption of new curricula, instruction, and routines that develop the strengths that all students bring with them to school.

Flexible Grouping for Mixed-Ability Groups

The Helena-West Helena School District (Number 2) in Phillips County, Arkansas, has approximately 4,500 students, 70 percent of whom are African-American, with a majority eligible for free or reduced-price lunches. The district serves the eastern part of Phillips County in an area that Mark Twain called "one of the prettiest situations on the river."

In 1979, schools in the district were desegregated and reorganized. In 1986, tracking students in rigid ability groups was abandoned as a district policy—"with some pressure from the Equal Education Opportunity Commission," recalls one principal who embraced the new practice even before the district did. Kenneth Murphree, principal at Woodruff School, serving fifth and sixth graders, had taught for five years under the tracked system. "We saw over the years how kids got locked in. They could never get out of those low groups," he says. Class placement in Woodruff's seven fifth- and seven sixth-grade classes is now done heterogeneously by the principal, using student test scores to create planned mixed groupings. All teachers are expected to teach all levels.

When Marcia Klenbort of the Southern Regional Council visited the district in 1990, she learned that within a teacher's individual class, students are further grouped in mixed-ability learning clusters. In Naomi Stevens's sixth-grade class, for example, the twenty-eight students sit in five cluster groups. "Each has a high and a low achiever, and the rest are just mixed in," says Stevens. Students at Woodruff stay almost the entire day with their teacher, leaving class only for music, art, or physical education during fourth period.

Not all the district's ten principals apply the new grouping methods as willingly or effectively as at Woodruff. According to Dr. Gail Cheney, who heads the district's Office of Curriculum, Instruction, and Staff Development, "There are a few who have it on paper, but when you look in classes, you can see that classes are ability grouped." In Cheney's view, the principals who abide by the policy are those who have the skills to make it work or believe that it is best for students.

Cheney's staff-development sessions encourage teachers to create a variety of groups in their classes at different times. "Use flexible grouping, rather than label or track students," Cheney advocates. Thus, she advises teachers, depending on the lesson, to use large-group instruction, ability groups, interest groups, social groups, project groups, skills groups, cooperative-learning groups, or groups clustered at random—perhaps placing students wearing green shirts, red shirts, or black shirts together on a given day.

Cheney, a former teacher of teachers and head of the Lab School at the University of Mississippi, is committed to the

process of staff development as a means of equipping teachers to
work with heterogeneous groups. Originally employed by the
school district to head the Gifted and Talented Program, she
stretched the program's philosophy and state funds allocated for
the top 5 percent of students included in such programs to
include a wider range of students. "Learning centers and hands-
on activities are effective means for *all* children's learning, not
just 'gifted and talented,'" Cheney asserts.

In the past several years, the school district has offered
strategy sessions and workshops for teachers in collaboration
with the district and the Great Rivers Teacher Cooperative.
Cheney is proud that all teachers can now select from a list of
teacher-created courses and enroll in them in blocks with their
grade-level colleagues. "We are not yet where we want to be with
hands-on materials used in classrooms, but we are so much
better," she reports. These efforts go a long way toward reinforcing flexible grouping as an alternative to rigid tracking.

Flexible grouping arrangements, when implemented in such a
way that students' primary identification is with a heterogeneous
group, have the support of research as an educationally effective
grouping strategy. For example, researchers at Johns Hopkins
University, working with the National Education Association,
have found that skill-based grouping can be effective when:

• Students remain in heterogeneous classes most of the day
  and are regrouped by performance level only in such subjects
  as reading and math
• Grouping results in reducing heterogeneity in the specific
  skill being taught
• Group assignments are both flexible and frequently assessed
• Teachers adapt the level and pace of instruction to accommodate students' differences in learning

In addition, the NEA suggests that high expectations for all students, a test-reteach-retest approach for correction of specific
learning difficulties, regular monitoring of learning, and absence
of negative stereotyping should all characterize a flexible use
of ability grouping. These practices appear regularly in the classrooms of untracking schools.

Controlled
Heterogeneity:
Willard Junior
High School

Without heterogeneous grouping, equal access to knowledge may be elusive. John Goodlad, for example, in *A Place Called School*, notes how disparities in terms of access to knowledge that begin with ability grouping in the elementary grades continue in the later grades, producing wider gaps in learning with every passing year. Goodlad also describes remedies that can reverse that pattern:

> The first corrective measure is agreement on a common core of studies.... The second corrective measure is the elimination of any arrangements designed to group in separate classrooms on the basis of past performance students presumably enrolled in the same subject. Students should be assigned to classes randomly in a way that assures heterogeneity. Only in this way can we have some assurance that grouping practices alone will not lead to different subject matter, different expectations, and different teacher treatment of students.... Classes of randomly assigned or heterogeneous students appear to offer the most equity with respect to gaining access to knowledge while still preserving the more advantageous content and teaching practices of the upper tracks.

In Berkeley, California, Willard Junior High School has followed Goodlad's suggestions with positive results. This urban school of some five hundred students, half African-American and one-third white, used to have four distinct tracks. But when the district's testing coordinator pointed out discrepancies between majority- and minority-student test results, a core group of teachers, including resource teachers, together with Chris Lim, the school's principal, decided to address inequality of access to learning head on. The group studied Goodlad's *A Place Called School*, Jeannie Oakes's *Keeping Track*, and the state department of education's report *Caught in the Middle* and slowly developed a plan for eliminating tracking at Willard. By 1991, except for three remaining math sections, the school had heterogeneous grouping in all core subjects. Also, grouping decisions were consistent with the school's statement of educational philosophy, which emphasizes teachers' commitment to equitable classes in regard to race, sex, and academic achievement.

As they implemented their plan, Willard staff focused first on developing a core curriculum based on standards set at the highest levels. As teacher Addie Holsing asserts:

> All students have the moral right to "Equal Access to Knowledge." All students should be taught the Advanced Curriculum in English with a backup week's head start if they read below the 36 percentile. All students carrying around the same book at the same time is a great democratizer.

Willard teachers also quickly began to assess ways of assigning students to mixed-ability classrooms. They recognized that creating heterogeneous classrooms required concrete support from administrative levels of the school to draw up a master schedule, determine the most favorable way to "heterogenize," balance mixed classes by hand if the district's computer could not handle heterogeneous distribution, and deal with parent and student questions about placements. They also realized that it would be tempting to allow random class assignments, and they observed:

> When the academic balance of a class is skewed, as it often is by random heterogeneity, our experience shows us that even the best teachers have trouble making CTBS [California Test of Basic Skills] growth for all. For instance, with too many low students, the academic level of instruction drops. With too many high students, the bottom few flounder helplessly while the teacher instructs the top.

Although Willard uses computer software to blend student groupings by academic performance, race, and gender, further balancing into small work groups within classes is also necessary. At Willard, teachers first form these groups early in the year by a quick reading of papers written by students on the first day of classes. Although teachers know that no method is ever foolproof and recognize that reshuffling will be ongoing, they have settled on two methods for initial in-class groupings. In the first approach, teachers put one "low" student in each group; then they put the strongest academic students with the lowest ones; finally, they distribute the "middle" students where they are needed to balance a group by gender and ethnicity. Using a second approach, Willard's teachers may take learning styles or personality into account, so that each group includes students who favor different learning strategies and so that all the extroverts don't end up in one group. As the year progresses, the composition of the small groups will change as teachers become more familiar with students' individual preferences and motivation as well as group "chemistry."

Over the years, Willard teachers have come to understand that specific structural and program changes are essential to make controlled heterogeneity work for all students. For example, Willard's untracking process emphasizes:

- Increased attention to individualizing learning so that students working at an accelerated pace have opportunities for enrichment while vulnerable students, including those whose first language is not English, receive additional support. All students are encouraged to complete "advanced" projects in English and history.

- Opportunities for students who score below the thirty-sixth percentile on the California Test of Basic Skills to enroll in an extra period of reading instruction, when they are exposed to literature a week *prior* to its introduction in their heterogeneous classes.

- Tutoring support in all classes, especially English. Willard has used extra funds to hire college students as tutors whose roles and responsibilities are clarifed in the school's Tutor Handbook.

- Expanding and strengthening teaching strategies through ongoing, multiyear staff development in cooperative learning, TESA, study skills, portfolio assessment in writing, Great Books techniques, and appropriate theories related to critical thinking and human intelligence.

- Annual all-staff retreats at the end of each summer.

- Scheduling to allow for common planning time and an extra preparation period for teachers.

- Preparation of teacher-developed guides for teaching mixed-level groups in core-curriculum subjects, which are then disseminated to all staff.

With the implementation of controlled heterogeneous grouping together with improved curriculum and instruction, Willard's principal Lim reports that achievement has "improved a lot" for average students, "a little" for high-achieving students, and is "way up" for other students—and differences in achievement by race have narrowed. The number of graduating eighth graders enrolling in college-preparatory English classes in high school has doubled. And with less work-sheet and rote learning, all students have more opportunities to apply thinking skills. Adds Holsing, "Perseverance and patience pay off; pursuit of effective teaching methods makes heterogeneity the easiest, most efficient, most enjoyable, and most effective way to teach."

*Multi-
dimensional
Intelligence
Groups:
Middle School
of the
Kennebunks*

In the spring of 1990, Sandra Caldwell, principal of the Middle
School of the Kennebunks in southern Maine, went with several
teachers to hear a lecture by Dr. Howard Gardner, codirector
of Project Zero at Harvard University's Graduate School of
Education. The teachers had read and discussed Gardner's
research on multidimensional intelligence at one of Caldwell's
"5:00 Reveilles," a regular, voluntary early-morning feature of the
school. Fired up after the lecture, staff began to consider how
they might help children and teachers alike approach intelligence, in Caldwell's words, as "a gift of possibilities."

In most schools, academic activities traditionally focus on
rewarding student performance in two areas: verbal-linguistic
and logical-mathematical. But Gardner's theory suggests that
human intelligence encompasses much more than is evident in
these two domains. Project Zero is currently researching seven
kinds of intelligence:

- **Verbal-linguistic:** Sensitivity to the sounds, rhythms,
  and meanings of language; awareness of the different uses
  of language
- **Logical-mathematical:** Sensitivity to, and capacity to identify,
  logical or numerical patterns; ability to handle long chains
  of reasoning
- **Musical:** Sensitivity to rhythm, pitch, and timbre; appreciation
  of forms of musical expression
- **Spatial:** Capacity to perceive the visual-spatial world
  accurately and to perform transformations on one's initial
  perceptions
- **Bodily-kinesthetic:** Ability to control one's body movements
  and to handle objects skillfully
- **Interpersonal:** Sensitivity to the moods, temperaments,
  motivations, and desires of other people
- **Intrapersonal:** The capacity to assess one's own feelings
  and the ability to discriminate among them and use them
  as guides to behavior; knowledge of one's own strengths,
  weaknesses, desires, and intelligences

Gardner's theory suggests that if students are allowed to build on
their strengths in an environment that respects all kinds of
learning, and if classroom activities can incorporate teaching
techniques and assignments that touch on all aspects of intelligence, everyone will be motivated to succeed.

Inspired by Gardner's theory, a few teachers at the Middle
School of the Kennebunks decided to try a pilot approach
designed to put ideas about multiple intelligences into practice.
First, they made spring visits to feeder elementary schools in
their district to explain the theory of multiple intelligences to all

incoming seventh graders and, with them, brainstorm examples of each type of intelligence. They then asked all students to write their thoughts about the presentation in "reflection journals" and announced that they would return after two weeks to learn reactions to the question: "What is the evidence you can use from your home, school, or community to tell us, show us, or involve us in who you are and how you are a multidimensional learner?" Interviews with individuals would not only offer middle-school staff the unique opportunity to get to know new students, but would also provide information to form the basis for the school's pilot multidimensional-intelligence classroom.

The student "demonstrations" at the feeder elementary schools revealed a wealth of talent unimagined by any school staff. One child labeled by his school as "nonverbal" played the cello for his small audience of teachers and reported that, unknown to school staff, he performed regularly with a local chamber ensemble. Some students described volunteer work in community programs and displayed boxes of skiing medals. Others told of their accomplishments in the interpersonal or artistic arenas. Another taught all the teachers how to weave potholders and friendship bracelets. At the end of the process, says Caldwell, "We knew our incoming students better than we knew our graduating eighth graders!" On the basis of the presentations, the school selected students representing a range of strengths and interests to comprise a pilot "multidimensional intelligence (MDI) cluster."

With a curriculum encompassing a diversity of activities to match the diversity of students' interests and talents, the MDI class has been an overwhelming success. On one day in this cluster, for example, students are busy working in small groups on their "family budgets." This budget is not for the 1990s but is part of a complex and engaging curriculum called Immigrant 1850, developed by Project Zero specifically to evoke a wide range of student intelligences. Using information on a computer disk, student partners "adopt" an Irish immigrant family and analyze historical data, examine a data base, and balance a budget with the information given. This day, students have *become* their families and, dressed in costume approximating photographs that they have studied, are having their photographs taken.

Over the course of the year, seventh-grade team leader and language-arts teacher Fran Farr may pick and choose among activities suggested by the Project Zero curriculum, or she may develop her own projects to expand the curriculum's core activity. Referring to recorded historical data, students may compile graphs or charts of employment opportunities of the 1850s, create three-dimensional models of housing of the nineteenth century, and compare prices and wages of the time with those of the 1990s. They may read articles from the immigrant community newspaper, with allusions to the current events of the time, westward expansion, and social conditions preceding the Civil War. They may write letters "home," present skits or plays for other classmates, interview contemporary immigrants or family members about their immigration experiences, or create a collection of artifacts to hand down to subsequent generations of their "family." On some of these projects, Farr and her students will work in collaboration with the computer teacher or the drama coach, all learning new skills that go beyond narrow language-arts assignments.

Do opportunities for learning in "multiple-intelligence groups" make a difference to students? As Judy Pace, teacher and educational researcher at Project Zero, explains, a curriculum based on the principles of multiple intelligences calls on students to use different kinds of strengths. Pace elaborates: "In project work, it's beneficial to have a group of students who bring a variety of intelligences to the tasks. Skills are embedded in a rich context, and diversity becomes a positive asset in understanding that context." At the Middle School of the Kennebunks, one student who was asked for a definition of MDI says easily, "It's when you're smart and you don't know it." Sandra Caldwell adds, "In our middle school, every single kid gets to be bright every single day."

Providing Compensatory Education in Heterogeneous Classes

In the 1960s, increased awareness of the learning gaps between rich and poor students resulted in a set of federal programs intended to help poor students catch up to their middle class peers. The most explicit of these programs, Chapter 1, offered resources to schools to provide "compensatory" or "remedial" services to low-income students performing below expectations. Whereas elementary schools have typically offered students services in "pull-out" programs, middle schools have tended to use Chapter 1 funds to set up separate classes for designated students, perpetuating the harmful consequences of tracking in the name of remediation.

Untracking schools, however, view segregative approaches as harmful to student learning. These schools have developed alternative approaches to reduce labeling and isolation of students from the mainstream. These approaches engage students, not with a low-level curriculum, but with a challenging and nurturing program designed to improve learning.

Plenty of the 1,375 students at the Louis Armstrong Middle School—I.S. 227—in New York City's Borough of Queens can use the extra help provided by Chapter 1. Likewise, at Western Middle School in Louisville, Kentucky, where 95 percent of the 820 students are eligible for free or reduced-price lunches, many require enriched learning experiences to offset the disadvantages of poverty. At these schools, educators have taken both large and small steps to ensure that students get this help without being publicly labeled or remanded to a low-status position, never to be retrieved into the school's mainstream.

Reorganizing School Routines

At Louis Armstrong, Chapter 1 integration begins by reforming the relationship of the program to the school's mainstream to reduce isolation of students. For example:

- Every child in need of Chapter 1 support is enrolled in heterogeneous classes for all subjects. In these grade-level classes, paraprofessionals work with children who need extra help, providing tutoring in language arts and math within each of the content areas.

- A flexible, nine-period schedule *also* allows students to receive an enriched curriculum during an elective time period. In this way, Chapter 1 provides *added* support rather than "instead-of" services, and students do not have to miss out on regular classwork as a condition for Chapter 1 help.

- Alert to the connotations of labels, teachers have changed the name of the elective-period Chapter 1 reading course from "Basic Reading/Writing," to "Power Reading," a title reflecting staff beliefs that students "know a lot more than we give them credit for."

- Staff have located Louis Armstrong's Chapter 1 computer lab in the school library—a "high status" setting—where students have immediate access to all academic resources available.

Enriching
Chapter 1
Curriculum

Reflecting its schoolwide goal of promoting the academic success of all students, Louis Armstrong has also beefed up the
Chapter 1 curriculum. Chapter 1 teacher Lynne Cohen and her
colleagues were concerned that low expectations for Chapter 1
students may have, in the past, locked these students into day
after day of work-sheet activities. As a result, they have redesigned the curriculum to expose students to "real" application
of language arts through approaches calculated to engage discouraged learners and boost advanced skills in reading comprehension and interpretation. For example, in Louis Armstrong's
Chapter 1 program:

- **High-interest literature has replaced work sheets for
  teaching reading.** Materials now include short stories by
  recognized authors such as James Thurber, Shirley Jackson,
  and Ray Bradbury as well as a series of multicultural books
  from New York City's Project Equal, a program to develop
  critical reading skills through an awareness of stereotyping.
  Students also keep reading logs, work in small groups to
  discuss questions of comprehension and interpretation,
  and do book reports.

- **Active learning approaches are the norm.** On some
  days, students may role-play characters from literature in
  "what-if" situations. At other times, students expand both
  their knowledge of the vocabulary and concepts that make
  up our "cultural currency" by reading from Marvel's high-
  level "Alf" comic-book series, identifying words or ideas
  unfamiliar to them and competing in a "scavenger hunt"
  to collect definitions of those references. As a result, they gain
  familiarity with terms that can be found in fiction, reference
  materials, or current events and learn to delineate both literal
  and figurative meanings of words like "Houdini," "Pygmalion,"
  "dance card," "lanolin," "The World Cup," "Kosher food,"
  "Mecca," "yin/yang," "star-crossed lovers," "Gettysburg" and
  "Butterfly McQueen."

- **Computer learning supplements instruction.** Students have
  exposure to computer-assisted instruction in a computer lab
  attached to the school's library. Activities include puzzles and
  problem solving, involving such assignments as designing
  crossword puzzles as challenges to fellow students.

- **Purposeful writing assignments have meaning beyond the scope of the classroom.** For example, students correspond regularly with boys and girls in "gifted" classes in another New York City public school—an assignment that provides a "real life" context for practicing communications skills, makes writing both more practical and pleasurable, and exposes students to high-quality work of their peers in a noncomparative way.

- **Staff actively involve parents in their children's learning.** Teachers and paraprofessionals meet regularly with parents and offer workshops designed to support parents as in-home teachers to strengthen learning. Efforts include read-aloud programs—the story of family relationships, *I'll Love You Always,* is a favorite—and a special library corner for parents. In addition, materials prepared for the "Parents as Reading Partners" program include a parent-student reading calendar and an annotated bibliography of children's books suitable for the age group and distributed to all parents.

Staff at I.S. 227 are thrilled with the new approach. Cohen reports that her students are "finally reading *real* books, sometimes for the first time in their school lives." And teacher Carmella Bowden notes other gains for the students: "The problem with pullouts for the low achievers is that if they were behind *before* they were pulled out, they're *surely* behind after," she says. She adds, "Now we're seeing our kids leave the program!"

Schoolwide Implementation of Chapter 1

Current Chapter 1 legislation throws open numerous possibilities for schoolwide reform of both grouping and curriculum in schools with a large majority of low-income students. Moreover, new regulations require *all* schools receiving Chapter 1 funds to show that the expectations for eligible students are equal to the expectations for all students. Schools are also required to show how the Chapter 1 program is coordinated with the "regular" program, allowing for development of both basic and advanced skills.

At Louisville's Western Middle School, schoolwide implementation of Chapter 1 is designed to:

1. Improve student achievement in basic and advanced skills
2. Provide activity-oriented instruction to promote problem solving, critical thinking, and practical uses of technology
3. Increase students' self-esteem by expanding opportunities for recognition
4. Increase students' awareness of cultural and career opportunities through field trips and "job shadowing"

5. Increase parents' understanding and skills to help students at home
6. Build positive home/school relations

Within this framework of objectives, Western's Chapter 1 staff have geared up to offer students more personalized attention while shaping curriculum around high-interest activities. Additional staff funded by Chapter 1 allows the school to reduce class size in reading to eighteen and in math to twenty students. A computer lab makes possible both computer-assisted programs such as Higher Order Thinking Skills (HOTS) and an evening Family Computer Program in which students teach computer skills to their parents both at the school and at home on lap-top computers available for loan from the school. In addition, a parent coordinator supervises the EPIC (Effective Parenting Information for Children) program in which students and parents together learn leadership and responsible parenting skills.

The addition of Patricia Futch, a science resource teacher, to Western's staff has been key in terms of ensuring that all students develop problem-solving skills through a meaningful curriculum. To meet goals of strengthening curriculum and improving students' thinking skills, Futch introduces enriched science content and methods into regular classrooms. A new microprojector, "grow lab," dissecting apparatus, and map-developing equipment upgrade activities of the in-class science curriculum to increase all students' knowledge of technology and science. Out-of-school interdisciplinary activities involve trips to local fossil beds and a nature center and include such challenging inquiry and writing assignments as determining the speed of a stream with a cork and fishing line.

Western Middle School's Chapter 1 Schoolwide Project has produced observable results. Project Resource Teacher Nancy Hack reports that parents are now in the school day and night to support student learning, the children show increased interest in research and reading, and CTBS scores have jumped decisively, with students making a 5.6-point Normal Curve Equivalent (NCE) gain from the first to third year of schoolwide implementation.

By allowing for greater program flexibility, setting higher standards for program coordination, and focusing on a curriculum that addresses advanced skills, schoolwide implementation of Chapter 1 makes pullout approaches obsolete. At Louis Armstrong, Western, and other like-minded schools, supportive organizational structures allow for the integration of students in need of extra support within grade-level classrooms, thereby promoting improved school climate and academic gains for all.

Integrating Language-Diverse Students

Imagine a classroom of twenty-six eighth-grade students, fewer than half of whom were born in the United States. Fourteen of them have a first language other than English, including Spanish, Vietnamese, Amharic, Chinese, and French. If labeled, these children might be placed separately in regular, gifted-and-talented, special education, or ESL programs. Here, with ongoing support for learning, they are working together on high-interest tasks that require cooperation in small groups to accomplish complex assignments.

Imagine small groups of four or five students within this classroom formed to include two students with strong reading and writing proficiency, one or two with strong cooperative skills, and one or two with either limited English proficiency or a defined learning disability. A change of grouping every three months expands student interaction; and occasional regrouping of two or three students for specific projects allows for participation on three different teams and in up to ten different activity groupings over the course of the school year. In this environment, young adolescents from all cultural backgrounds can learn to take risks, question, explain, discuss, and hypothesize while gaining enhanced self-acceptance, confidence, independence, and cross-cultural awareness in the process.

Imagine, finally, a classroom in which all students are developing written and oral skills in English beginning from their own individual level of competence. Feedback to support learning comes from teachers who introduce, facilitate, and enrich assignments; from students working in small groups who critically analyze their own writing and the writing of their peers; and from technological aids, including computers and video equipment, which allow students to monitor their own progress. In this classroom, the children can engage in activities regardless of their level of English and are pushed to develop beyond that level in order to improve their communication with their classmates.

At the Davidson Middle School in San Rafael, California, learning like this is the hallmark of the school's MacMagic Program. Developed in partnership with Lucasfilm Learning, the program combines a creative-thinking curriculum based on computers and audiovisual aids—the *Mac* component—with an explicit commitment to encourage student learning through the cooperative interaction of children with different cultural perspectives, language backgrounds, and abilities—the *Magic* component. Scheduled during a daily 145-minute time block, the program does not encompass a full day, so participating students can both interact with others from different cultures within this heterogeneous classroom and also realize their membership in the wider life of the school during the remaining part of the day.

Within the three-period time frame, students are exposed to a richly textured curriculum that integrates eighth-grade language arts with social studies. MacMagic students experience writing, speaking, listening, and reading activities not simply as important ends in themselves—to improve pronunciation, for example—but also as a means of understanding complex ideas. For example:

• Within the context of topics such as world geography, archeology, and anthropology—which are explored through literature, computers, or current events—students compile "word banks," write dictionary meanings for all words, interview one another about the meaning and use of "banked" words, and are tested on spelling and word usage.

• After reading stories aloud as a class, students then work in small groups to answer prepared questions analyzing character and interpreting plot. Further, based on reading autobiographical literature such as *Geronimo: His Own Story*, students individually design a storyboard to illustrate the significant events of a life, incorporating visual icons into their descriptions.

• A reading of the story "Boy of the Painted Cave" forms the basis for exploring imaginary cultures created by student teams and described in terms of visual clues related to a culture's geographic environment, food, division of labor, tools, weapons, and belief systems—all topics that students have discussed in detail from the reading. Once each group's "culture" is developed, other groups examine the "discovered" cave paintings, hypothesizing about the course of that culture's development in response to given environmental conditions.

• Regular current-events activities require students to prepare handwritten summaries of news events of national or global importance and deliver presentations before the whole class.

Beyond activities like these, the learning of Davidson's MacMagic students develops through the use of computers, video equipment, and tape recorders. Because *all* students—regardless of ability or English proficiency—encounter hurdles as they master the intricacies of the MacWrite, MacPaint, and HyperCard software programs, they must constantly use one another as resources. Moreover, as Elly Pardo, MacMagic's program evaluator, states:

The computer is a nonbiased tool. It does not comment on an individual's accent or ability to speak and write; nor does it judge the quality of an individual's work. On the contrary, the computer provides the same opportunity for all users to be expressive and to create attractive text and graphics. For a second-language learner or a learner with language-processing difficulties, the computer then is a valuable aid for expressing thoughts, ideas, and information.

However, as important as the computer, camera, and tape recorder are to the success of the program, it is the pairing of these technological aids with a multidimensional and multicultural curriculum that is key. This curricular context supports and challenges all students to excel, especially those who are vulnerable because of limited English proficiency. One such student noted:

[This class] helped me have courage to do the things I wanted to do. I got a lot of help, and I wasn't embarrassed to talk in class. I had more courage to tackle harder problems. [The] MacMagic [class] wouldn't let you leave tasks. Everyone had to do the work. There was no special treatment because you were not a native speaker. All the kids were treated the same.

Robert Vasser, Davidson's principal, emphasizes that because MacMagic promotes learning based on the common ground of *ideas* and *communication,* all students' contributions are accepted and appreciated. To the extent that the program deemphasizes the acquisition of remedial English in favor of equal access to a challenging and engaging content, students from diverse language backgrounds in particular thrive. As Vasser reports, "The program is finding a better way to assist ESL students acquire language and critical-thinking skills by mainstreaming them successfully in a class where they can be like everyone else."

Indeed, Davidson's MacMagic approach conforms to five prerequisites for effective language learning. As summarized by Pardo, school conditions that enhance such learning include:

- Opportunities for language-minority students to communicate with native speakers
- Opportunities for second-language learners to interact purposefully and appropriately, strengthening students' understanding of *how* to say *what* to *whom*
- Learning environments that build on a context of meaningful real-life experiences and encourage communication about these experiences in a culturally appropriate way
- Opportunities for learning-by-doing, with a focus on acquiring language through projects that require interaction with the real world
- Opportunities to apply new language learning in a wide variety of situations, each of which encourages development of different kinds of vocabulary, linguistic expressiveness, and conduct, so that students learn to test out and refine their responses to diverse situations

As Davidson Middle School's experience demonstrates, heterogeneous grouping of students of diverse language backgrounds can provide such opportunities. But this approach requires abandoning the notion that students must learn English *before* they can engage in academic content of any complexity. It also entails adopting a nontraditional curriculum that emphasizes both thinking and problem-solving skills and capitalizes on, rather than stigmatizes, student differences. Under these conditions, integration of students learning English with their English-proficient peers enriches the academic life of everyone.

Integrating Disabled Students

The 1970s witnessed a major change in public-school enrollment in the United States. For the first time, large numbers of children with disabilities entered the educational system, protected by Public Law 94-142, the Education for All Handicapped Children Act. This act established that all students have a right to an adequate and appropriate education in the public schools. Just as civil-rights laws of earlier decades had established that separation of students by race undermined equal educational opportunity, P.L. 94-142 asserted that students with disabilities are entitled to educational programs on equal terms with their "typical" peers. This federal law and supporting state laws have complemented a movement toward integration of disabled citizens into all aspects of society.

P.L. 94-142 and its attendant assumptions have played a dramatic role in shaping the course of untracking at Rundlett Junior High School in Concord, New Hampshire. This Monday, the daily seventh-grade team meeting opens with a discussion of the logistics involved in organizing some 110-odd students for the upcoming canoe trip, but quickly moves on to focus on of the needs of Aurora, a student with autism whose new schedule now fully integrates her into the team's regular classes.

At Rundlett, approximately 170 of the school's 1,000 seventh, eighth, and ninth graders have disabilities that call for learning strategies as diverse as their needs. And at this school, all these students receive the support that they require in "regular" classes rather than in a separate resource room. The common planning time available to teachers is critical to the integrity of Rundlett's goal of fully mainstreaming all students with disabilities into the school's heterogeneous classes. The regular meeting of teachers with a special educator makes this goal workable.

Today teachers question their "generic" special education colleague about Aurora's Individual Education Plan (IEP). Although they have learned something about autism, they are only beginning to get to know Aurora. They wonder what particular needs they should anticipate, and they listen carefully as their specialist makes suggestions about how to encourage Aurora's participation in class. None of these teachers has prior experience teaching a student with autism, but each one is poised to begin, bolstered by the support of the specialist, assured that they will receive the extra help of an aide in Aurora's classes, and in agreement that the education of students with disabilities is as much their responsibility as that of any "special" teacher.

The planning period is over, and the teachers move on to their classes. In the hallways, one student in a wheelchair and another with crutches mingle with their classmates and change classes easily in the single-story building. Although many students with IEPs are enrolled at Rundlett, those with less visible disabilities are impossible to identify in the heterogeneously grouped classes. The availability of an extra adult in many classes is what makes possible the full participation of these disabled children in settings with their grade-level peers.

For example, students in Steve Potoczak's social-studies class are focusing on the geography of the Carribbean, a topic enriched by a reading of Theodore Taylor's novel *The Cay* and supported in class by Joan Urbach, the reading teacher. In this class, Potoczak and Urbach have adopted a co-teaching model, with each covering different parts of the curriculum that they have designed together. English teacher Jean Cannon, on the other hand, coaches her eighth graders in vocabulary and an analysis of conflict in *Watership Down*, while an aide circulating among small student groups poses questions and ensures that those who need individualized intervention receive it in accordance with their IEP. In other classes, single teachers benefit from consultation with a specialist who advises them on how to adapt classroom management or testing approaches to facilitate learning for students with particular disabilities. In still other classes, a second teacher may play the role of "superstudent," detecting student confusion about explanations of complicated information and asking for the rephrasing of material to clarify understanding for all students.

Aurora is late to Leah MacLeod's third-period English/ language-arts class, but without making too much of the fact, MacLeod urges her to join the class. Today a substitute aide accompanies Aurora to help her adjust to the new schedule. Aurora watches attentively as small groups enact the myth of Perseus and the class discusses the power of the oracle in predicting and determining events in Greek mythology.

With the presentations complete, MacLeod concludes the class with a reading aloud of the story of the race of Atalanta. As students gather in a circle, Aurora chooses her seat next to MacLeod. Aurora's eyes follow her teacher as the story unfolds; her shoulder just slightly touches MacLeod, and she reponds with a smile to the tone of suspense and excitement in the reading. MacLeod later explains that the students in the class understand how important it is to Aurora to be able to sit close to her teacher, and they concede this place to her. The special education liaison further clarifies that Aurora's interest in closeness signals an acceptance of others—itself an essential ingredient for learning the skills that she will need as an adolescent in the real world.

What makes integration work at Rundlett? Over the years, the school has nurtured a coherent set of beliefs that support the full integration of students with disabilities into the school's mainstream while implementing specific structures that make the education of all students the responsibility of all teachers. Most important, the school's philosophy affirms the value of the school as an inclusive community and the belief that the role of schools in a democratic society is, in the words of former principal Christine Rath, "to develop responsible productive individuals committed to caring for each other and contributing to the wellbeing of society." Likewise, desired outcomes of learning— "common skills, knowledge, and attitudes that we believe all students who complete ninth grade can achieve regardless of diverse backgrounds and experience, learning rates and styles"— reflect expectations that "students should understand and accept individual differences, acquire a sense of community, and demonstrate behaviors that contribute to their community... be sensitive to others; respect the rights, opinions, and values of others; and be willing to share skills with others."

At Rundlett, scheduling and staff relationships also support an inclusive school community. For example:

- A strong instructional team includes special education teachers as full members of the team rather than clustering them as a separate "adaptive education team."
- Flexible block scheduling includes common planning time for each team so that teachers can discuss strategies to promote inclusive learning.
- The pairing of language-arts/reading teachers with content-area teachers builds support into the regular classroom which, in turn, reduces the need for referrals for special education.
- Support from the district's director of special education allows for the use of special education funds for the assignment of specialists and in-class aides to many classrooms.
- Small study-skills groups, similar to teacher-advisory groups in other schools, build in additional learning time for all students.
- Specific outcomes are cited for all courses but can be modified to account for students' special needs.

Finally, Rundlett's experience illustrates how the untracking of mainstream classrooms and the integration of students with disabilities complement each other. Indeed, untracking is virtually a prerequisite for the successful integration of students with disabilities into the life of the school; the two efforts are not only philosophically compatible, they must also necessarily intersect as a practical matter. For example, when tracked schools try to integrate students with disabilities into their mainstream, students needing special education support may be incorporated into the lowest track only. As a result, integration may only reinforce the high concentration of vulnerable students in one classroom that is little different from a special education resource room. On the other hand, when special education students are integrated into a heterogeneous mainstream, their numbers in classrooms are dispersed and do not overwhelm "regular" teachers, making integration more easily implemented *and* more true to the mission of inclusive schooling.

Multiage Grouping: Promoting Learning in Familylike Groups

At the Bennett Park Public Montessori School in Buffalo, New York, groups of students, whose ages range from eleven to thirteen, are working alone or in small groups of three or four. Walls are covered with student work, maps, graphics, and information charts. During the morning, the teacher assists one student at a project for a time, then moves on to a dialogue with another one, asking questions that will lead to discovery of a skill or comprehension of the content of the work at hand. Later, the teacher coaches the group as they work together to solve a problem, and still later, she gathers together another small group to ask them to describe what they have learned in a specific assignment. The grade assignment for these students is hardly relevant; what matters here is how individual students are learning.

Sometimes, untracked schools evolve as much by the coincidence of political circumstances as by design. Such was the case with Bennett Park. Indeed, the 580 students at Bennett Park, 56 percent of whom are African-American or Latino, have never been grouped by ability, although nearly half are eligible for Chapter 1 services. Rather, the norm at the school is multiage grouping—a practice that reflects the diversity in a family or neighborhood of children with similar interests.

Established in the mid-1970s during the years of desegregation in Buffalo and in the shadow of a teacher strike threatened in response to job cuts, the Bennett Park School opened with certain advantages. It already had a supportive constituency of parents drawn from families whose children had attended an ungraded inner-city Catholic school, which had been closed. The teachers' union was willing to support the model as a way of preserving jobs, and, coincidentally, the superintendent at the time was on the lookout for promising approaches that would serve as magnets in the overall desegregation effort.

Although multiage grouping is not a new concept in Montessori schools, the notion of ungraded classrooms was new to public schools in Buffalo. Consequently, because the teachers who came to the school had little experience with heterogeneous grouping of any kind—let alone multiage classrooms—most needed preparation for teaching in this setting. As the school's program director explains, "Many were coming from traditional lecture, rote-learning classrooms. The training taught them the 'how's' and 'why's' of the Montessori method. If they weren't enthused about it, we knew it wouldn't work as a shared method throughout the school."

The school took advantage of professional standardization and stipulated that teachers had to be recertified by the American Montessori School Association through participation in an intensive year-long training program. This training and subsequent experience made teachers converts to the multiage grouping approach. Says one of them:

> Students really are responsible for their own work. By individualizing assignments and by promoting cooperative learning activities, we don't face the daily problem of kids being bored by meaningless repetition of lessons. Teachers here do not want to return to tracked classrooms.

The overall mission of the school is to provide an academic community where respect is mutual and students will learn how to think productively, how to access information, how to manage time for a variety of learning experiences, and how to share their questions and achievements. The school believes that these goals can best be met in multiage groups in which children always have access to older students whom they can look up to and younger ones who can look up to them. These groupings encourage teachers to build on students' individual strengths through lessons that require the individual development of learning competencies rather than fit students into a grade-level slot.

Once the district gave the go-ahead to the incorporation of Bennett Park into the public school system, there was simply no debate that it would be a school without tracking. Indeed, both the core beliefs and organizational features of Montessori schools support multiage grouping and make tracking a virtual impossibility. These include expectations that:

- Montessori teachers will facilitate learning through a wide variety of approaches.
- Teachers will assess individual student progress at various stages of the school year.
- Teachers will abandon traditional "isolationist" habits in favor of participation in team planning.
- School problems will be solved by teachers working on committees that may include students.
- Although teachers will introduce new lessons to small groups of students, students will set their own learning pace themselves through using skills in each subject area.

- Activities for mastering the lesson will be multidimensional. Manipulatives, graphics, writing projects, reading selections, experiments, and discovery labs are developed by teams of teachers as they prepare to engage their students in learning.
- Chapter 1 teachers will work with small groups of Chapter 1 students primarily in regular classrooms rather than in separate settings.

According to staff at Bennett Park, multigraded classrooms fit especially well in untracking schools, enhancing learning for all students. Says one teacher, "We do so many good things in the workshop setting. Older kids help younger kids and vice versa. Students share work and projects. They rely on each other for insight and editing help." Multiage grouping does not mean that students or teachers are off the hook when it comes to grade-level assessments, however, and mutual support is apparent, even as students engage in the tedious task of reviewing for city-wide standardized tests. For example:

- In a multiage science class, Mike, the teacher, explains, "We're just applying what you've learned to new questions. Let's do this another way. Remember the lab that we did on ionization? What did we figure out?" Students share their memories of individual experiments. Two students who had performed several experiments read conclusions from their notes. The class is alive with students responding to the teacher's questions. Then Mike says, "Okay, let's look at the exam again." Together students begin to answer the questions. Mike asks why they choose specific answers. Students sort through their notes together, and draw on examples that are applicable to test questions.

- In a multiage English class, the teacher explains how a standardized test may present students taking any grade-level exam with a question like: "People have conflicts that change them. Choose two characters whom you've read about and explain what conflict changed their lives. Be certain to explain the change that occurred." Students begin to check their reading logs in search of characters to use as examples. They bring up the characters' names, the works in which these characters appear, and refer back to the question. Then they name the conflict and the change and work at mapping this information. They are at ease in asking for help from one another as they fill in information gaps. The teacher circulates among the students who, as they practice writing, ask one another process-oriented questions: "Who's the speaker? Who's the audience? What's the purpose?"

Recent reports on multigraded classrooms support the grouping of students across diverse age levels. For example, a study by the Appalachia Educational Laboratory and the Virginia Education Association noted that 76 percent of teachers in multiage classrooms cited learning benefits for students including increased motivation for both younger and older ones, greater independence in work habits, and improved socialization. In a review of the literature of multiage and multigrade groupings, David Pratt found evidence that multiage groups offered academic, social, and emotional advantages—the greatest of which may ultimately be increased attention to students' individual needs. As Pratt asserts, "Even the least radical multiage structure, the split-grade classroom, can deal much more flexibly with both faster and slower learners [than age-segregated grades.]"

The experience of multiage grouping at Bennett Park confirms these advantages. Principal Jan Dumbkowski says:

> Our overall goal is to promote a shared language of respect for persons, property, and learning. This is a daily process. We work hard to know students' names and work. We discourage competition and encourage cooperation. We keep our doors open; students address teachers on a first-name basis. We have some daily routines and schedules, but we view every action as a piece of the whole-school program. Multiage grouping really allows us to maintain our focus on the relationships between our teachers and individual students as the most effective route to success.

Grouping for Diversity as a Way of School Life

Grouping for diversity in the middle grades does not follow a set pattern or formula. Rather, grouping assumes a wide variety of forms, with variations as different as the configurations of students in each school. Grouping variations in untracking schools emerge through a teaming structure that allows teachers to implement and develop various approaches on a pilot basis. Teams in untracking schools are vehicles for promoting both academic learning and the personal and social growth that all adolescents need in an increasingly diverse society. At the same time, teams also foster the professional dialogue essential for teachers' own development as learners and problem solvers.

Schools committed to extending opportunities for students to learn from one another in heterogeneous groups find a number of ways to do so. Their approaches may include flexible grouping strategies, multiage grouping, or controlled heterogeneity; they may involve integration of students whose first language is not English or those with disabilities. The success of these groupings, whatever form they take, will depend on administrative leadership to make scheduling changes and provide teacher support along with the implementation of an innovative curriculum that is inviting to all learners.

4 • High-Level Curriculum for Heterogeneous Groups

What the best and wisest parent wants for his own child, that must be the community want for all of its children. Any other ideal for our schools is narrow and unlovely; acted upon, it destroys our democracy.

—John Dewey, *The School and Society*

Untracking involves more than the regrouping of students. It also demands innovations in curriculum and instruction to offer all students the learning experiences often reserved for the "high" students. These innovations organize learning around investigation and discussion of meaningful problems, are multidimensional, and involve students in hands-on activities that offer diverse routes to knowledge. Often new curriculum is teacher initiated; sometimes it is borrowed from other schools or bought as part of a package. In some schools, teachers have abandoned curriculum organized by isolated subject area in favor of bridging subjects through thematic approaches. In almost all cases, effective implementation of these alternatives involves focused professional development at the school level.

Designing a challenging and interesting curriculum for everyone leads many untracking schools to extend the learning opportunities frequently reserved for students labeled "gifted and talented" to all those in heterogeneous classes. This strategy is not one of watering down traditional curricula to an "average" level; rather it aims at adopting approaches often available only to the "high" groups and making them accessible to more students. As Karla Deletis, superintendent of schools in Wellesley, Massachusetts, asserts, "My perspective is that we have to 'raise the floor,' *and* 'raise the ceiling.'" John Delaney, principal of the Parker Middle School in Reading, Massachusetts, adds, "Whenever we have a choice about what curriculum to adopt, we choose the most challenging, the one we would assign our most facile learners."

With this standard in mind, some untracking schools have designed their own challenging curricula for all students. Others have adopted ready-made approaches to broaden access to a meaningful curriculum for everyone. Whether adapted from other schools or homegrown, curricula for diverse learners all offer a context for intensive classroom inquiry, dialogue, and discussion to engage students and teachers in conversations about ideas of interest to both.

Meaningful Curriculum for All Students

> The human mind hungers for meaning and will impose it whenever possible. That is why the random lists so dear to the psychological researchers' hearts are hard to remember until a pattern, no matter how bizarre, can be discerned in them. Unrelated lists of words and facts are hard to learn. Skills in and of themselves have no meaning and cannot engage the students' minds.
>
> —Council for Basic Education, *Off the Tracks*, 1989

The realization that children in lower tracks or ability groups simply do not receive either the curriculum or instruction that is fundamental to a meaningful education is a major impetus for curricular reform in many untracking schools. Educators in these schools reject the assumption that only some students can venture into the realm of complex ideas while others must review basic skills over and over before being allowed to experience a more conceptual curriculum. Instead they insist that a conceptually oriented curriculum that offers all students equal access to knowledge represents the broadest and most meaningful arena for learning. In fact, curriculum based on thinking skills is more closely attuned to the ways that children learn. As researchers Barbara Means and Michael Knapp point out in their work on teaching advanced skills to disadvantaged students, all students, regardless of their diverse background or understanding of *basic* skills, enter school with significant intellectual strengths and skills in regard to *thinking*—in communicating, comprehending complex situations, making inferences, and coming to conclusions.

With an emphasis on intellectual development and the teaching of thinking skills, curricular approaches for heterogeneous classrooms build on these strengths. Curriculum in untracking schools is typically thematic, interdisciplinary, experiential, hands-on, and project oriented. It is often focused on real-life situations and designed to develop skills leading to good citizenship. Taken together, these characteristics provide a framework for challenging, "high content" learning that is rich in meaning for a diverse group of students.

What is the best curriculum for diverse students? Educator John Arnold, for one, defines it as one that, first, explores substantive ideas from a wide variety of perspectives; second, engages students in reflecting upon the values embedded in the issues and ideas studied; and third, relates to the needs and interests of students, helping them better to understand themselves and the world around them. Jeannie Oakes and Martin Lipton elaborate:

> A rich and balanced curriculum runs counter to rigid standardization. It weaves together large units of knowledge rather than stringing along bits and pieces of facts; it mixes abstractions with concrete experiences and children's informal knowledge of the world. The teacher offers a variety of ways for students to learn complex ideas. Teachers who respond to the richness of their own experience and knowledge as well as to the diversity of their students will not all be on the same page at the same time.

If all students are to participate fully in life in the twenty-first century, they need a curriculum that both expands meaningful learning opportunities to those who have been excluded from these opportunities in the past and also enriches school life for everyone. In response to this need, Johns Hopkins researchers Joyce Epstein and Karen Salinas call for a curriculum that ensures that minority and low-income students have access to "gatekeeping" courses that lead to higher levels of knowledge and also incorporate advanced skills, multicultural perspectives, technology, computer-based instruction, and real-world service projects into every aspect of student learning. This dual focus on "new access" and "new content" is a hallmark of meaningful curriculum in untracking schools.

Thinking Skills:
A Cornerstone of Meaningful Curriculum

A primary goal in choosing curricula and teaching methods
in the middle grades should be the disciplining of young
adolescents' minds, that is, their capacity for active, engaged
thinking.... A disciplined mind connotes a disposition toward
inquiry, discovery, and reasoning across all subjects.

—Carnegie Commission on Adolescent Development,
Turning Points, 1989

Fundamental to the mission of many untracking schools is the
goal of fostering higher-order thinking among all students. But
what does "higher-order thinking" really mean? As the Council
for Chief State School Officers (CCSSO) notes:

Researchers do not agree on a precise and complete definition
of higher-order learning, but they do agree on key characteristics of higher-order thinking. It is complex; yields multiple
solutions; requires interpretation and the use of multiple
criteria; involves uncertainty and finding structure in apparent
disorder; demands self-regulation of thinking processes; and
requires considerable mental effort.

CCSSO points out that subject matter curriculum is natural territory for teaching thinking because reasoning involves thinking
not in the abstract but about *something.* Moreover, making
thinking skills part of instruction in *specific* disciplines is a way
of ensuring that the subjects will be taught at a high level.

This is not to say that untracking schools abandon a commitment to teaching basic skills. Many do, indeed, reschedule time
and reallocate resources to ensure that students deficient in
these skills receive the support and attention that they need.
What these schools do *not* do is use students' weakness in basic
skills as an excuse for withholding challenging and interesting
curriculum. Instead, all students are challenged to apply thinking
skills in every class—including in such courses as home economics (at Pioneer Valley Regional School) and in technology
classes (at Rundlett Junior High). Furthermore, curriculum is
organized so that students of all learning styles and abilities can
acquire the kind of knowledge and skills that tracked schools
have traditionally reserved for "advanced" students.

At the John Glenn Middle School in Bedford, Massachusetts,
the program in critical and creative thinking is crafted with an
eye toward improving reasoning capacities. Classes here are concerned as much with the *process* of learning as the content of it,
and the school's goal of fostering critical and creative thinking

among all students involves teaching thinking skills as part of the curriculum at every grade level. This focus becomes clear in the school's mixed-level social-studies classes taught by Salvatore Fiumara and Linda McGraw. For example:

- **The emphasis is not primarily on what students are saying so much as on why they are saying it,** with the teacher probing for the reasoning behind the statements. Moreover, when one student asserts herself, Fiumara follows up by saying "Now, see what she has said. Sam, can you paraphrase that?" and then, "Janine, give me two facts to support her statement." After being asked to list items that our current society has "inherited" from Roman civilization, and having cited architecture as one example, Fiumara queries the students, "*How* do we inherit architecture?"

- **Students are challenged to make a connection between the class discussion and their own lives.** When asked, "Where have you seen the word *heritage*?" twelve-year-old Joshua, an African-American student, replies, "On a rap album. The Europeans stole the heritage and soul of black people who came from Africa." In responding to Joshua's personal understanding of the abstract and intangible nature of the concept, and challenging his ability to generalize from the culture of ancient Rome to present-day African-American culture, Fiumara immediately follows up by revealing "My ancestors came from Sicily" and asking the class to "match what Joshua said to your own heritage."

- **Students are asked to consider facets of one particular topic—the contributions of ancient Rome to contemporary society, for example—by arranging them in categories of their own choosing.** Creating a taxonomy develops understanding of the context and meaning of each item, as opposed to rote memorization of particular lists.

- **Students are asked to discuss their heroes, then called on to *make generalizations* about them.** When they use their list to generalize that most are leaders, politicians, and male, Ms. McGraw exclaims, "Okay, now you guys are thinking!" Students are then asked to *make predictions* based on their generalizations. At this point the teacher takes the opportunity to ask students to speculate about whether history might change with the presence of more women on future lists.

- **Students are exposed to simulations that foster empathy with other groups.** McGraw's class is divided into "plebeians" and "patricians," with the former required to do the homework of the latter as well as their own. In class, they discuss three questions: 1) What did you do about the assignment? 2) What else could you have done? 3) How do you think the "patricians" or "plebeians" felt? With only one exception, no "plebeian" had done the added work and all resented the extra burden, with more than one "plebeian" asking "Do we *have* to do this? Will we get a bad mark if we don't?"

- **Students experience opportunities to develop specific skills in problem solving.** Working in four small groups, the boys and girls are asked to imagine that they had been on a ship and are now stranded on a desert island. They must consider three issues: 1) What problems are you going to encounter? 2) What are the causes of the problems? 3) What solutions can you come up with? Students are instructed in the skill of brainstorming, and the teacher moves from one group to another acting as a facilitator rather than as "the one with the answer."

The thinking-skills curriculum at the John Glenn Middle School helps students learn that most problems offer many possible solutions and that the process of coming up with the answers is at least as important as the answers themselves. With questions taking precedence over answers, student participation in these heterogeneous "thinking classes" is high, and the atmosphere is often charged with the kind of electricity that accompanies genuine discovery.

Professional Development for Thinking-Skills Teachers

For many teachers, a thinking-in-content curriculum poses new challenges; at John Glenn, a peer coaching model has been a key to support in making this shift successfully. Five teachers who attended intensive programs devoted to teaching thinking skills now act as "coaches" for their colleagues. Along with the principal, Laurence Aronstein, they regularly convene small groups of teachers in day-long meetings to devise ways to incorporate particular thinking skills like predicting, classifying, sequencing, and making assumptions into the curriculum.

A typical peer-coaching session at John Glenn begins with an overview by Aronstein, who is himself deeply committed to the school's goal of infusing thinking skills into every lesson in every classroom of the school. In this session, teachers will focus on "goal setting" as a thinking skill. Aronstein first sets out the agenda for the group of peer coaches and learners assembled in his office: they will clarify and analyze what the skill involves, then brainstorm how teachers can incorporate this skill into their lessons.

In the discussion that follows, teachers agree that goal setting is a *process* that begins by assessing the situation under study, continues by constantly retuning original goals, and ends by attaining the redefined goal and establishing a feedback loop to make possible a reassessment of the situation and establishment of new goals. Once they outline this framework, they delineate several related characteristics of goal setting in terms of an interconnected web of various goals; the importance of context, or a "family" of goals; the possibility and consequences of failing to achieve goals; the necessity of taking risks; and the inevitability of uncertainty.

The freewheeling discussion moves on to how teachers can promote better thinking on the part of students. Teachers mention "wait time" as critical for allowing students to reflect on answers to particular questions and cite the value of modeling good listening skills through eye contact and attention. They consider how and when to use reflective questioning, asking students, "*Why* did you say...?" or "Tell me how you got from point *x* to point *y*." They discuss using analogies to students' prior knowledge and experience, and they agree on the importance of establishing a nonjudgmental, nonthreatening atmosphere to facilitate learning.

In fact, this meeting itself models the valuing of ideas. Although the principal acts throughout to clarify thinking and reflect questions back to the teachers, the democratic tone of these sessions conveys an appreciation of each teacher's contribution. Aronstein himself makes a timely analogy: "Too often," he says, "we think of teacher-student dialogue as a tennis match, rather than a volleyball game, in which more people can participate." It is the latter metaphor that defines the climate of this session.

Following the group discussion, teachers and coaches pair off for ninety minutes to develop their own "infusion lessons." To stimulate the teachers' planning, Aronstein offers the example of setting up a simulation in a current-events class in which students experience goal setting in terms of the aims of the different parties—the United States, Israel, and the Palestinians—in the Middle East negotiations. Whatever the lesson, teachers will incorporate what they have learned into the content area and will plan to model the component thinking skills that they identify.

Toward the end of the day, the group reconvenes to report on the teacher-coach meetings and discuss additional ways to foster the skill of goal setting in their lessons. The participants leave with concrete plans for teaching the skill in their content area; sometime during the subsequent week their peer coach will visit their classrooms to observe and comment on their lessons. A follow-up meeting will give teachers and coaches an opportunity to think through the new ideas and problems that their lessons generate.

John Glenn's staff-development initiative rests on the observation of educator Arthur Costa that teachers are more likely to emphasize thinking skills if they are in an intellectually stimulating environment themselves. Teachers engaged in active learning that builds on prior knowledge and experience can refine new knowledge and assimilate new concepts through application to their own context. Expectations for teachers' capacity to grow are high; it is assumed that every teacher can learn new approaches. Dialogue promotes this growth, and techniques of modeling, coaching, and reflective thinking that are used to promote student learning also serve to stimulate teachers. The success of the approach, in short, is as strong as its commitment to practice what it preaches.

Philosophy for Children

When you see slow learners or disadvantaged students drilling and drilling, when you see the monotony and the drudgery, you begin to think that nobody cares about making school interesting for these students, that nobody cares about having them voice their opinions or enjoy learning. But if you talk with them—ask them about fairness or friendship or why the world is the way it is—you discover that they've been mute and inarticulate all this time only because nobody's ever taken the trouble to consult with them.

—Matthew Lipman, Institute for the Advancement
of Philosophy for Children

What is the purpose of life? What gives life meaning? These philosophical questions need not be restricted to college classrooms; in fact, they are of intense interest to children at all grade levels.

Steve Willette's heterogeneously grouped study-skills class at the Livermore Falls Middle School in Maine is reading aloud from *Harry Stottlemeier's Discovery,* one of the texts from Philosophy for Children's curriculum for the middle grades. As they read one by one, students encounter the dilemma of the story's main character: Should Dale salute the flag in school to express loyalty to his country, or should he respect his parents' objections to the Pledge of Allegiance based on their religious belief that the flag salute is a form of idolatry—the equivalent of "bowing down to a graven image?"

Students volunteer their perceptions and interpretations of the dilemmas that the story raises, and Willette writes on the blackboard:

1. What does the Pledge of Allegiance have to do with religion?
2. If everyone believes in something, does that make it right?
3. Dale's father said he isn't supposed to bow down to other gods.
4. Dale wants to respect his parents, and he wants his parents to respect him.

By now, students have become used to the "discoveries" contained in episodes from the fictional life of Harry Stottlemeier and his friends as they struggle with problems concerned with truth, friendship, differences in kind and quality of experience, loyalty, and justice. As Willette asks questions designed to catalyze debate, students uncover these issues through discussion and apply skills of logic and philosophical inquiry to justify their positions. In subsequent lessons, students come to grips with the ways in which each story may have meaning for their own lives:

> WILLETTE: Okay, let's look at some of these questions. If everyone believes in something, does that make it right?
> AMY: Well, if the majority believe in something, I don't think that makes them right because the *minority* might be right. They just didn't have enough people that believed in it. But then, the minority might *not* be right....
> TOM: I don't think because a lot of people believe something that that makes it right...'cause some people believe killing people's right. That doesn't make *that* right. But we can't say that's wrong.... We can't really tell. To *us* it's wrong, but to somebody else, it might be right.
> LENA: I don't think it's, like, true. Because a lot of people might believe in drinking alcohol or something like that, and the majority of people do it, but that doesn't mean you have to. It doesn't mean that it's right.

The discussion continues, punctuated with questions from Willette: "Do you want to make any other points about that?" "Do you have any other examples we could talk about?" "Anyone have a response to that?" When students exhaust their discussion of each question, Willette moves the focus on to the other topics, concluding:

WILLETTE: Dale wants to respect his parents, and he wants his parents to respect him.
CORRINE: Well, Dale wants to respect his parents in the way that he wants to believe in their religion, and Dale wants his parents to respect him in—I don't know—in a way that he can do things he wants to do, so he doesn't exactly have to do everything they do.
WILLETTE: Anyone agree with that? (*He waits.*) Anyone in that situation?
KELLY: You're supposed to respect your parents, and most of us do, but they should listen to us, too.
WILLETTE: Why should they respect your opinion? What's your reasoning? Aren't they older? More experienced?
AMY: I think they make judgments like about what happened when they were kids. But it's different now.
JOSEPH: I agree a lot with what Kelly said. If your parents say something to you, and you don't agree with them, you should have the right to disagree with them....

Explicitly designed to foster students' reasoning skills through philosophical inquiry and dialogue, Philosophy for Children's twelve-grade curriculum assumes that students will develop critical thinking skills through classroom discussion that allows them to reflect on the human experience, ask one another for opinions and evidence, listen carefully, and build on one another's ideas. At the middle level, the curriculum follows two novels, including *Harry Stottlemeier's Discovery*. The situations that Harry and other characters encounter provoke discussions that allow teachers to introduce topics such as making immediate inferences from a single premise, drawing syllogistic inferences from two premises, recognizing consistencies and contradictions, making connections, discovering alternatives, and constructing hypotheses. Questions such as "What is thinking?" "Why are some things called 'good?'" and "Is there a right way to think?" stimulate debate that is both philosophical and sequential. As teachers encourage students to respond to and explain their points in dialogue with one another, all participate in a "community of inquiry" based on values of independent thinking and respect for the opinions of others.

Because Philosophy for Children is structured to promote thinking in a variety of modes, students of all levels of ability develop basic and advanced skills. Indeed, evaluation studies have documented gains in both reading and reasoning skills for participating students. At Livermore Falls Middle School, where *Harry* is one sixth grade text, students' test scores have improved in the areas of critical thinking, reading, language, and math—an outcome that suggests that learning to think philosophically is preparation for thinking in other disciplines as well.

At Livermore Falls, Philosophy for Children is part of the regular reading and study-skills curriculum. The school's experience confirms that the program need not be offered solely to "gifted" students, whom some may view as the only students "ready" for the challenge of wrestling with complex ideas. On the contrary, Matthew Lipman insists:

> Philosophy is very appropriate for the whole range of students. I don't think that ordinary children are incapable of thinking about complex matters. Kids who may be doing badly in school can argue with the manager of a professional baseball team about whether a player should have been suspended or whether somebody should have been sent up to bat. They can cite the batting averages, fielding averages—the kind of criteria a manager uses to make such decisions. Children do that sort of thing very well when there's sufficient motivation and incentive.

"[Philosophy for Children] works even better with mixed-ability groups than with homogeneous groups," he concludes.

Junior Great Books Curriculum

> One of the most crucial ways in which a culture provides aid in intellectual growth is through a dialogue between the more experienced and the less experienced, providing a means for the internalization of dialogue in thought. The courtesy of conversation may be the major ingredient in the courtesy of teaching.
>
> —Jerome Bruner, "Culture, Politics, and Pedagogy,"
> *The Relevance of Education*, 1973

Given the chance to examine challenging literature and engage in meaningful discussion about what they have read, all students can develop habits of intellectual thought necessary for lifelong learning. This is the basic premise of the Junior Great Books Program, an inquiry approach to learning that provokes students in heterogeneous classes to ponder complex ideas.

At the Parker Middle School, teacher Pat Zona's seventh-grade reading students perform at a wide range of levels, but as one observes them seated in their prearranged circle of desks, it is impossible to identify the "high" or "low" readers. Zona starts the class by checking to see whether everyone has read Max Steele's "The Cat and the Coffee Drinkers"—a short story about a class of kindergarten students and Miss Effie, their teacher—at least twice. She asks students to spend five minutes jotting down their thoughts about one discussion question, using passages from the story to support their ideas. She also instructs them to set a goal for themselves for the number of times each would like to respond during the class.

Zona then refers to the discussion question:

ZONA: The title of the story is "The Cat and the Coffee Drinkers." Why is learning to drink coffee black one of Miss Effie's most important lessons?
STUDENT: Drinking coffee makes kids more mature.
ZONA: What do you mean by "mature?"
STUDENT: Since grown-ups drink coffee, she wanted the children to drink coffee and be grown-ups and mature.
STUDENT: But at that age you're supposed to have fun, and you're not supposed to be grown-up.
ZONA: So why does Miss Effie want five-year-olds to be grown-up?
STUDENT: I think it might be due to the time period—the Depression. They needed to learn these things.

Mary, another student, says that she thinks the children need to feel important. She refers to the fourth paragraph on page 106 and reads to the class: "Her firm words gave us a warm feeling and from that moment on, the schoolroom became a special safe and rather secret place." Aaron, another student, then asks why it is so bad for a teacher to teach things that have little to do with school.

Ms. Zona listens to responses from other children. Returning repeatedly to the original question, a number of other questions arise, and Zona continues to provoke thinking about the story with questions that follow up on the children's former answers and that she herself finds of interest: "Why does Miss Effie teach the kids how to put the cat to sleep?" and "Why does Miss Effie teach the children to do chores before they learn to read?" and "Why is it that Miss Effie never smiles?"

And discussion continues: "She was sad but couldn't show it," suggests Stanley. Malcolm remarks that Miss Effie couldn't let anything out, while Kristal speculates that Miss Effie had mixed emotions and refers the class to page 113, pointing out that Miss Effie loved the cat, but she didn't show any feelings toward it.

ZONA: So why does Miss Effie teach things that don't usually come up in a classroom?
STUDENT: I think she went too far in treating the kids like adults.
ZONA: What do you mean by "too far"?
STUDENT: I'm not sure exactly. But in kindergarten, children need to learn to play.
STUDENT: I think she was preparing the kids for the real world. You need to learn how to clean when you grow up.
STUDENT: And the kids were having fun while learning to sweep and dust; and that's what kids need—to have fun.
STUDENT: I think helping kids learn about the world is what education is all about.

As the class ends, Zona asks students if they have lived up to their goals for class participation. One student is especially proud of herself because she passed her goal and vows to do even better the next time.

What is a "Junior Great Book"? It may be fiction or nonfiction, a short story, novella, or excerpt from a longer work that fits four criteria promoting intellectual exchange and habits of inquiry. Specifically:

- Selections must lend themselves to extended interpretation by virtue of the ambiguity of meaning inherent in the selection and the richness of evidence that can support complex and diverse interpretations. Even with several readings of the story, characters' motives may remain unclear, and certain aspects of the story may continue to provoke curiosity.

- Selections must raise puzzling questions for teachers as well as students. In shared-inquiry discussion, teachers and students collaborate in exploring the "why's" of a story. Students look less to the teacher for answers and take more responsibility for their own learning.

- Selections are necessarily limited in length so that students can read and reread stories, examining details, hypothesizing, and pointing to evidence in the story to support their interpretations.

- Selections are age appropriate but also appeal to teachers. Some selections may have been written for adult audiences but appeal to young adolescents because of the theme, such as Toni Cade Bambara's story "Raymond's Run" or "The Cat and the Coffee Drinkers."

The Junior Great Books Program is designed to help students learn to interpret a text by participating in "shared inquiry": the teacher asks questions to prompt student discussion about a central problem of meaning in the selection. Interpretive questions that highlight this problem have more than one plausible answer that can be supported with material from the text. As students exchange perceptions and opinions, they develop habits of listening to others, weighing merits of opposing positions, seeking evidence to support interpretations, and reconsidering their original perspectives in light of others' views.

At Parker Middle School, English Department Chairperson Jeff Cryan is especially enthusiastic about using the curriculum in heterogeneous classes. He says:

> In homogeneous groups, the discussions used to drag; there
> wasn't a spark. But in the discussions in heterogeneous
> classes, the best thing about them is the mix of perspectives....
> The kids ask questions because they're really curious, not just
> for the grade.

As a "thinking skills" curriculum that meshes with most schools' "regular" offerings and ensures that all students receive instruction in advanced skills, the program has produced significant benefits in a variety of settings. For example, the director of a reading program serving both academically accelerated and academically disadvantaged students in District 29 in New York City reports that students have shown "monumental gains," with as much as a seventeen-point increase in standardized-test scores. And in Pennsylvania, one elementary school piloting the Great Books Foundation's Junior Great Books curriculum designed for daily, whole-class use found gains of over two grade levels in vocabulary and reading comprehension. After one year in the program, which is designed for classrooms in which students read at different levels, 50 percent of students considered "remedial" tested out of that classification.

The experience that these schools have had with the program is testimony to the value of the curriculum for all students. As Steve Craig, editor at the Great Books Foundation, emphasizes:

> Any student can participate in Junior Great Books. When
> you offer students interesting, substantive literature and the
> chance to talk about it in a context where their opinions
> matter, then everybody benefits. Students learn that thinking
> and talking about literature is fun, and teachers see that
> shared inquiry makes it possible for everyone to succeed.
> Everyone is challenged, and students' confidence—as readers,
> as thinkers, as members of a community—just soars.

The HOTS Program

When differences between low-achieving and high-achieving students are dramatic, it may be important to expend extra time and resources helping students who are furthest behind their grade level catch up with their peers in a setting designed especially to address their needs. The Higher Order Thinking Skills (HOTS) program is one successful approach both to focusing on these students and making their move into a "high-content" mainstream successful. HOTS is a general thinking program designed to help students deal with several concepts simultaneously, engage in dialogue about ideas, think in terms of general principles, and pursue ideas to their logical conclusions. Designed to close gaps in learning and to prepare students for a thinking-in-content curriculum, it offers a challenging approach for schools seeking a "gifted approach for at-risk learners."

At the Fowler Middle School in Maynard, Massachusetts, teacher Sally Cotter sits at the "thinking table" with six of her Chapter 1 fifth-grade students. On the front blackboard, Cotter has written "Guess the Number—Day 1." This is the first day of what will be a week-long discussion about "predicting" as a thinking skill. Cotter writes three numbers between one and ten using three separate slips of paper and asks the students to take turns guessing each of the three numbers. The students need four tries to guess the first number, one to guess the second, and three to guess the third. With this introduction, Cotter initiates a discussion on the difference between guessing and predicting. Over the next week students will learn skills in predicting themselves as they work with various software programs together and in pairs.

HOTS presumes that students are academically "at risk" in part because they have not learned skills of reflective thinking. To teach these skills, HOTS curriculum is designed around conversations about problems posed by computer games such as "Murder by the Dozen" or "Where in the World Is Carmen San Diego?" In these conversations, teachers critique students' responses in a coaching, nurturing way. As Stanley Pogrow, developer of HOTS, explains:

> The goal [of HOTS] is to create an ongoing, powerful learning environment in which students begin to discover thinking through the social process of having adults react to their ideas. It is not a process of adults' teaching something, but rather of reacting to students' ideas and students' attempts to construct meaning. By experiencing adults' reacting to their ideas in a consistent way, students slowly begin to get a sense of what it means to understand something.

These conversations mirror the ad-hoc style in which parents use general events as an opportunity to query their children.... These questions and subsequent discussions develop a sense of what understanding is. Instead of a dinner table, and discussions about events of the day, HOTS uses computers, and discussions about what happened on the computer screen the previous day.

The HOTS curriculum encourages teachers to use carefully worded questions to probe students' minds about how they reached particular conclusions, why their answers are correct, or why they are incorrect. Through computer simulation, students learn to make decisions based on evidence gathered and consequences predicted. For example:

- In a sixth-grade class, students work as a team of three to travel the Oregon Trail, making collaborative decisions about provisions and routes. They must read words, write down any that they do not understand for later discussion, and explain the decisions that they make in terms of the consequences of those decisions.

- In a seventh-grade class, students collect clues related to a "murder mystery" and decide which clues should be selected over others. Students keep records of their attempts to solve the mystery and learn to refer to previous attempts as they practice the problem-solving skills applied to other situations.

- In an eighth-grade class, students determine the best strategy for raising money for bus fare home by selling six apples. They discuss pricing strategies in terms of how to determine the amount charged for each apple, whether it would matter if the number of apples available to sell were increased or decreased, and reasons for raising or lowering the price.

In discussions about these experiences, students learn that thoughtful answers require more than one word; that problems often generate more than one right answer; that specific examples are different from general principles; that you can learn something from wrong answers; and that persistence leads to improvement. HOTS students share these insights with classmates on "Invite a Friend Day" when they select a friend from outside of the HOTS class to join them in the "HOTS lab." Follow-up studies of HOTS suggest that after two years of the program, low-performing students do not need additional remedial services, and many attain "honor roll" status in their school.

Despite its success, as a pullout program, HOTS risks the liabilities of labeling and in-school resegregation inherent in any program that separates students from the mainstream for catch-up work. At the Prescott Middle School in Baton Rouge, Louisiana, principal Anna Bernard has come up with an obvious solution: Make HOTS available to every single student who wants to take it by offering it as an elective course in thinking skills! Ms. Bernard explains:

> The first year, our HOTS lab was the program of choice for students who failed any one of three parts on our state-mandated exam. It was a terrific success. We never had any student try to get out of the program, and if we suspended HOTS students, they would refuse to go home until they had taken their HOTS class.
>
> We were impressed! When we looked at the program, we saw there was no need to limit it to a few students. We applied for a special grant, and the second year we were able to double the class, and now we offer it to anyone who wants to take it.

At Prescott, the HOTS lab has seventeen computers, a resource that allows at least that number of students to work with a teacher and aide during each period of the seven-period day. Anna Bernard rejects the notion that only a few selected students should benefit from a new program. "If it's here, it's open to everyone," she says. Like all classes at Prescott Middle School, which has replaced remedial classes with a single, multidimensional curriculum for all students, HOTS classes are heterogeneously grouped. Bernard explains:

> We have "honor roll kids" and kids with behavioral problems all in the same class, and you can not pick these kids out. It's a different learning atmosphere. In HOTS, there's a clean slate. There's no past garbage. Everyone starts off equal. After a week or so, they learn how to cooperate. The teacher did not have to send one child to the office from the HOTS class the whole year.

Bernard and her teachers give HOTS credit for a positive change in classroom attitudes of their students. Bernard notes:

> HOTS has really improved student attitudes toward learning. You know, if you go into many traditional classrooms, kids are asked to raise their hands and speak out. But if children have a long record of failure, they are hesitant to risk. HOTS encourages kids to take chances, to make guesses. You can walk into a HOTS class, and the kids want to tell you what they *predict* might happen if they do one thing or another. They learn to learn from their wrong guesses, and they get support for taking risks.

She concludes:

> These kids have lots of problems, but they have so many
> abilities that have never been tapped. A lot of kids have not
> been contributors, but HOTS changes that. After two weeks,
> the kids learn they can help one another. By the end of the
> semester, they can do anything.

Thematic, Interdisciplinary Curriculum

In adopting heterogeneous grouping, many schools wrestle with
the problem of how to reorganize curriculum so as to provide
various points of entry into learning for students of different
levels while maintaining high standards. One way to do both is
to organize curriculum thematically to provide a meaningful
context for practicing basic skills and thinking critically.

*Thematic
Curriculum in
Language Arts
and Literature*

In 1984, when teachers at Pioneer Valley Regional School formed
a committee to study heterogeneous grouping, many by their
own description were "working sixteen hours a day to make
tracking work." Suggestions for reform proved threatening
to some, and nowhere was this more the case than in the
English Department. After much debate and some hurt feelings,
Pioneer's English teachers did agree to "try it," but with reserva-
tions. As teacher Sylvia Gallagher says, "I predicted the most
horrible things. I said, 'I can't teach *Ivanhoe* to everyone!'" Today,
says principal Evrett Masters, "I think we would have a revolt on
our hands if we were to revert to a tracked school." That revolt
might be led by Pioneer's English teachers who have designed
a thematic curriculum that is as exciting for them as it is for
their students.

The ticket to successful heterogeneous grouping in Pioneer's
English/language-arts classes has been a teacher-developed curriculum conceptualized around broad themes. Textbooks have
disappeared; literature is the basis for all learning. Whether in
Amy Mann's class where discussion revolves around Dreams of
the Depression, in Gallagher's unit on folktales, Roger Genest's
interdisciplinary class on Shakespeare and the Law, or Karen
Morgan's unit on Elders in Literature, students read, write, communicate, develop vocabulary, hone grammar skills, and think
within a context that lends meaning to skill building. Reading
encompasses "the classics," young-adult and contemporary fiction, and literature in translation. Assignments call for informal
and formal writing in creative and expository modes. Whatever
the assignment, all students have access to the same high-level

curriculum and the opportunity to learn in a variety of ways. Says Mann, "Thematic curriculum is absolutely the way to go because everyone has a point of reference. You can work off it and modify it so that all kids can excel."

Within a thematic context, students select their reading not according to predetermined ability but based on their own interests. For example, whether pursuing units on Native Americans, Censorship and Banned Books, or mysteries, students in Karen Morgan's classes are required to read one "anchor book" which provides a framework for discussing plot, character, and theme. But students must also choose additional novels from selections that Morgan pulls together from the school library, her personal collection, and ten-cent finds from yard sales and flea markets. Morgan explains, "With this system, I have to be on top of what every student is reading. If someone's bored, I jump in. Whatever their level, the kids are never allowed to stop reading."

Morgan's sense of trust in students' own choices has developed with experience. At first, she distributed books according to her own perception of ability. But that changed. She explains:

> Students knew exactly what I was doing. I found I'd made a
> mistake thinking I could restrict their reading. So the next
> year, I put all the books on the table and let the kids choose.
> What happens is that they make their choices according to
> their interest in the story. Some very good readers choose
> "easy" books, but that's all right because they still have to think
> about the *ideas* in the story, and they still get pleasure from the
> literature. And some kids you'd never expect choose the harder
> books. One of my poorer readers chose to read Conrad
> Richter's *Light in the Forest*. It took him all semester, and at
> the end he said it was the most awesome book he'd ever read.
> I never would have assigned that book to him. None of my
> kids is ever without a book to read.

In Pioneer's classes, all language-arts activities relate to the reading theme. Practice using prepositional phrases and new vocabulary evolves from the novels that the students select. Likewise, writing assignments reinforce reading so that, for example, a unit on Native Americans may involve composing original legends, researching and writing about a particular tribe, drafting a letter to a guest speaker about the impact of the philosophy of a native culture on a student's own life, or taking a woodland walk and reacting to and writing about nature as an indigenous American might.

Assignments like these mesh with work done in the school's Writing Lab course, a quarter-long introduction to computer-assisted writing required of all eighth graders. The work is subject to peer editing, and Morgan expects her students to edit each paper two or three times. She explains:

> I pair students myself, first a pretty good writer with a not-so-good writer, then equals with equals. The third time I put them in a group of four. This way the low-level students get to see what good writing looks like. And the good writers learn to critique and think about matters of purpose and meaning and choice of words.

Just as Pioneer's curriculum offers students of all levels of ability the opportunity to approach challenging content across thematic bridges, thematic organization also allows for diverse modes of learning. As Genest notes, "In themes we try to accommodate many areas of interest and many types of learning materials to appeal to all types and levels of learners." Mann further explains how both individual and group work is structured into classroom activities:

> The cycle moves from individual, to small group, to large group, and returns to the individual. This can work with any text and with any theme. It works beautifully in a heterogeneous classroom because it allows for choice and mandates working together for maximum comprehension. For example, once students have worked together on the anchor piece, their next reading might come from a list of five novels, perhaps [in a unit on Survival], *Lord of the Flies, The Miracle Worker, Anthem, When the Legends Die,* and *Kidnapped.* Groups form randomly as students choose the book they want to read. I do limit groups to a five-person maximum. Then it is my job to set a time line for reading, responding, and small- and large-group work.

Mann explains that sometimes each group may work on understanding a single element such as the use of symbols, character development, or the evolution of conflict. At other times, content becomes a vehicle to discuss and deepen student understanding of how literature can convey different perspectives of such concepts as love, family, community, courage, or justice. Groups must report to the whole class about the story, and individuals are responsible for writing analytical papers on each novel. In addition, everyone keeps "response notebooks" which contain their personal responses to each chapter and notes relating to the theme that they are following. These notebooks allow Mann to monitor student work and progress.

Likewise, Gallagher's unit on folklore combines individual, small-group, whole-group, and cooperative learning, as well as independent study to provide an in-depth approach. The unit begins with a visit from a local storyteller. As students move into the theme, they might explore Animal Tales, beginning with one story that they already know and using it as the foundation for whole-class discussion of, perhaps, the use of animals as symbols. In small groups, students choose a proverb or "lesson" from a list created by Gallagher, discuss the proverb, and brainstorm a plot line involving animals as characters. Then, after each student writes an individual folktale and presents it to the small group, the group chooses one to read to the whole class. Eventually all stories are bound in a volume for next year's class.

In Gallagher's classes, thematic curriculum allows grouping to vary according to the assignment. Sometimes each student in a group will read a different Arthurian legend, then present the legend to the small group to create a broader understanding of common aspects of the genre. At other times, the entire class will read one book but will work in small groups to explore different concepts such as good and evil or loyalty and disloyalty.

Themes also lend meaning to writing and language-development activities. As students write their own legends explaining the origin of the Connecticut River in their journals, incorrectly spelled words become individual spelling words assigned for study. Themes further promote thinking skills as, for example, in Gallagher's use of African dilemma tales to stimulate discussion of the appropriateness of different decisions in different cultures or individual projects researching of creation myths from different cultures.The unit culminates in an oral storytelling event.

If Pioneer's English teachers were at first hesitant about thematic curriculum in heterogeneous classrooms, they are now sold on its advantages. Morgan says, "I have never had kids producing so much, reading so much, using critical thinking so much." Mann adds:

> A thematic approach to teaching literature…stimulates a heterogeneous group to do the real analytical work we crave from our literature students because inherent in this approach is choice. Many interesting and diverse pieces of literature can be offered to students. Not everyone has to read the same thing, as long as the piece has to do with the theme. Not only does reading different material create choices for students, but it also mandates that students learn to see connections and patterns in literature. Such learning, I believe, is the thematic approach's most important value.

*Making
Themes
Interdisciplinary*

Early adolescence is an ideal point at which to present students with learning activities that cross all disciplines—science, math, social studies, and language arts—and also knit those disciplines into themes that develop critical thinking skills. For example, Islander Middle School principal Sue Galletti describes central, interdisciplinary themes at work in mixed-ability classrooms at that school:

- In the sixth grade, one connecting theme is Ships. Students read *Treasure Island,* and as they read that novel, they observe sections of the old movie and analyze differences in character development. Students role-play as portions of the book are narrated, write in journals, and develop vocabulary and spelling words from the literature. They learn geography and history by tracing the path of ships on a map and study the history of schooners and parts of ships. Using fractions and measures, students cut ropes and do rope tying. They connect science with the "Voyage of the Mimi," a thematic, packaged curriculum. A guest speaker discusses the history of schooners, and students make a field trip to visit the *Wanona,* a local ship. A second sixth-grade theme is The Renaissance through which students' study of Leonardo Da Vinci incorporates learning in art, the history of inventions, geography of Italy, and science of oceanography, while developing the concept of "rebirth of knowledge."

- In a seventh-grade classroom, the connecting theme is The Pacific Northwest Region. As students study the climate and physical geography of the region, they read appropriate novels such as *I Heard the Owl Call My Name,* which blends the traditional culture of the Kwakiutl people with the present urban culture of Vancouver, British Columbia. Students delve into topics of prejudice, international trade, use of symbols and themes in literature, and a comparison of two cultures. Spelling and vocabulary words come from reading, writing, and research assignments on these topics. Students develop graphs which compare and contrast trade between Canada and the United States in terms of dollar amounts and types of goods.

- Democracy, with a focus on citizens' rights and responsibilities, constitutes one theme of an eighth-grade classroom. Daily review of global, national, and local news models the obligation of citizens to stay informed about current events. Debate and expository writing necessitate research and evaluative thinking about current issues. Political cartoons stimulate students to measure public concerns and analyze trends. Literature such as *Animal Farm* and *Salem, Massachusetts* provide a literary analogy to the development of government and the protection of individual rights. Students invite police officers and lawyers to visit to explain search warrants, free-speech regulations, Miranda rights, and other principles of the Bill of Rights.

Galletti explains that these and similar integrated units involve students in learning basic skills and concepts through activities that engage different learning styles and develop more complex thinking and problem-solving skills. Although curriculum still incorporates subject material, it is not driven by a single textbook. Instead, many resources enrich learning in various parts of the curriculum, which are woven together to deepen understanding.

Thematic curriculum in heterogeneous classrooms also ensures that all students have access to "high content" that incorporates thinking assignments into every single class. For example, at Central Park East Secondary School, students may investigate interdisciplinary themes such as energy conservation, political power and change in American history, or stability and change in non-western societies over a period of one year. Whatever the theme, focused questioning serves as the route to deeper understanding. Teachers ask students over and over again to consider questions related to:

- **Viewpoint:** From whose angle or perspective are we viewing the topic at hand?
- **Evidence:** What do we observe or know about the problem and how reliable is the evidence?
- **Connections:** How do aspects of each topic fit together? What are causes? What are effects?
- **Conjecture:** What about the situation could have been different "if only…?"
- **Relevance:** Why does what happens in a topic matter? Who cares?

As they become accustomed to questions like these, students of all backgrounds learn to think in order to understand. As one Central Park East student states, "It's different from a tracked school. In our school, the teacher makes *everyone* think from different perspectives before we judge them."

Making Themes Multicultural

A thematically organized curriculum is also an ideal vehicle for introducing materials from a variety of cultural perspectives into classroom learning. Themes such as "Native Americans" can incorporate materials on indigenous cultures not only of North America but also of Central America, South America, and the Caribbean, and thereby reflect a broader range of cultures that may also more closely mirror the heritage of students' own families. Thematic learning may trigger explorations of art, architecture, geography, anthropology, or archeology—and, in turn, lead to an examination of community, family, or power within a particular culture. In like manner, a theme like Survival can incorporate literature on American slavery, war, the Holocaust, or immigration into discussions about the struggles of individuals and communities against social adversity. Journeys and Quests may consider similarities and differences in Homer's *Odyssey, The Epic of Gilgamesh,* and Toni Morrison's *Beloved* and offer opportunities to apply concepts not only through an examination of history and literature but also by studying current events, visiting art or photography exhibits, writing letters on behalf of a prisoner of conscience, or interviewing community or family members.

As themes are developed to reflect a diversity of cultural perspectives, possibilities for learning are opened up that appeal to the diverse student body of the classrooms of the 1990s. In the process of expanding the learning context to include experiences that students can recognize as close to their own, multicultural themes offer building blocks critical to the acquiring of new knowledge. At the same time, thematic curriculum opens doors to the use of materials and activities—for example, oral histories, field trips, guest speakers, music, videotapes, pen pals—that make learning more accessible to more students.

*Using
Curricular
Themes
to Merge
Academic and
Occupational
Learning*

Thematic curriculum can also be a bridge between academic and vocational learning. At Cambridge Rindge and Latin School in Massachusetts, for example, the technical-arts curriculum for ninth graders interested in exploring occupational education does just that. To break down barriers between two tracks that are often seen as incompatible, teacher/curriculum consultant Adria Steinberg and a team of technical-arts teachers at the school have fashioned a curriculum organized around an in-depth study of their 100,000-person, multiethnic city.

Throughout the year, Cambridge itself is the "text" as students examine the architecture and design, services, people, neighborhoods, industries, and trades of their city and participate in projects that expose them to the vocational areas offered at the school while maintaining their full participation in academic subjects. Projects involve not only "shop" skills in word processing, graphic arts, carpentry, drafting, electronics, or metal work, but also skills in literature and language arts, mathematics, and science. Student work results in "artifacts" of the city: maps, scale models of interiors and exteriors, photographs, tapes, oral histories, and painted backdrops. During the year, ninth graders present their work to real audiences composed of community decision makers for discussion and feedback.

Curricular integration at Cambridge Rindge and Latin also prepares students for work and community settings where life is not divided into isolated topics and moves vocational education from a focus on occupationally specific, narrow, skill-based training to one that addresses all aspects of a given industry. For example, construction activities in the shop program are coordinated with academic studies of homelessness, local zoning regulations, and the history of tensions between logging and conservation interests and with extracurricular activities in dramatic arts.

Thematic learning at Cambridge Rindge and Latin ensures that students who learn with their hands have access to knowledge equivalent to that offered to those who learn in more traditional ways. This approach also realizes the vision of the program's executive director Larry Rosenstock who insists, "Vocational programs shouldn't be places where students have less or inferior access to knowledge. In this program, students just gain knowledge in a different way."

Experiential, Hands-on, Project-Oriented Curriculum

Human beings learn more readily from *doing* than from seeing or hearing alone. This principle underlies much of the curriculum in heterogeneous classrooms. In the mixed-ability classes at the Middle School of the Kennebunks, teachers are putting this principle into daily operation through their science curriculum known as Fundamental Approaches in Science Teaching (FAST).

Today is the final day of the marking period at the school. In Mike Denniston's science class, it is a day of reckoning. In this class, the students have been studying concepts of buoyancy, volume, mass, and density. Rather than memorize *"D=m/v,"* however, and let it go at that, the students have been coming to grips with these concepts through a very particular and concrete assignment.

Using materials of their own choosing, they have designed a model submarine. Today, they will hand in their submarine model, drawing, and explanation of its operations to Denniston. They will also demonstrate the operation of their model for the entire class of twenty-three seventh graders. According to specifications, the submarine must rest on top of the water in a fish tank for five seconds, submerge, remain on the bottom of the tank for one minute, rise to the surface, and repeat the cycle. The assignment has endless possible applications, with plastic bottles, aluminum drink cans, film canisters, medicine bottles, yogurt cups, used batteries, and keys among the materials chosen for submarine bodies and ballast.

Roger Twitchell, Science Department chairperson, first suggested adopting FAST for all students as a way of improving science learning in heterogeneous classes. "FAST is great for all kids," he says. "I have kids with retardation working with gifted kids. All of them open up to the lab assignments because everyone can be involved in a different role. What happens is that they all take more responsibility."

Increased student responsibility for learning does not, however, reduce teachers' responsibilities. In fact, the importance of the teachers' questioning during the course of the project makes FAST teacher intensive, but not teacher centered. Twitchell explains that the style of questioning is both demanding for the teacher and challenging for students:

The questioning is extremely important. You use open-ended questions such as "What do you think is happening?" or "What would happen if…?" as much as possible. When you close a question, the "average" or "remedial" kids quit the first time they get the wrong answer. By redirecting the question, the "gifted" kid has to keep working harder to articulate why something does what it does, and the other kids are encouraged to keep going until they have a deeper understanding of the concept.

Denniston is a persistent questioner of his students who, one by one, come to the front of the class to explain their models. Nicole sets her submarine on the water's surface. She has made her model from a clear plastic bottle weighted with washers, filled with vinegar and raisins, and punctured with a straw into which she feeds a spoonful of baking soda. Denniston asks for more specific explanations:

Okay, Nicole, tell us what's happening…. What are the air bubbles doing? Why are the air bubbles increasing? What's happening to the mass? How much does an air bubble weigh? How much space does it take up? What's happening to the volume? If something takes up more space than it weighs, what does that do to the density? So what's happening when the bubbles pop off? What do you think would happen if you cut the straw in half? What would happen if this tank were deeper?

Later, Dan is back for a second try with his design, a high-bouncing ball with a string of safety pins attaching the ball to a weighted plastic cup containing Alka-Seltzer and perforated with three holes, one pierced with a straw. Denniston begins:

What do you have, Dan? What did you do compared to last time? You added some weight? What did that do? What's going to make it go down this time? What's going to bring it back up? What's going to get it down again?

The students are gathered close, some sitting on their desks. They watch as Dan's "submarine" remains halfway submerged in the fish tank. Denniston again asks:

Anyone have any thoughts about what's happening? You think the ballast is too *light* this time? Would it matter to shorten the safety pin "string"? What might help it go down better? Dan, you almost have it, but you have to go back to the drawing board. Perseverance pays off, though. It's definitely an improvement.

FAST's emphasis on increasing the capability to perform basic lab skills, use symbolic tools of science, and understand fundamental concepts of modern science overshadows any imperative to find "the one right answer." Twitchell says:

> I don't tell the students that the formula for density is $D=m/v$, but the kids do learn to talk about "grams per millimeter." FAST helps give all this meaning: "What happens to density when mass changes? What happens to volume? What happens if we change the density but not the mass?" Students have to demonstrate that they know what density is in these terms not that they have memorized a formula.

Often it is the "gifted" children who initially resist this approach. As Twitchell explains, "Kids who are used to getting the "one right answer" are no longer kings of the class. It's hard for some. This year I had a student who refused to ask any more questions after he realized that I would just throw them back at him. He had to change. Now he loves it. He comes in and asks, 'What's the challenge of the day?'"

FAST was developed by the University of Hawaii's Curriculum Research and Development Group expressly for use in classes with a wide range of abilities. With an overall emphasis on physical, biological, and earth sciences and their relation to the environment, grades six through eight focus on ecology and the environment, while grades eight through ten emphasize matter and energy. Although FAST does not require extensive lab facilities beyond heat, running water, and bench space, students do spend 60 to 80 percent of their time in a laboratory or on investigations in the field. The remaining time is devoted to analyzing and interpreting data, reviewing literature, discussing findings, and writing or sharing reports.

Donald Young, codirector of FAST, summarizes the program's main strengths:

1. Students learn by doing. They learn how science develops new knowledge.
2. Students develop an understanding of basic science concepts. They progress through a sequence of laboratory and field activities that build on concepts and skills that have come before.
3. Students develop basic thinking skills and creative-thinking skills. FAST encourages them to wrestle with problems and pursue their hunches by trying various solutions. Instead of giving answers, the teacher poses the kinds of questions that scientists ask as they attempt to solve similar problems.
4. FAST has proven effective in developing science concepts and skills among students of all ability levels.

Training and consultation by teleconference is provided by the University of Hawaii, and teachers from the Kennebunks find this support invaluable. Twitchell also notes that participation of teachers as a team in the training provides a foundation for continuing collaboration as the curriculum is implemented. "We're really a team now. We like working together," he says. "We're at school doing our own experiments until five P.M. every day."

FAST was originally funded by the National Science Foundation (NSF) which has continued to support the development of hands-on science curriculum for heterogeneous classrooms in the middle grades. Additional NSF-funded science curricula, some still in a field-test stage, also show promise for heterogeneous classes. These include:

- **Human Biology Middle Grades Life Sciences Project**
  of Stanford University, which offers an interdisciplinary
  approach to the teaching and learning of science specifically
  for students of varied backgrounds and abilities. Designed
  thematically both to stimulate students' interests in science
  and to help them address serious social, behavioral, and
  health problems, the twenty-four-unit curriculum can
  stretch over two to three years to combine the hard sciences
  with social sciences in a focus on adolescent development.
  Interdisciplinary units may involve language-arts, math,
  home-economics, or health teachers in challenging activities
  which include lab work, writing, role-playing, debates, and
  group work. Materials include a textbook and teacher training
  materials for implementing hands-on activities that build on
  innovative, complex instruction approaches developed by
  Elizabeth Cohen of Stanford.

- **"Insights,"** a thematic curriculum building on heterogeneous
  cooperative-learning groups developed by the Educational
  Development Center (EDC) in Newton, Massachusetts, targets
  the needs of all early adolescents while specifically addressing
  urban students. Based on a broadly focused study of the
  human body, module topics include "You Are What You Eat,"
  "Meeting Our Needs," "Designed for Motion," "How Do
  We Know Anything—Perceptions," "Energy, The Source
  of All Action," "Music to My Ears," and "Connecting with
  Our World." Activities incorporate skills and concepts from
  other disciplines and blend with videotape and software
  applications. New curriculum for grades seven and eight
  builds on a framework developed for earlier grades.

- **"Models in Physical Science,"** an activities-oriented curriculum applicable for grades six through nine, was developed by the Children's Museum of Boston and uses topics such as "Inks and Paper," "Ice Cream Making," "Tops and Yoyos," "Salad Dressing Physics," and "Houses, Bridges, and Towers—Investigating How Structures Stand Up." The aim is to involve students in experiential activities with real-life materials that will lead to an understanding of concepts of physical science. The curriculum includes guidebooks and kits covering eight topics, each centered on enough activities for fifteen to twenty sessions of in-depth learning on that topic, and involves intensive teacher-led discussion. Teachers' guides and kits marketed through Cuisenaire coordinate with video-tapes produced in collaboration with public television.

- **"National Geographic Kids Network,"** developed by the Technological Education Research Centers (TERC), is a telecommunications-based science curriculum project that extends the program's elementary-grades curriculum into seventh, eighth, and ninth grades. Similar in format to the elementary-grades program, the curriculum engages students in local environmentally oriented experiments. Data from those experiments will then be shared on a computer network. Working with their "research teammates," students also compare data from their own class with those of others. The curriculum encompasses units in the earth, biological, and physical sciences and includes a software package that permits communication with other students via computers and modems.

Susan Snyder of the NSF is enthusiastic about the potential of these curricula in heterogeneous classrooms. Indeed, NSF has funded several of these projects expressly for mixed-ability class-rooms—"the wave of the future," according to Snyder.

Project-Oriented Activities for Heterogeneous Groups

> I often hypothesize that people probably learn more from the few projects they do in school than from hundreds and hundreds of hours of lectures and homework assignments. I imagine that many people end up finding their vocation or avocation because they stumbled into a project and discovered they were really interested in it.
>
> —Howard Gardner, *Teacher* magazine,
>   November/December 1991

In untracking schools, teachers have discovered that hands-on project assignments allow students of all ability levels to develop understanding of subject matter in heterogeneously grouped classrooms. Projects also provide a meaningful context for studying one topic in depth while at the same time learning basic skills. As one student at a heterogeneously grouped middle school admitted, "I just don't write easily, and it's hard for me to write a lot. But I like to talk and learn." Multidimensional learning projects can develop the skills of children who read and write well and of those who also "like to talk and learn." For example:

- At heterogeneously grouped Columbus Academy, a New York City public school, 180 middle-grade students explore the evolution of communications technology in a three-part course. First they review basic scientific discoveries related to communications technology. They then visit communications facilities to see modern communications technology in action. Finally, teams of students create their own video, film, and audio projects.

- At the Crossroads School in New York City, 100 sixth, seventh, and eighth graders gain hands-on experience with video equipment in all their classes. They produce their own video programs and study how video is used on TV for maximum effect. Teachers also learn to use video equipment and explore the use of video as a tool to enhance staff development and assess student performance.

- At the Louis Armstrong Middle School, English teacher Fran Corvasce uses a project called "Community Historians: Talking City Blues" to help heterogeneously grouped students become oral historians and cultural journalists. Drawing from the experiences of their own relatives and neighbors, they create monologues for dramatic performances, school publications, readings, and a school exhibit. Part of an ongoing collaboration with oral historian Arthur Tobier, this approach, says Corvasce, "helps kids know where they are in the historical process." She adds, "I got some of the best interviews from kids who had poor writing and test taking skills, but who had good ideas. As long as you can talk, listen, and use a tape recorder, you can succeed. The writing skills follow."

Learning for Life:
Linking Student Concerns with Social Issues

I wish I knew why the world has so many problems and why the different countries just can't get along. I wish I knew why people treat the earth the way they do, spraying aerosols into the atmosphere, ruining the ozone, burning trash, filling landfills, using up all our natural resources.

—Middle-grade student, quoted by Lee McDonough, "Middle-Level Curriculum: The Search for Self and Social Meaning," *Middle School Journal,* November 1991

Most discussions of curriculum reform tend to focus narrowly on improving the quality of what is taught in English, math, social studies, and science. Even those who have come to believe that new curricula must expand to include thinking skills usually consider these to be within the boundaries of the traditional academic subjects. However, some educators now question whether a separate-subject approach is appropriate for young adolescents and suggest that middle-level schools in particular should reposition subject matter within a broader curriculum reshaped to connect students' personal concerns with larger social issues.

Educator James Beane, for example, proposes using the full range of young adolescents' concerns—the need to understand physiological changes and develop a personal identity; concerns about social status, peer conflicts, and authority; and preoccupations with friendships, changing relationships with adults, economic roles, and commercial pressures—as a springboard for launching curriculum that encompasses a variety of social concerns across subject areas. He argues that combining the developmental needs of students with parallel social issues can establish a foundation for investigating such broad themes as Identities, Independence and Interdependence, Conflict Resolution, Justice, and Caring—themes that in total become a "living" curriculum.

Within the context of studying the *common* needs, problems, and concerns of young people and the larger world, students can learn skills of reflective thinking, critical ethics, problem solving, and social action. Moreover, this general curriculum can become a vehicle for communicating enduring concepts of democracy, human dignity, and diversity. Beane argues further:

> Surely there must be a way for the middle schools to offer early adolescents something more deeply human than they do now, more relevant, more compelling, more truly educative.... [That way] is to open the hearts and minds of young people to the possibilities for a more just and humane world—a world in which human dignity, the democratic way of life, and the prizing of diversity are more widely shared and experienced. In doing this, we would surely find our work more complete, more coherent, and more satisfying.

Beane's emphasis on curriculum for democracy, dignity, and diversity is thoroughly compatible with a paramount goal of many untracking schools: to foster a community of learners committed to realizing both individual and shared achievement. For example, principal Kay Goerss of West Windsor-Plainsboro Middle School in New Jersey, reports that that untracking school will implement a thematic curriculum aligned with Beane's proposals by 1995. West Windsor-Plainsboro has already developed an interdisciplinary curriculum for its heterogeneously grouped seventh grade, including a one-month period during which students choose for themselves a set of social issues that they want to study in depth. Working cooperatively in teams, students incorporate learning in all subject areas to produce detailed magazines on each topic. Goerss explains:

> The magazines pull all the subject areas together. Students have to use math skills to produce charts, tables, and graphs to illustrate their topic. They use research in social studies and science to gather and organize information, and their literature selections—the school uses reading workshop, writing-across-the-curriculum, and whole-language approaches—include readings on biracial families and family interaction, economics, the environment, and problems of segregation and integration. It's different from year to year since it all grows from the kids' deciding what social concerns they're going to look at.

At West Windsor-Plainsboro, week-long schoolwide projects also promote interdisciplinary activities having to do with social concerns that touch on all parts of the school's curriculum. For example, just prior to the winter holidays, a focus on cultural diversity extends to physical-education classes where students learn games from around the world.

Activities such as these acknowledge that adolescence is a time of increasing curiosity about the world beyond students' immediate families. Eager not only to learn *about* life's problems but also to address these problems in an immediate way, young-adolescent students are ready to experience the responsibilities of citizenship in a democratic society. Curriculum that builds on this assumption not only capitalizes on students' developing interest in the wider world; it also harnesses youthful idealism and energy for improving the world.

Practicing Citizenship Skills in Heterogeneous Classrooms

In Marsha Bailey's sixth-grade class at the Holyoke Magnet Middle School, classroom mobiles illustrate environmental themes, and wall posters include a portrait of the Reverend Dr. Martin Luther King, Jr., and a nautical chart of George's Bank, a rich North Atlantic fishing ground. Magazines in Spanish and English and literature like Nicolasa Mohr's *El Bronx Remembered* and Rudyard Kipling's *Captains Courageous* invite students to settle into cozy beanbag chairs for a good read. This afternoon, however, students are poised for a group discussion preliminary to episode five of the "Voyage of the Mimi" curriculum, part of a larger focus on learning about ocean ecology.

Bailey begins by asking her students to conjecture why an oceanographic research expedition might want to scrape the bottom of the ocean and what researchers might discover there. But one student's suggestion that researchers might find garbage among the treasures of the sea reminds others of an earlier discussion about environmental devastation of another sort. "Oh!" exclaims one student. "I just remembered. I was going to ask. Do you remember the Mitsubishi letters? I have one!"

Over the course of the year, Bailey's heterogeneously grouped class, including students from some of the poorest families in the city, has followed environmental issues through a study of different ecological systems. As part of their focus on the world's rain forests, they considered allegations that multinational corporations have contributed to deforestation, and they have written letters to alleged violators. Now one, the Mitsubishi Corporation, has responded, and Bailey asks students to read aloud from the replies: "Mitsubishi only uses a small amount of tropical timber.... The real damage to the rain forests is being done by the many people who live in them.... We work to make sure that trees that are cut are replaced...." The letters are form letters and printed on paper labeled "recycled."

The children are immediately thoughtful in response to Bailey's discussion questions: "So what is the Mitsubishi Corporation saying?" "What is their position?" "Do we know that to be true?" "What do we have to do to be sure?" "What's one thing we can do?" The students are thoughtful before they answer:

LEISHA: "You know how they said they're planting trees again? Well, we could find out if that's true. We could ask for pictures."

JESUS: "But we have to be careful. They could send us pictures of someplace else, and we wouldn't know."

FRANK: "If we want to call them, there's a number on the letter. What would we say?"

BAILEY: "So you can ask for more information?"

The students nod. They think for a moment. Then...

JAIME: "Also, how do we know it's really recycled paper?"

SARA: "We can feel it. Remember when we made paper how it felt?"

BAILEY: "Does all paper feel the same? Are there different grades? Different weights? Is that the best evidence?"

LEISHA: "I think we could call a recycling company to see if they've made a delivery to the company. Then maybe they have and maybe they haven't. Or, are there people who would be interested in writing to Greenpeace again? Or calling the company? Can you write that phone number right away?"

BAILEY: "First of all, remember it's a 212 number. You have to talk with your parents first, tell them your concerns. And you have to let them know you want to call. You don't pay the bills. Also you want to write down your questions first so that you are prepared. And take notes."

JESUS: (*Jumps up to the blackboard.*) "Do you have his telephone number and his address?" (*He writes the number and address for the entire class.*)

BAILEY: "Those people who received letters... How did it make you feel?"

SARA: "Interested. I want to know more."

MARTIN: "I feel happy they wrote back and they care about our statements."

JESUS: "Important... I feel important."

It is no accident that the teaching in this class supports what James Beane has called "authentic" middle-school curriculum that "combines the *common and shared* concerns of early adolescents and the larger world." At the Holyoke Magnet Middle

School, teachers explicitly value the goal of empowering their students as learners and consciously adopt a curriculum that has meaning for the immediate lives of the children. As Bailey explains:

> Students of this age need to feel part of something. They need to feel important. We are looking for curriculum that is more like what society is dealing with now. We have bad days, but we are having many more days where we see kids discriminate between and develop ideas and be loving. This can only help our kids deal with the academic and family and economic issues they face every day.

Curriculum focusing on activities to develop citizenship skills is especially compatible with mixed-ability classrooms. Learning in heterogeneous groups contributes to an understanding that everyone has an equal right to have his or her opinions heard and that students are responsible, as citizens, for speaking out and learning about issues that affect the community at large. In the process, the children learn that they can influence the social conditions that shape their own lives.

Resources for a Curriculum Focusing on Social Concerns

From the students' perspective, curriculum "rich in meaning" should link learning with the real world. Emerging supplementary resources for heterogeneous classrooms, many designed by community organizations, are now available to help schools include compelling life issues as part of their classroom curriculum.

Facing History and Ourselves

Facing History and Ourselves is an interdisciplinary curriculum focusing on questions of bigotry, racial and ethnic prejudice, and intolerance in society through studies of the Nazi Holocaust. It encompasses issues such as abuse of power, unquestioning obedience to authority, and the choices available to resist social abuse. Methods of inquiry and analysis probe such questions as "How is an environment of mass conformity and racism created in a society?" and "Why and how did some individuals defy the power of the state despite the dangers that they incurred?"

For untracking schools interested in developing a curriculum focusing on social concerns, Facing History offers an obvious bridge between the lessons of the Holocaust and the lives of students in the world today. As educators Martin Sleeper, Margot Stern Strom, and Henry Zabierek explain:

Facing History and Ourselves identifies universal concerns of adolescents—loyalty, peer-group pressure, scapegoating, labeling, conformity, and belonging—and uses them as pathways on which the students can encounter history and then travel back and forth between the past and the present.

Primary-source materials help students examine recurring notions of conformity, responsibility, and the link between thought and action. Students also relate the adolescent theme of identity to stories of real people whose lives in Europe of the 1930s were not too different from theirs. *Choosing to Participate,* a resource book of case studies of citizenship in American democracy, encourages students to think about their own civic responsibility to participate in current affairs.

Teaching Tolerance

A second resource for linking student concerns to social issues is *Teaching Tolerance,* published by the Southern Poverty Law Center in Montgomery, Alabama. Based on the understanding that tolerance can be taught, not just talked about, this biannual magazine for teachers is full of invaluable suggestions for classroom activities, book reviews, and leads to resources. These suggestions are helpful both to schools enrolling diverse populations and to more homogeneous schools where teachers want their students to learn respect for cultural differences. Highlighting ready-to-use ideas and strategies, the magazine is designed to offer "a source of encouragement for the thousands of teachers who are working to build communities of understanding in their classrooms."

Food First

A third resource for developing a curriculum focusing on social concerns is the Institute for Food and Development Policy, known as Food First, which is dedicated to public education about root causes of global hunger and culturally appropriate approaches to development in third-world countries. Food First's award-winning curricula include two comprehensive packages for heterogeneous classrooms.

Food First Curriculum for grades three through eight links the development of basic skills and students' everyday experiences with global concerns. Six illustrated units in a 146-page curriculum span a range of compelling topics including the path of food from farm to table, why people in other parts of the world do things differently, and how young people can help make changes in their communities.

Exploding the Hunger Myths: A High School Curriculum helps students critically assess global issues related to world hunger, food production and distribution, food aid and economic development, and population. The curriculum is interdisciplinary, and students explore each issue while applying language arts, math, social studies, biology, geography, and environmental concepts. "Action activities" including role-playing, simulations, interviews, and writing stimulate an understanding of the underlying causes of hunger and potential solutions.

National Association for Mediation in Education (NAME)

NAME, a national network for educators and community mediators, is a fourth major resource for schools implementing conflict resolution and peer mediation as approaches to encourage citizenship skills, recognize students' roles in school decision making, nurture a democratic school climate, and foster skills in problem solving among all students. NAME's clearinghouse of books, manuals, and articles pertinent to the field includes William Kriedler's *Creative Conflict Resolution* and David and Roger Johnson's *Creative Conflict*. A bimonthly newsletter, *The Fourth R*, provides a forum for research findings, summaries of curriculum models, and descriptions of student- and teacher-developed approaches.

With the question "Why can't countries and people get along?" nagging at the minds of many students who may experience conflict as a "normal" part of their own lives, NAME meets the needs of untracking schools that recognize that conflict-resolution programs have a place in the curriculum. In fact, these programs are uniquely suited to untracking schools in that the values underlying conflict resolution in school—an appreciation and respect for differences and an emphasis on personal responsibility for behavior—mirror those that inspire heterogeneous grouping. Moreover, parallels between conflict resolution and thinking skills emerge as students in training as peer mediators learn to identify common ground, think analytically, generate options and alternatives, and find win-win solutions to complex problems.

Project Public Life

A fifth resource, Project Public Life, located at the University of Minnesota, helps citizens develop as powerful actors in public problem-solving. Public Achievement, one of the project's activities, specifically involves teams of adolescents in designing and implementing strategies to address problems in their own communities and present their work at citywide Youth and Democracy Conferences and training sessions. Based on ideas and themes developed with over 1,000 young people from across the country, Project Public Life's handbook, *Making the Rules: A Guidebook for Young People Who Intend to Make a Difference*, helps young people act effectively in the arena of democratic politics by stressing citizenship activities that extend beyond voting. Themes focusing on "Discovering Your Self-Interest"; "Stepping Into Public Life"; "Encountering Diversity"; "Building Power"; and "Go For It!" all include stories, lessons, and exercises that can be used to set the stage for projects that involve student/citizen participation.

Taken step by step, the activities in *Making the Rules* prepare students to work as part of a team, identify an issue that is important to the team, and define a problem that the team would like to solve. Taken as a whole, the set of exercises taps into the idealism of young citizens. As student participants at the 1989 Youth and Democracy Conference wrote in an anthem composed collectively with Minneapolis singer-songwriter Larry Long:

> It's our thoughts
> It's our future
> Our voices and our lives.
> We are young,
> But we're not children
> We're fighting for our lives.

The Kids' Guide to Social Action

What happens once students are ready to attack a community problem that they have identified? After research on issues relating to the environment, drug abuse, discrimination, hunger, or homelessness has been completed, what comes next? Teacher Barbara Lewis provides some answers in the form of a resource guide called *The Kids' Guide to Social Action: How to Solve the Social Problems You Choose—and Turn Creative Thinking into Positive Action*. As Lewis says, "The real world is chock-full of real problems to solve: real letters to write, real laws waiting to be made, real surveys to analyze, real streams needing monitoring, scraggly landscapes in need of artistic attention." Based on her classroom experiences with "academically talented" students, activities in *The Kids' Guide to Social Action* are even more appropriate for heterogeneous classes where the classroom itself more closely reflects that "real world."

The guide is organized into five parts: creating projects that make a difference; skills needed to accomplish those projects; legislative advocacy; resources for more information; and tools for social action. Activities develop problem-solving skills in fund-raising, media relations, interviewing, writing letters to the editor, and lobbying. Along the way, students may write a press release or execute and compile results from a citizen survey, putting to use basic and advanced skills as they communicate with different audiences, analyze issues, and apply new knowledge.

Exercising Citizenship Through Meaningful Community Activities

> Let the skills of problem solving be given a chance to develop on problems that have an inherent passion—whether racism, crimes in the street, pollution, war and aggression, or marriage and the family.
>
> —Jerome Bruner, "The Relevance of Skill or the Skill of Relevance," in *The Relevance of Education*, 1973

In addition to engaging mixed-ability groups of students in the pressing issues of the broad society, activities that link schools with community organizations provide multidimensional routes to learning about social concerns affecting students' own neighborhoods. For example:

- At Louisville's Western Middle School, the school's science curriculum connects hands-on projects to environmental concerns in the larger world. Students have landscaped the school yard; "adopted" four acres of rain forest through the Nature Conservancy with money raised from the collection of recyclable aluminum cans; and won first prize in a districtwide collection of yellow pages for recycling. In addition, students make field trips to nearby Indiana farms to glean excess food for distribution to Kentucky Harvest, a network of local soup kitchens.

- At Crete-Monee Junior High, all eighth graders fulfill a community-service requirement prior to graduation. In addition, students and teachers alike "think globally and act locally" by recycling all paper and avoiding all Styrofoam products in cafeteria and classroom activities. In addition, the young people make significant decisions concerning planning and implementing group projects that have consequences in the real world. For example, a student board of directors elected by classroom planned a fund-raising project then decided how to spend the $600 raised to benefit others in the larger community.

- At the Middle School of the Kennebunks, every teacher-student advisory group chooses a "Kids Care About..." service project to meet a need that the boys and girls identify. Projects include contracting with disabled adults to do chores and errands; working at a soup kitchen for homeless people; making baby quilts to distribute to hospitals throughout the country for AIDS and drug-addicted babies; conducting auctions to raise money for Toys for Tots, the Salvation Army, and a local children's home; raising money to defray medical expenses for a classmate burned in a fire; and sending books to children in Kinshasa, Zaire.

- At the Louis Armstrong Middle School, students in the Home and Career exploratory classes participate in the Early Adolescent Helper Program and visit a nearby nursing home and day-care center twice a month. In addition, sixth graders with learning disabilities tutor first graders from a nearby elementary school; others take responsibility for maintaining the vest-pocket park across the street from the school.

- At Chestnut Street Junior High School in Springfield, Massachusetts, Community Service Learning is an integral part of the curriculum, not an "add-on." Every year, students choose work on community-service projects at agencies ranging from the Red Cross to the New England Puppet Theater, including the popular "Brothers and Sisters" program which counters gang expansion in the neighborhood by involving young adolescents as tutors and mentors for children in younger grades.

- At the Dudley Street Neighborhood Initiative in Roxbury, Massachusetts, a heterogeneous group of students ages ten through nineteen has worked with architect Gail Sullivan to design two community centers slated to be built in the neighborhood. Student groups first planned how space should be used in the facility, visiting buildings designed for similar use in the greater Boston area to generate ideas. Applying math skills, small groups then designed the centers themselves, with older students preparing scaled models of buildings for two separate sites. Says Sullivan, "Often the students who had the strongest visual and spatial ideas were the ones who had been in remedial programs for years. One thought he was really stupid because his basic skills were weak. But he had enormous talent. He should be an architect."

These activities affirm the capacity of adolescents to develop an awareness of their responsibilities as citizens of democratic communities and of the wider world. Adults can open doors of opportunity to help students realize these roles through activities that prepare them for *life* in the twenty-first century—not simply for the next grade.

Multilevel Groups, Multifaceted Curriculum

Schools that move to adopt heterogeneous grouping also understand that curriculum must reflect a commitment to all students. These schools move toward curriculum that emphasizes thinking skills as the common ground of learning for everyone. A focus on thinking skills in the middle-level curriculum does not circumvent basic skills; rather it sets out a meaningful context for learning and reinforcing these skills through a variety of activities.

Effective curriculum in heterogeneous classrooms is often thematic, experiential, and project oriented; it may incorporate multicultural activities through an interdisciplinary focus. Whatever the framework, curriculum for heterogeneous groups offers multiple routes to learning, engages students in dialogue with the teacher and one another, and takes advantage of diversity in the classroom by encouraging cooperative learning. As important as covering specific content in traditional subjects represented by reading lists or numbers of assignments is, developing dispositions for inquiry among all students is equally important. Only then can a foundation be laid for further learning throughout life.

5 • Instruction and Assessment for Heterogeneous Classrooms

We need classrooms in which beauty is savored, truth
honored, compassion practiced, and fellowship engendered;
classrooms where creativity is encouraged, where youngsters
are assisted in dreaming of a better life, classrooms that are
laboratories of living rather than places in which teachers talk
and students listen.

—John Lounsbury, *Middle School Journal*, November 1991

Heterogeneous grouping calls for changes not only in curriculum but also in instruction and assessment. No longer can
instruction assume a single pace geared to the "average" student
within a particular ability level. No longer can the teacher be
positioned as the sole source of facts, information, and ideas.
Instead, classes that treat students as individuals rather than as
categories require the orchestration of all the resources of the
school and community so that there are *multiple* routes to
learning. Fundamental to changes in instruction and assessment
in heterogeneously grouped classrooms is a shift from an
emphasis on teaching to an emphasis on learning.

Educators in untracking schools stress that a student's ability
to learn may ultimately be as important as any particular body of
knowledge that he or she *has learned*. Teachers in these schools
are less purveyors of answers and more directors of learning—
coaching students to formulate questions, tolerate ambiguities,
interpret meaning, and generalize to develop new hypotheses
based on their observations. They are using innovative
approaches such as cooperative learning, complex instruction,
Foxfire, and peer and cross-age tutoring to complement these

techniques. And, reflecting more multidimensional instruction, they are developing new assessment strategies that necessarily move away from the testing of facts toward approaches that evaluate thinking and problem-solving skills as part of the learning process itself.

Differentiated Instruction for Diverse Learners

Teaching in classrooms with children at varying stages of mastering skills and knowledge can be hard work for teachers who must account for the learning of all their students. In planning for diverse groups, increasing numbers of teachers are guided by the belief that approaches often characterized as "good for the gifted" are also effective for lower-achieving students. As Sue Carrel, a math teacher from Glenbard West High School in Glen Ellyn, Wisconsin, wrote in a Letter to the Editor of *Educational Leadership:*

> Instruction in the high-ability group should not be labeled "gifted" educational instruction; it is simply *good* educational instruction that should be offered to *all* students in the same setting.
>
> I should know. I received my M.A. in Gifted Ed. at Kansas University in 1982. Throughout my course work, the question that kept nagging me was "But aren't these just good educational techniques for all students?" I was taught techniques labeled "differentiated instruction geared for the gifted student," which included 1) how to create an atmosphere that fosters creativity, 2) the steps for creative problem solving, and 3) strategies to help students produce a project to present to an audience. All these techniques are just as applicable to a ninth-grade pre-algebra class as they are to my freshmen honors algebra class. Having been trained in cooperative learning and other so-called "gifted" educational techniques, I bet I could teach low-, middle-, and high-ability students some good geometry in a heterogeneous setting, and everyone would benefit in more ways than one.

Successful heterogeneous classrooms rest on the tenet that "good teaching" encompasses a variety of techniques. At Tate's Creek Middle School in Lexington, Kentucky, teachers Dorie Combs, Elizabeth Barrett, and Julia Robbins are acting on just this proposition. These teachers have identified methods that allow them to work successfully with a seventh-grade cluster that blends students described as gifted, general-advanced, basic, and learning disabled. The adaptations that they make in traditional instruction to individualize learning within their classrooms allow students to reap the benefits of belonging to a heterogeneous group. These adaptations include:

- **Personalized assignments.** Two days each week are assigned to reading and writing workshops involving literature of students' own choosing. All students complete identical assignments ("Describe the sequence of events leading up to the conclusion..." or "Describe how the traits of the main character affect your book's plot..."), although they may be working from different texts that reflect similar themes but represent different levels of difficulty.

- **Personalized teacher-student correspondence.** Teachers ask students to write regularly in literature logs and journals in response to "prompts" such as "Do you like what is happening in this novel and why?" in reading or "If they were to mummify you tomorrow, what five possessions would you want buried with you and why?" in social studies. Teachers then write detailed comments directly in response to student work.

- **Questioning.** Teachers direct questions of varying degrees of difficulty to students according to their level of understanding.

- **Direct teaching of study skills and note-taking strategies.** Teachers offer special cross-disciplinary workshops to teach such skills as semantic mapping and outlining that strengthen the organizational skills needed for all subjects.

- **Use of learning centers.** Teachers use classroom work stations to define assignments for varying levels or learning styles. For example, an assignment focusing on "cause and effect" might engage students working in small groups with different sets of materials collected at different tables. Or one learning center might include earphones for students who need tapes to prompt them as they follow assigned reading.

- **"Mailboxes" with leveled materials.** When students have extra time, they can choose extension assignments from "mailboxes" containing materials of varying levels of difficulty.

- **Differentiated testing.** Recognizing that the purpose of evaluation is not to "get" students but to assess learning, teachers may work with special education resource teachers to individualize tests for different learners. For example, tests can be redesigned to vary the amount of white space on the test paper to make the questions more comprehensible for students with learning disabilities. While distributing questions, teachers can avoid labeling by pointing out that different versions of the test discourage cheating.

- **Grading.** Teachers can broaden grading criteria to focus on individualized learning objectives, especially for students with Individualized Education Plans who are integrated into "regular" classes. Other approaches include establishing standards of competence, asking students to redo work until they have mastered objectives, and giving grades that reflect effort.

In the heterogeneous seventh-grade team at Tate's Creek, teachers select from these approaches as needed. Combining these adaptations with cooperative learning, they have been able to boost the achievement of students at all levels of learning.

Educators in other untracking schools build on research to develop their own strategies for improving achievement of all students. Rejecting instruction that focuses on parts of a subject at the expense of the whole, memorization of facts apart from their context, and a narrow emphasis on basic skills to the exclusion of inherently challenging assignments, these teachers choose approaches that add meaning, coherence, and depth to learning. The approaches that they use focus on an orientation to whole concepts *prior* to breaking the larger learning focus into parts and creating learning situations that relate directly to students' interests and real life.

For example, researcher Martin Nystrand of the University of Wisconsin suggests offering whole texts to read rather than lists of vocabulary or phonetic combinations remote from any meaningful context. He also recommends writing assignments that encourage students to communicate ideas within their real-world context. Some of his specific suggestions include:

- Interweave writing, reading, and classroom talk so that students can relate continuously to what they have already learned. For example, teachers may facilitate classroom discussion before introducing a reading or writing assignment, have students write about what they discuss, and follow up by discussing what they write about. During classroom discussions, teachers can incorporate previous students' answers into new questions.

- Enhance authentic communication by building students' concerns into discussions and assignments. Put greater priority on thinking than remembering. "Authentic" questions that probe for students' opinions—"Do you think the main character did the right thing?" and "Could this happen today?"—help students relate to, discuss, and interpret meaning.

- Provide opportunities for "real writing," including journals, to encourage habits of frequent, regular writing, with teachers responding to content only and students receiving credit but no grade; learning logs in which students summarize and formulate written opinions of their readings; and position papers in the form of essays, news stories, letters to the editor, or a letter to a public official in which students take a stand and explain their views.

- Introduce literature—including Shakespeare—by exposing students to the entire work in its context. Use dramatizations, videos, or field trips to full-scale productions to expose students to the overall drama of plot, characters, and theme. Only then is a closer reading of particular parts likely to make sense.

Nystrand notes that approaches like these can be equally effective with learners of all levels; in fact, many of his suggestions sound remarkably like "good teaching" practices that appear both in upper-level and effective mixed-ability classes.

Cooperative Learning: A Powerful Strategy for Heterogeneous Groups

- In a seventh-grade language-arts class at the West Baltimore Middle School, the room is humming as Joan Taylor's thirty-five students pair off to review the use of similes, metaphors, and personifications in their original poetry. Today they are sharing their poetry with a partner for enjoyment and critical evaluation. Using their structured "Evaluation Guide," they discuss questions such as "Did the poem appeal to the senses… Which ones?" and "Was there evidence of descriptive language…clear use of a simile?" and "Was there a comparison/relationship shown…and did they make sense?" and "Was the poem fun or compelling?" Taylor moves about the room, conferring with pairs, occasionally silencing the whole class to remind students, "Remember to share, don't interrupt, honor the opinion of your partner." Reveling in the language her students have produced, she says, "It's as if they've had a bird released from inside themselves…. They're beginning to see their 'mind movies' come alive."

- Across the hall, Regina Valentine's thirty-seven seventh graders are going over their predictions based on their halfway-through reading of "Thank You, M'am" by Langston Hughes. Referring to their Word Mastery List, for which students have reviewed and defined antonyms for new vocabulary words, Valentine takes them back through the predictions that they have made based on the story's title and the vocabulary and asks them to discuss the question, "Are these predictions true so far?" Then moving on to the list of antonyms, Valentine asks her students to work in their groups to match student-created antonyms with the story's vocabulary. As they finish, each group submits its completed match to the teacher. An anticipatory silence prevails as Valentine announces "Not quite, keep trying!" and the room buzzes again until another team submits its entry. The winning team will be eligible to receive a "Big O" pass, which team members can trade in any time for a night free of homework or cancellation of a tardiness detention.

- In a nearby classroom, Thelma Watford's thirty-four seventh graders have already read Borden Deal's short story "Antaeus" silently to themselves, then orally with a partner. Halfway through, the pairs have answered questions related to the story, described the characters and setting, and predicted how the narrative's problem might be resolved. Student pairs have also identified new or difficult words related to the story— "antique," "resolute," "calculate," "contemplate," "desecrate"— and have practiced using these with their partners. Today they have moved to the next step in their "reading process" and are working in small groups to write out their thoughts about the story.

With 1,500 students in sixth through eighth grade, size alone makes West Baltimore the sort of urban school where a teacher might remain stuck forever in old ways of instruction. At best, teachers in such a setting might be tempted to try something new behind the closed door of their own classroom. But in these language-arts and English classes, cooperative learning, not traditional instruction, is the rule, not the exception. Adopted first in the school's sixth grade, then in the entire seventh and eighth grades, cooperative learning is now the instructional norm in reading, writing, and literature classes that include as many as thirty-seven students.

In this school, English classrooms are defined by the habits, language, and techniques of cooperative learning implemented in the form of the Student Teams/Reading (STR) and Student Teams/Writing (STW) approach. For example, in one classroom, a prominently displayed poster reads:

Team Manners
1. Talk quietly.
2. Be respectful.
3. Stay with your group.
4. Talk only to your group members.
5. Listen.
6. Follow directions.

The vocabulary of cooperation sets the tone in some classrooms where teachers have posted a list of character traits valued in their classes: "Cooperation, honesty, kindness, courtesy, responsibility, consideration, enthusiasm, fairness, patience." In others, logos, signs, and symbols dangle from the ceiling pipes indicating the nature of the cooperative-learning activities: "Brainstorming"; "Think—Pair—Share"; "Roundtable"; and "Jigsaw." Posted on the walls are "Word Mastery" lists, with vocabulary generated collectively from textbook stories and from students' own work. Alongside these are clues to the assignments, such as a poster entitled "Two Ways to Write Meaningful Sentences."

Cooperative learning at West Baltimore reflects teachers' commitment to deepen students' engagement in learning by developing their reading, writing, listening, and speaking skills as an integrated body of communications skills. Their approach links practice in reading and writing skills with a study of good literature anthologized in Scholastic's *Scope English Anthology—Level 1,* including stories by authors such as Maya Angelou, William Saroyan, O. Henry, and Langston Hughes. Whether students are working on language mechanics such as punctuation; writing poetry or meaningful sentences; or reading literature for theme, character, and comprehension, certain routines are consistent across all English classrooms at the school. For example:

- **Student "teams," usually of four students, are heterogeneously grouped so that one "high," two "average," and one "low" student work together.** Team composition changes every six to nine weeks so that students get used to working with different people. Desks are clustered, with a dictionary distributed to each team so that students can work together freely. Teams adopt their own distinctive names and descriptions such as "The Magnificence Kids: Magnificence is our name; thinking is our fame."

- **The expectation of peer review prevails, and students are explicitly instructed in skills of cooperative reviewing and editing.** Teacher Julia Young, for example, addresses the objective of critiquing meaningful sentences by coaching her students: "If you tell someone 'That's a dumb sentence,' how do they feel? Sad? Dumb? Right. That's why you say 'That sentence needs some work.' That's how people learn." Thus, while students are held accountable for their own learning, they also take responsibility for helping one another.

- **Students clearly understand the objectives of the work that they are assigned in the writing or reading process.** In every language-arts classroom at West Baltimore, teachers post "Objectives of the Day" for all to see. For example, the blackboard of Regina Valentine's classroom reads, "We will… 1) compare and contrast writing styles of Langston Hughes, O. Henry, and William Saroyan; 2) discuss the words of the new mastery list; 3) complete steps 1, 2, and possibly 3 of the reading process." At the beginning and end of each class, teachers refer explicitly to the objectives: "Let's see how we're doing and where we're going next.…" If students complete the activities early, they are directed to additional independent reading of their choice.

- **Instruction moves from a teacher-based focus to a partner- or group-based focus to independent learning and includes direct instruction in reading comprehension.** Weekly instruction reflects research findings that comprehension can be taught as a separate skill. Thus, cooperative learning does not completely substitute for direct instruction but reinforces and enhances teacher-transmitted knowledge.

- **Rewards both for individual student effort and for teams are built into learning.** At the end of three class periods, teachers give students a comprehension test on the story, a test on writing meaningful sentences for each vocabulary word, and a test of their oral reading of the words on the Word Mastery List. Students are not permitted to help one another on these tests. The test scores, along with compositions and book reports, are major components of weekly team scores. In addition, teachers regularly acknowledge teams that have worked together well in class and have successfully competed as teams to complete an assignment. Teams that meet an average criterion of ninety points or better on all activities are designated SUPERTEAMS; GREATTEAMS are those with eighty- to eighty-nine-point averages; teams that receive fewer than eighty points are designated GOODTEAMS, and all receive certificates of recognition. Over the term, as the compositions of teams change and students' work improves, virtually every student is cited on a SUPERTEAM.

Robert Stevens of Johns Hopkins University, developer of West Baltimore's new language arts/English curriculum, explains how students respond to cooperative learning:

> What do kids catch on to? First, they learn they can do things in class that are fun. Then they learn that if they work on the assignments, they will be recognized for their accomplishments. And once they get actively involved, they begin to realize that they like this author or that author, and that they like learning, and that there are intrinsic rewards to their schoolwork.

Research over the last decade has demonstrated that cooperative learning has had a positive impact on student achievement, attitudes toward school, and peer relations. So far, at West Baltimore in particular, researchers from Johns Hopkins have found that students in STR achieve at significantly higher reading levels than similar students who are exposed to traditional instruction. At the classroom level, teachers say simply, "We love it," and students say, "This is different from other years. It's fun. You learn more.

In fact, success is built into the design of the approach. As Bob Stevens explains, "The whole system is designed around mastery. If you do everything you're supposed to do, there's no need for failure. You should have every kid succeed. Everyone can be a winner."

Characteristics of Cooperative Learning

The most commonly mentioned teaching change in untracking schools is the shift from traditional teacher-centered instruction to cooperative learning. What does such a change entail? Dr. Robert Slavin of Johns Hopkins describes some of the characteristics of cooperative-learning classrooms:

- Heterogeneous grouping, including special education students, is the norm.
- Teachers and students share leadership appropriately.
- Activities emphasize task accomplishment and maintenance of skills.
- Students share responsibility for one another's learning, with the most effective learning evolving from positive interdependence among students.
- Teachers observe and intervene, teaching social skills directly.
- Students are held individually accountable for performance.
- Groups reflect on their effectiveness.

A number of well-researched cooperative-learning approaches fit these characteristics; many have become widely used in untracking schools, where teachers report that they prove especially effective for students who have experienced little success in traditionally organized classes. West Baltimore has adopted one model known as Cooperative Integrated Reading and Composition (CIRC), in which students work in mixed-ability teams on reading and writing assignments. CIRC has been found to promote the achievement of students at all ability levels, including very high achievers, more effectively than traditionally taught homogeneous classes.

Cooperative-learning models—including CIRC, Learning Together, Group Investigation, Jigsaw, Team-Games-Tournament (TGT), Student Teams-Achievement Division (STAD), and Team-Assisted Individualization (TAI)—offer teachers a repertoire of strategies to accommodate wide-ranging differences in skill and achievement levels in mixed-ability classrooms, including those integrating special and general-education students. Common to all these approaches is the expectation that all children will gain both academic and social skills by sharing information, knowledge, and personal viewpoints while completing a group task.

Incorporating Cooperative Learning into Teachers' Repertoire of Skills

Effective implementation of cooperative learning depends in large part on the professional-development opportunities that are offered to teachers. Because it can take up to two years for teachers to feel fully comfortable about incorporating cooperative learning into their repertoire of instructional approaches, untracking schools often find themselves approaching staff development in ways that provide ongoing support, as was the case at the Parkman Middle School in Milwaukee. Here, after teachers decided to eliminate tracking, they began to explore cooperative learning as a means of stimulating higher order thinking on the part of their students. What came first, though, was a change in teachers' attitudes and preparation for this new instructional methodology.

Parkman is located in a predominantly African-American, working-class community. Student enrollment numbers some 600 with average class size at 29. Fifteen percent of the students participate in special education programs, 81 percent are eligible for free or reduced-price meals, and many come from one-parent families. These challenges prompted Parkman teachers to search for instructional practices that would set a standard for high expectations and provide the requisite social and academic support.

At the start of the 1989–90 school year, then-principal Dennis Schumacher along with several staff embarked upon a training program in cooperative learning. Many of the teachers were veteran educators who were most comfortable with traditional instructional methodologies. However, knowing that if teachers were going to be effective in heterogeneous classrooms they would need to utilize a variety of instructional strategies, Schumacher first offered several awareness-building sessions on cooperative learning.

Initial training occurred when thirty teachers attended an informational lecture on cooperative learning. Following this orientation, five staff members took part in an in-depth cooperative-learning seminar in San Francisco. Subsequently, knowledge and support for cooperative group learning spread slowly throughout the school. When the next in-service opportunity was offered, seventeen teachers, approximately 35 percent of the faculty, volunteered for training. Consistent with the training-for-trainers model, these seventeen returned to Parkman and established a comprehensive program for other staff members interested in using cooperative-learning strategies.

To balance and sustain the changes in pedagogy at Parkman, one faculty trainer, Belle Tomasello, has been designated the school's cooperative-learning "implementer." She is responsible for ensuring that cooperative-learning approaches, once accepted, are used appropriately in the classroom. To this end, Tomasello engages in modeling sessions with teachers in their own classrooms and follows the progress of faculty trainees, providing additional support and assistance as needed through monthly meetings on classroom-management strategies and development of learning units. Tomasello and interested teachers also produce a cooperative-learning newsletter featuring instructional tips and anecdotal information.

As a result of this approach to staff development, Parkman teachers can now employ an array of teaching strategies that are well suited to the broad mix of students in their classes. Teachers have reached consensus on common "ground rules," such as making students individually accountable for work completed in cooperative-learning groups, and they agree that it is up to each teacher to determine when the use of cooperative-learning methodologies is appropriate. Since the establishment of the cooperative-learning training program, participating faculty members have observed better retention of subject matter, higher motivation, peer mediation and tutoring, and improved discipline among their students—effects that, in turn, sustain interest in staff development.

Other untracking schools have applied variations on Parkman's approach to staff development. For example, at Crete-Monee Junior High, most teachers first learned about cooperative learning through a series of dinner workshops scheduled from 4:00 to 7:00 P.M. over seven consecutive weeks. Principal J.T.

Crawford explains that teachers there learned that "for the cost of sending a couple of staff to national seminars, we found we could bring in an outside expert with close to a national reputation and provide dinner, too." He adds, "And the payoff is greater because we get more staff on the same wavelength more quickly."

Interested educators and parents can keep abreast of developments in the field of cooperative learning through *Cooperative Learning* magazine, which collects current information on theory, research, curricula, instruction, concrete suggestions for classroom activities, and staff development in this methodology. In addition, teachers who seek further training can turn to the regional networks of the International Association for the Study of Cooperation in Education; the Johns Hopkins University Center for Research on Effective Schooling for Disadvantaged Students; Resources for Teachers; and the Cooperative Learning Center of the University of Minnesota. Many trainers believe that staff development in cooperative learning is most effective when implemented in the context of specific subject areas.

Evaluating Cooperative Learning in the Classroom

Although research has clearly demonstrated the benefits of cooperative learning, sometimes teachers feel the need to assess its effects for themselves in the classroom. At the Louis Armstrong Middle School, seventh-grade science teacher Nanda Sundri, for one, wanted to determine the impact that cooperative learning was having on her students. She had already observed progress in terms of motivation and class participation, and she had noted that students were taking on new roles as tutors, guides, and friends to classmates with whom they found themselves involuntarily grouped. But she also wanted to assess academic changes, so she decided to use end-of-unit test scores as "before" and "after" points of comparison.

In all classes, the less-successful students showed gains. Moreover, in some classes, improvement was dramatic for all groups. Of her thirty-one students in one class, for example, fifteen had scored below 60 percent before the introduction of cooperative learning; whereas afterwards, only four remained in that range. At the same time, seven had scored above 80 percent while working in simple groups; whereas fifteen scored about 80 percent (and eight above 90 percent) after Sundri introduced assignments in which students were more responsible for one another's progress.

Experiments like these offer powerful evidence to skeptics that shifting from a teacher-centered classroom to a more student-centered one can improve learning for all students. Their example can also prod others to try similar approaches.

Complex Instruction

I need motivation to do the work. If someone asks me to help,
that starts the motor in my brain working. That's why when
Samantha asked me for help, I helped her, and then could
do my own.

—Eighth-grade student, *Boston Globe,* 16 July 1991

Richer diversity in the nation's public schools, particularly as
far as students' language backgrounds are concerned, makes
paramount the need for instruction that is effective with heterogeneous groups. At Stanford University, Dr. Elizabeth Cohen,
Beatriz Arias, and other researchers at the School of Education's
Program for Complex Instruction have taken the urgent implications of this diversity to heart. Since 1979, their work developing
a set of research- and experience-based techniques for heterogeneous classrooms has formed the foundation for a teaching
approach called Complex Instruction.

As Cohen and Arias have noted, "Even the popular recommendation of cooperative learning for heterogeneous classrooms
does not remove the problems connected with status differences
between students." Thus, the unique focus of Complex Instruction is on improving the achievement of children who are often
assigned limited social status in their classrooms. These include
students whose ethnicity, language accent, perceived academic
or reading ability, popularity, or length of time in the United
States makes them vulnerable to reduced expectations in terms
of academic performance. Specific techniques create changes in
classroom organization and management, introduce a multiple-
ability curriculum, strengthen teacher-student interventions to
reduce status differences, and support teaching staff.

What goes on in these classrooms? First, in classrooms using
Complex Instruction students are clustered in small, heterogeneous work groups. They are *required* to talk with and help one
another to complete the task assigned at each learning center. All
written instructions and materials are presented in relevant languages as well as pictographs, and conversation in both English
and other languages is encouraged.

Although reading, writing, and computation are at the basis of
each assignment, tasks themselves focus on solving problems
that are inherently interesting and conceptually demanding. The
exercises may repeat concepts, yet each demands different
media, modes, and kinds of intelligence. "Tasks should be open-
ended so that precocious students can carry them further, while
less-mature students can complete the tasks on a simpler level,"
emphasizes Cohen.

Second, in Complex Instruction classrooms, the teacher must *explicitly* instruct students in the *process* of learning and working in groups, even before they begin their learning-station assignments. The participants also agree to two rules: "You have the right to ask anyone else at your learning center for help" and "You have the duty to assist anyone who asks for help." These rules both maximize student involvement and limit classroom-management problems. In addition, rotating assigned roles, including that of "facilitator," promotes greater interaction and achievement.

Third, Complex Instruction calls on teachers to employ two specific techniques called "status treatments," which are *explicit* teachings about ability. The first, the Multiple Ability Treatment, holds that successful completion of assigned tasks requires many different skills, not just reading and writing. Teachers specifically identify all the skills necessary to complete a task, then directly announce to the class: "No one person is going to be good at all these abilities, but everyone will be good at at least one." The second, called Assigning of Competence to Low-Status Students, requires teachers to observe low-status students for demonstrations of competence at some intellectual ability that is necessary for the completion of the assignment. Then the teacher must remark on this ability within hearing distance of other children, explaining what the particular student did and why this specific skill is valuable in the adult world. By using these techniques to equalize and increase student interaction in diverse classrooms, teachers have realized significant gains in achievement by low-status students.

With clear evidence that Complex Instruction results in higher academic achievement and social acceptance of low-status students in heterogeneous classrooms, a growing network of practitioners trained in this methodology now focuses on sharing and refining strategies. *Complex Instruction News* features tips from teachers, principals, and researchers, and teachers are increasingly inspired to develop their own multiple-ability curriculum. For example, in California, the Teachers' Curriculum Institute (TCI) has used principles of Complex Instruction and cooperative learning to develop a history and social-studies curriculum. TCI's United States History curriculum, Making History Come Alive for Diverse Learners, builds in activities that require students to work individually, in pairs, in small groups of four or five, and in large groups. Building on Complex Instruction, cooperative learning, and the work of Jerome Bruner and Howard Gardner, the curriculum is compatible with major textbook series and includes interactive slide-illustrated lectures, experiential exercises, skill-building tasks involving primary sources, response and problem solving, and meaningful writing assignments.

Like its curricula, TCI's integrated approach to staff development is created and run by teachers, for teachers. TCI's *Manual for Teaching the Multiple Ability Classroom* includes rich examples of activities and materials that comprise a multidimensional curriculum, suggestions for developing teamwork and promoting a productive classroom climate, samples of overhead transparencies for teacher training, and advice on funding innovative curriculum with existing resources. These materials illustrate the ways in which effective instruction for heterogeneous groups and a multidimensional curriculum together create a powerful learning environment.

Foxfire: Promoting Student-Centered, Democratic Learning

FOXFIRE: An innovative approach to teaching which has left me in a state of awe, utter exhaustion, renewed fervor, and feeling like an eagle with a broken wing, waiting to soar above the clouds, but feeling like I've only reached the treetops at times.

—Amy Blanchard, *Foxfire* teacher, Southern Middle School, Louisville, Kentucky

What kind of teaching is an effective match for the imagination, energy, and enthusiasm of young adolescents of mixed academic backgrounds? In 1988, the Rural Cultural and Organizing Project (ROCC) of Holmes County, Mississippi, began to explore this question through several projects involving low-income African-American eighth and ninth graders in the production of materials related to their own local history. These projects, each with its own personality and history, fall within the philosophical context of the democratic, experiential education of teacher Eliot Wigginton's *Foxfire* approach.

In Holmes County, *Foxfire* inspired ROCC Education Project staff to launch an ambitious summer project for an academically mixed group of thirteen- to fifteen-year-olds, including some solid "A" and "B" students along with others who had failed most of their courses the previous year. With a mini-grant from the *Foxfire* Teacher Outreach Project, the group set out to document the experiences of Holmes County residents during the Depression.

How did the approach work with this diverse group of young people? Teacher Jay MacLeod reports that, at first, the grouping of students from all points on the "ability spectrum" did not go smoothly:

> What happened was we had a rebellion. The best students at first rebelled against the collective process. They wanted their own projects. But it happened that we put some of the less accomplished kids together and they were the first to interview the sharecroppers, and they did a great job. In fact, they got out ahead of the others, and that helped the better students see that everyone had something to offer and to see that some kids who aren't such great students may be better than they are at putting people at ease.

During the first week, students defined the steps of their project: selecting people to interview, drawing up the interview guide, conducting the interviews, transcribing, editing, doing a follow-up interview, writing the introduction, drawing illustrations, typing the interview into columns, and laying out the final copy for the printer. Describing the project, MacLeod explains:

> Interviewing is the crux of the whole project, and the students spent countless hours honing their questioning techniques. Instead of writing out the questions, the students learned to construct an interview guide—a series of prompts to guide the interview. This ensures that the students *listen* to their sources as they speak and can follow up on what's being said....

The young people prepared thoroughly for their interviews, learning to avoid "yes/no" questions, ask follow-up questions, and probe their subjects for anecdotes and elaborations through practice on their parents, teachers, and one another. The first interview broke the ice sufficiently to increase the students' confidence that they could collectively resolve whatever problems emerged—even when a solution might require two days of debate about whether, for example, they should change spellings of words to reflect local dialect and pronunciation. They discussed errors in subject-verb agreement and other grammatical gaffes that surfaced in the interviews. They learned lessons in grammar, punctuation, capitalization, and spelling. They debated what to do about "cuss" words. They struggled with transcriptions. Together they learned about the power of language and learning and their own capacity for producing high-quality work.

As MacLeod emphasizes:

> Otherwise defeated by a blank piece of paper, many students
> positively enjoyed transcribing their tapes. Some of their
> efforts were superhuman. Joseph went home to his three-
> bedroom house that accommodated twenty-one people last
> summer and returned the next day with fifty-one pages of
> transcription. Another student who had failed seventh grade
> two years running went home with his taped interview and
> came to class the next day with a twenty-five page transcrip-
> tion, written by flashlight in the bed he shares with two
> nephews. Because those hours of labor were perceived as
> personally relevant and as a step in the creation of a tangible
> product of value to the community, motivation was not
> an issue.

With the interviews completed, the time came to edit. Students
labeled each topic covered in the interview in the margin. They
crossed out extraneous words and eliminated muddled or boring
materials. They spread the entire interview on the floor so that
whole sections of the material could be moved to make the flow
smoother. The process was not easy, but the students slowly
learned to articulate their reasons for organizing, grouping, and
sequencing material. As they struggled with editorial decisions,
they assumed a greater sense of pride in the product that they
had created. Again, MacLeod reports:

> It is absolutely crucial that the students be firmly ensconced
> in the driver's seat throughout this whole process. Having the
> students work through and democratically resolve questions
> and problems as they come up can be tedious and time-
> consuming, but there is no substitute. As Eliot Wigginton
> points out in his course guide, the creation of a final product
> is a means to motivate and educate the students. The extent to
> which I lay my hands on that product and supply those skills
> necessary for its creation is the extent to which I diminish not
> only the project's power to motivate, but also its ability to
> educate and excite anyone but me.

Finally, with the aid of a word processor, students worked
through the whole project, interview by interview, printed out
each one again, repeated the editing process, and wrote an introduction. They printed out their pieces in columns, chose a title,
selected photos, prepared illustrations, and sat down to lay out
the final copy for the printer. According to MacLeod:

This layout task, like those of interviewing, transcribing, taking photos, and drawing pictures, tends to break down the hierarchy of competence among the students. "High academic achievers" often become impatient and frustrated trying to cut and paste their interview so that the margins are uniform and straight, while those who struggled with editing and writing their introductions often turn out to be natural paste-up artists. This reshuffling of the hierarchy works wonders for students' confidence, often inflating and deflating in just the right proportion.

Even when the summer program was officially over, students continued to work in groups after school and on weekends. They still had to select a name for the magazine (*Bloodlines* was the winner), line up a printer, distribute the finished product to the media, and arrange for sales. With *Bloodlines* a success, there was no stopping the students. They then went on to complete a history of the Civil Rights Movement in Holmes County, *Minds Stayed on Freedom*, which was published as a second magazine as well as a book, and a videotape, "Struggle for Equality in Holmes County: 1860–1960," produced with the local high school.

The students' own words leave little doubt that these *Foxfire*-inspired learning experiences had a profound impact on their young lives:

Minds Stayed on Freedom lets you see
Our people's struggle to be free.

A 200-page book is what we made,
And we didn't do this to get paid.

Eighteen of us came together,
Wrote a book that will last forever.

Movement veterans we did interview;
Research, transcribing, and editing, too.

We worked hard to get it right,
It often took both day and night.

The book was not done at a rapid rate,
But in the end it was worth the wait.

Our cultural heritage we must find,
So our generation won't be blind.

Listen! Once our old folks die,
They won't be able to testify.

And when they are put in the ground,
It's like a library has burned down.

Our past is distorted and denied
But we need it for our cultural pride.

The keys to tomorrow and today
That's what history can convey.

We interviewed our local folk
About the past they plainly spoke.

Minds Stayed on Freedom is the book.
Study it, read it, at least take a look.

—Roderick Wright, Youth of the Rural Organizing and
   Cultural Center, Holmes County, Mississippi, 1990

The *Foxfire* approach is not new. Developed in the mid-1960s by Eliot Wigginton with students in his high-school English classes in rural Georgia, *Foxfire* has flourished, gaining support among teachers in all parts of the country through regional networks of educators trained in *Foxfire* principles. These principles, embodied in *Foxfire* core practices set forward in *Hands On: A Journal for Teachers,* Spring/Summer 1990 issue, emphasize the democratic relationship among all members of the learning community; high standards and expectations for student work; a learning process that is both reflective and action oriented; and meaningful projects that connect classroom activities with the surrounding community.

As Marcia Klenbort of the Southern Regional Council points out, the principles underscore the fact that *Foxfore* does not have as much to do with *content* as it does with the *process* of learning within a particular context. She notes:

What I find most interesting about *Foxfire* now is that it is
widely misperceived to be a way of teaching children about
folklore or about writing. Instead, it is really a means to
democratize the classroom, putting into the hands of students
the means by which they take charge of their own learning.
Student initiative and teaching run high in classrooms where
teachers have studied *Foxfire* techniques. Not accidentally,
Foxfire teachers probe their own learning desires and
activities. They are willing to be taught by their students.

With the understanding that the core practices are fluid guide-lines, not rules, the Jefferson County public schools in Louisville have incorporated *Foxfire* as part of a major professional-development initiative in that district. Louisville's *Foxfire* teachers meet frequently to reflect on the ways in which core practices are shaping their instruction. Also, their local network, Louisville Area *Foxfire* (LAF), produces *LAF Lines,* a teacher newsletter that describes activities like those of Southern Middle School where student projects have included the production of a videotape on law enforcement and a performance of an original play on child abuse.

"Philosophically, tracking goes against the whole notion of *Foxfire*," asserts Allan Dittmer of the University of Louisville. So it makes sense that *Foxfire* principles would be able to shape a student investigation of tracking itself. This is just what happened at Martha's Vineyard Regional High School in Vineyard Haven, Massachusetts, on an October day in 1988, when one student's question to teacher Dan Sharkovitz triggered a *Foxfire* project. "Ever notice that the ones you let go [to the bathroom] are also the ones who are well dressed?" queried the student. The question provoked a discussion that covered several days about differences in the treatment of "brains" and "lubers," a name that some students in the school's auto-mechanics program have given themselves.

As the inquiry progressed, energetic discussion resulted in a group decision to write letters to the principal and plan a public talk show focusing on issues of school fairness. Preparation for the event involved writing invitations, interviewing administrators, researching articles about tracking in professional publications, keeping journals, and learning to use video equipment.The public presentation itself resulted both in an invitation to address educators at Brown University and in an ongoing legacy of communitywide discussion about equity in the school.

Experiences like these demonstrate that *Foxfire* can work effectively with adolescents who learn at varying rates. *Foxfire*'s perspective on student development emphasizes education as one means to realize a more effective, humane, and democratic society. But teachers as well find renewed commitment from *Foxfire*'s insistence on teaching as an evolving art. As Dittmer stresses:

> It is essential to appreciate the notion that teachers are uniquely different, so you can't standardize *Foxfire* core practices. The wonderful thing about the practices is that they are changing all the time. They always have to be adjusted to the comfort zone of teachers.

Peer and Cross-Age Tutoring

Untracking schools often describe one unintended consequence of heterogeneous grouping: increasing numbers of students helping others through informal tutoring arrangements. These schools note the potential of peer and cross-age tutoring to reduce the isolation of groups of students from one another and to strengthen the school as a community of learners.

For example, as "manager" for her school's football squad in Lakewood, New Jersey, student Dale Weschler was responsible for keeping weekly statistics and baking brownies for the team. She describes what happened when she also became an impromptu peer tutor for team members:

> My duties expanded when, for the first time in years, the principal's office was going to enforce the athletic eligibility requirements. No one had ever cared about the players' far-below-average grades until then. Instantly concern arose because the coaches were faced with two-thirds of their team about to be declared ineligible. So they recruited a member of the math department and me, a solid math student, to start intensive tutoring in a frantic attempt to raise the players' grades.
>
> The guys on our football team were in the bottom two tracks of our school and had the same poor grades—lots of "C"s, "D"s, and "F"s. They neglected to see the value of getting good grades and getting an education. More importantly, in my opinion, their teachers were never particularly concerned with the progress of those students, particularly boys who weren't adept at math or didn't care about schoolwork. They were labeled "Dumb Jocks."
>
> When I first began, the guys had a hard time with a girl tutoring them. They gave me a lot of grief for being smart, especially in a subject where excellence has been traditionally reserved for boys. Finally I got fed up with trying to help a bunch of ungrateful, pigheaded boys and told two of them: "When the day comes that you don't have to worry about getting benched because of your grades, then you can give me this grief. All I'm trying to do is to keep you playing ball." From that afternoon onward, I never heard another joke or disrespectful comment.

Twice a week we worked through problem after problem. I think that just having someone sit down, take the time, and really look at the problems with them was effective. As a fellow student, I knew how to relay the material so that it was understandable to my peers. Despite my harsh statement to them, I was respected and could convey the material to them without seeming like a "teacher." They realized I was tutoring because I wanted to help, and I wanted to see them all playing ball. It wasn't something I had to do.

The grades improved on the first tests after our intensive tutoring began. Surprisingly enough, my tutees' grades improved drastically. The math teacher succeeded at getting all his tutees average grades, but my tutees got "A"s, "B"s, and a few rare "C"s. I was proud, the players themselves were amazed, and I think the math teacher was a little perturbed. He just didn't understand how my tutoring worked so well. I think the key to my success was I taught how I liked to learn, not how I was told to teach.

As a peer tutor, I gained a great deal of self-confidence in my knowledge of math and in myself. Holding your own in a roomful of uncooperative boys wasn't easy, but it was a great, fun challenge. I learned what my capabilities were as a tutor, and the guys learned that studying wasn't all bad—there were some advantages to getting good grades.

Peer tutoring is a terrific experience for everyone involved. For the tutor, it provides the opportunity to help others and test your own skills. For the tutee, it provides an alternative, more personal way to learn, which many students need. For both, it bridges different tracked students together and forms a bond between them. Peer tutoring helps break the cycle of stereotypes such as the "Nerd" and "Dumb Jock."

Peer tutoring should not be seen as a substitute for equal access to high-quality curriculum or teachers' attention. Moreover, as a strategy designed to supplement classroom teaching, peer tutoring is not necessarily easier to implement than any other new instructional approach. Peer tutors need training, scheduling support, and follow-up. Still, the potential is great for peer and cross-age tutoring to break down social barriers, reduce isolation, and enhance friendships while also providing academic help for individual students.

Peer and cross-age tutoring in untracking schools occurs both formally and informally, and although the body of evidence supporting academic gains for peer tutors and their tutees is not large, published studies note significant effects. For example, Henry Levin and his colleagues at Stanford found that a well-structured cross-age tutoring program involving older students

working with younger ones led to higher achievement for both
tutors and tutees. In fact, dollar for dollar, researchers determined that cross-age tutoring produced more than three times
the learning as did lengthening the school day. In another program described in the *Harvard Education Letter* of March 1987,
teenage tutors labeled "emotionally disturbed" showed gains in
academics, attendance, and discipline, with their averages on
tests rising from 60 to 85 percent. At the Intercultural Research
Development Project in San Antonio, Texas, a cross-age tutoring
program involving dropout-prone youth as tutors also resulted in
improved attendance, academics, and discipline among tutors.
These results suggest that a shift in roles of lower-achieving students can improve learning dramatically.

Professional Development for New Instructional Techniques

Although untracking can proceed more smoothly when teachers
have some time to practice new instructional approaches, sometimes plunging into the challenge of teaching mixed-ability
groups can, in itself, stimulate interest in adopting new techniques. At the Pioneer Valley Regional School in Northfield,
Massachusetts, English Department chairperson Roger Genest
describes how changes in grouping and instruction benefited
from teachers' planning for change.

Genest was head of his school's Teachers' Association when
several teachers in the building started a push for heterogeneous
grouping. He says, "I wanted to keep tracking—I taught honors
courses then." Then one year, a professor from the University of
Massachusetts was invited to teach a course called Models of
Teaching for a group of fifteen teachers at the school site. By
then, the guidance counselor and several other teachers,
including the special education and remedial-level teachers, had
been busy dropping copies of research articles on the harm of
tracking into faculty mailboxes, and, says Genest, "I knew in my
heart of hearts that we had to change our grouping practices."
That year Genest and other teachers volunteered to teach one
ninth-grade class composed of four students each from the
honors, college, general, low, and special education tracks.
Genest says:

That class became my control group. As part of the U-Mass. course, I videotaped that group, and it became obvious that the problems were *my* problems, not the students' problems. Within the control group, I observed that real solutions to problems were coming from students in the general and low tracks. The honors and college-bound students were simply repeating material they already knew, parroting back what I had said. The low- and general-track students questioned them and forced these "academics" to move away from that position. Now the "academics" had to clarify what they meant and put their ideas in their own words and in terms everyone could understand. And I had to move away from a teacher-centered classroom model.

At the end of the year, Genest assessed his students' learning through a series of papers graded by outside educators. Much to his surprise, members of the mixed-level class scored equal to or above their homogeneously grouped counterparts in five of six areas including essay content, essay structure, and concepts of literature.

These days, the entire English Department at Pioneer is converted to teaching heterogeneous groups. Genest explains:

Education is what a student can *do* with the information, not how much information a student has. You have to see it to believe it. *All* our classes are academic now. *Every* student has to work at the academic level, but the students receive every tool they need to get through. We use a lot of cooperative learning. For two special education students, I taped the lesson for them. Every student uses Writer's Helper. They all learn from the writing process. The only way you can tell a special education student with a writing assignment is through his or her spelling.

Students who would be labeled "general" or "low" grow enormously, and the upper-level students have to do a lot more work. Now they go through six Shakespeare plays in eight weeks! Former honors students now work at a much higher level and produce work for the class—their peers—not the teacher. These students used to work for the teacher and his or her deadlines. Now assignments are set by the whole class, and the work is published. There is a much higher level of synthesis, more operating at a higher level, more group participation.

To a great extent, successful implementation of heterogeneous grouping at Pioneer has rested on the willingness of principal Evrett Masters to share decision making with teachers, including those who resisted change at the early stages. "Our teachers, because it was their idea, have a vested interest in its success," says Masters.

Genest makes additional suggestions to nurture teacher readiness for heterogeneous grouping and to make the transition to untracking classes. He recommends:

- Offer a course like Models of Teaching or suggest that teachers read the *Models of Teaching* text by Bruce Joyce and Marsha Weil.
- Provide many opportunities for teachers to experiment so that they begin to learn how students learn.
- Put teacher observations/evaluations on hold during the transition to heterogeneous grouping so teachers feel that they can fall flat on their faces without fear of sanction.
- Don't force anyone to change.

At Pioneer, changes in instruction develop hand in hand with grouping innovations. For example, some years Genest may co-teach a unit on Shakespeare and the Law with social-studies teacher Joe Nowicki. As student groups meet in "defense" and "prosecution" teams to prepare for a mock trial of Hamlet charged with the murder of Polonius, they must consider questions of motive, emotional state, and justifying circumstances. Teachers further their own growth through discussion among a wider community of educators, both by means of their own magazine, *The Pioneering Practitioner: A Journal on Heterogeneous Grouping, Cooperative Learning and School Change*, public visiting days, and teacher-sponsored conferences.

Assessment Strategies
for Heterogeneous Classrooms

We must constantly remind ourselves that the ultimate purpose of evaluation is to enable students to evaluate themselves. Educators may have been practicing this skill to the exclusion of learners; we need to shift part of that responsibility to students. Fostering students' ability to direct and redirect themselves must be a major goal— or what is education for?

—Arthur Costa, *Educational Leadership*, 1989

Curriculum and instruction that emphasize multidimensional aspects of learning demand approaches to student assessment that are equally complex and multifaceted. As schools begin exploring alternatives to tracking, it becomes obvious that traditional approaches to assessing student progress reveal much less than we need to know about learning. Standardized, multiple-choice tests, in particular, may focus on memorization of specific facts; however, they are not designed to reveal the process of students' thinking, their approach to solving complicated problems, or their inclination to form hypotheses or ask probing questions. Likewise, in schools gearing up to offer an enriched curriculum and instruction to everyone, straightforward number or letter grades are unlikely to gauge the true breadth or depth of students' progress, effort, or contribution to the learning of others.

In keeping with the more complex instructional approaches necessary for heterogeneous classes are a set of more complex assessment approaches, usually called performance assessments, with a particular focus on evaluating what students can *do* with their learning. A shift to performance assessments may both stimulate and respond to change in curriculum and instruction.

In the view of many educators, heterogeneous grouping and more complex student-evaluation strategies are integrated parts of a single package. As Susan Harman, formerly a guidance counselor at New York City's Central Park East School and currently a curriculum and evaluation consultant, points out:

Many teachers don't have much experience with evaluation approaches that don't have some kind of disastrous consequence for kids. But if you're not testing to sort students into groups and you're not worried about what's going to happen or where you're going to put a student based on this or that test, you can afford to look honestly for strengths and weaknesses and really use your evaluation for designing the best instruction.

Untracking schools, then, are faced with the task of developing alternative assessment strategies that are closely tuned in to more recent views of human intelligence and more multidimensional goals for student learning. New approaches must reflect the variety of intellectual habits, skills, or attitudes that are to be fostered among all students. And teachers must coordinate new assessments and strengthened instruction with the ultimate purpose of assessing all facets of learning without interfering in the learning process itself.

Classroom-Based Assessment Tools

The children in Launa Ellison's multigrade classroom at the Clara Barton Open School in Minneapolis, Minnesota, where fifth, sixth, and seventh graders form a semicircle around their teacher. Although it is the last week of school, and a special day at that, her children quiet down instantly when asked to do so. "How are you today?" Ellison opens. "Do we have lots of fives?"

At Clara Barton, children and adults alike use a one-to-five scale as a method of self-evaluation rather than an externally applied grading system. When Ellison asks for their assessments, opinions, and feelings in relation to this scale, they welcome her questions, and their hands shoot into the air. Ellison then explains the day's assignment: a year-end reflection on the year's work. Today they are to respond to certain reflective questions about the year by decorating a mobile with either words or pictures. This assignment, like others, calls on students to evaluate their own learning and reflect on its meaning for their future.

Adrian, a fifth grader, is, like most of her classmates, having trouble balancing her mobile. Whenever it is balanced, she adds another decoration and throws the whole thing out of kilter. Although Ellison is circulating around the room responding to students' questions with questions of her own that provide clues for the children to discover answers for themselves, Adrian is determined to resolve her balancing problems on her own. Compounding her dilemma is the fact that she had so much to say that her mobile is now bigger than she is. She stands on a chair to see if it balances properly; it doesn't, but she is having difficulty fixing it with only one hand.

Adrian now pulls her chair over to the open closet door and, using the chair as a ladder, hangs the mobile from the door top. She is now free to balance her mobile with both hands. She decorates her mobile with squares including these:

- My evaluation of the year: 100
- My feelings about the year: Good, Bad, Happy, Sad, Fun, Exciting, Boring
- My problems: Fights, Arguments, Disappointments
- My accomplishments: Going to Valley Fair, Lake Day, All the field trips

At Clara Barton, each morning includes a three-hour period to work on or discuss the day's topic. Today is no exception, except for the greater buzz of activity as lunchtime approaches and students prepare for visitors—their parents. Achievement Day at the school is a day when students summarize the experiences of their year for their parents. The day takes on an air of celebration as children lug around their portfolios to show their parents, and parents carry around their lunch bags to share with their children.

Portfolios in Ellison's class are collections of student work for the entire year, from first attempt to final copy. Among the wonders that they contain are narratives—fiction and nonfiction alike—and artwork, with most products combining the two. Some contain, for example, a series of reflections on current events such as Operation Desert Storm. Others require a process of self-reflection, stories that are themselves about thinking about writing a story. In the case of every child, the portfolios show change and improvement in the quality of work throughout the year. As parents and children pore through the folders, students describe why they have chosen particular pieces of work as representative of their best efforts and explain why and how they have improved. During this special day, the children can tell their parents the story of their year so that together they can appreciate their accomplishments in a formal way.

Ellison uses a portfolio-evaluation method instead of a grading system to encourage her middle-grade students to work in order to expand their learning and improve their skills, not to earn a magical grade. Because work is collected over time, portfolios can reflect growth and development—in breadth and depth—over a semester or year. Unlike a staged performance or one-shot event, portfolios can reflect both the *process* of learning as well as the outcomes and can emphasize the ongoing nature of the learning focus. Developing a portfolio requires students to reflect continuously on what they do, assessing ways in which work calls for improvement or changes in perspective. Portfolios also offer evidence of improvement as a result of effort and strengthen self-esteem by providing a concrete record of accomplishment.

The use of scales instead of grades contributes to this process. Over the course of a project, students participate in review meetings with Launa and their classmates. These meetings focus on such questions as "How far are you in your report?" and "How far are you in understanding this material?" on a scale of one to five. Students use their own capacity for self-assessment to evaluate the quality of their work, and because the project reflects their own interests, and because the work must satisfy the high standards of the students rather than the external "A," there is a striving for fives.

Self-assessment techniques can enhance a sense of responsibility in both academic and social arenas. At the Barton Open School, the spirit and practice of self-assessment extends to the school's commitment to helping students internalize high standards of academic achievement and conduct and develop "dispositions" for learning that can serve them throughout their lives. On a scale of one to four—representing assessments of "Hardly ever," "Sometimes," "A lot," and "Always"—students answer the question "How Am I Doing?" in relation to a set of clear expectations such as:

1. Be prepared for learning by having appropriate materials.
- I have my own things to write with.
- I have my assignments done on time.
- I bring books, papers, etc., to class when I have been asked to or am expected to.

2. Listen to, learn from, and be courteous to others.
- I listen to others without interrupting them.
- I learn from others.
- I am courteous to others.

3. Respect school and personal property.
- I use school materials carefully.
- I return things that I borrow.

4. Respect the rights of others. Act in physically and verbally appropriate ways.
- I am a helpful member of my class.
- I respect other people's feelings.
- I respect others' physical space.

5. Use your time wisely. Stay on track.
- I finish my work when I am supposed to.
- I control my socializing.

6. Do your best work always.
- I always put my best effort into my work.
- I am proud of my work.
- The time I put into my work shows in its good quality.

7. Use your best judgment when making choices for yourself.
- I choose good options.
- I help to make Barton a safe place to be.
- I make choices that help me achieve my goals.

One obvious benefit of the combination of portfolios and self-assessment scales is the tangible evidence of improvement. These approaches encourage students to become their own best critics. At the same time, the emphasis on effort and improvement reinforces curriculum and instruction designed to help students take responsibility for their own learning. In mixed-level classes like those at Barton, innovative assessments both reinforce the goals of learning and personalize that learning for every single student.

Emerging Assessment Strategies for Heterogeneous Classrooms

The task of developing assessment approaches that match learning goals for all students in breadth, depth, and complexity is not easy. Thoughtful prioritizing, planning, and execution are required. Additional staff development is also needed so that teachers are truly informed consumers of alternatives.

Most of all, new approaches to assessment cannot take place apart from changes in curriculum and instruction. As Ruth Mitchell of the Council for Basic Education cautions:

> What we learn from the history of schooling in the United States is that the system is a package deal; you buy all of it or none of it. Changing it means offering another package. For this reason, attempts to assess programs or students by using performance assessment without changing anything else in the system are doomed to failure.

Judith Arter of The Test Center at the Northwest Regional Laboratory goes one step further in emphasizing the relationship between assessment and teaching. She notes:

> Most alternative assessment approaches have their greatest potential use in the classroom as an integral part of instruction. If teachers do not understand how they can be misled by poorly conceived tasks and fuzzy criteria, and how extraneous performance requirements can affect student performance, then their daily ability to make judgments about student needs and progress will be inadequate.

To assist teachers in understanding new strategies, The Test Center offers a wealth of materials and technical assistance. Center staff also monitor developments in the field and present conferences on appropriate methodology to help educators better understand the purposes and components of good assessment approaches.

Based on their experience, Arter and her colleague Vicki Spandel have developed guidelines for implementing alternatives to standardized testing, particularly portfolios. While cautioning against an overzealous rush into uncharted waters, Arter and Spandel note that many of these alternatives can:

- Move beyond evaluating mastery of facts to describe students' thinking skills and habits, including persistence, flexibility, motivation, and self-confidence and to capture a richer array of what students know and can do than is possible with multiple-choice tests.
- Monitor work process by tracking students' use of different strategies for solving problems.
- Align assessment tools with valued learning outcomes.
- Provide realistic contexts for work, so that schools can examine what students know and can do in real-life situations.
- Provide students with a basis for self-monitoring and effective feedback.
- Integrate assessment with instruction.

However, the promises of new assessment approaches are often more easily stated than realized, and some of the traps inherent in standardized tests, such as the danger that they will not accurately represent the knowledge of all students, are not eliminated just by virtue of adopting alternatives. For these reasons, the Test Center staff, including Arter and director Richard Stiggins, emphasize that four basic components distinguish good assessments from inferior ones. These are:

1. A clear conception of what is to be measured, including agreed upon, explicitly stated criteria that constitute the basis for discussion among teachers and students about how student work is adequate and effective and what can be done differently in the future.
2. A clear purpose for assessment, whether to show growth or change over time, to show the process as well as the product of learning, to document achievement for independent-study credit, or to communicate with parents and other teachers.
3. Selection of assessment techniques that match the target and purpose of learning.
4. Minimizing factors that could lead to misinterpretation of results.

Within these guidelines, a variety of alternative methods, used separately or together, can enrich the repertoire of educators responsible for evaluating students in heterogeneous classrooms. These include:

- **Teacher Reports Based on Observation:** Teachers record daily observations of students' work in logs, which, over time, come to represent rich and detailed collections of information. These logs can be used to develop an anecdotal report card (with essay descriptions of a child's progress rather than number or letter grades) or to prepare for an extended parent conference.

- **Interviews and Conversations with Students:** Interviews with students have the potential to involve students in their own assessment of learning. Teachers at the beginning of the year may ask students what they want to learn during the year; as they proceed through the year, they follow up with questions like "Have you learned what you want to learn?" or "How will you go about learning more about this topic?" or "How do you select and judge books you've read about this topic?"

- **Projects and Demonstrations:** Students are asked to pull together all they have learned in one particular arena and demonstrate their learning in a public forum for teachers, parents, other students, and community members. Students must consider how best to communicate the extent of their learning and may choose to present their work in one or several forms ranging from oral presentations, written summaries, performance, or debate to a science project, play, oral history, or photography exhibit. A joint teacher-student evaluation conference may then focus on a discussion of the project development process, the presentation itself, and the individual effort involved.

In untracking schools, these approaches diversify assessment to match multidimensional curriculum and instruction. While each has potential for heterogeneous classrooms, they require teachers, administrators, and policy-makers to have a thorough understanding of both the promises and pitfalls of such alternatives. Again, as Arter and Spandel note, a grass-roots effort of informed practitioners participating in the development of alternatives, has the best chance of establishing a basis for improved large-scale assessments that match new teaching goals.

Exhibitions and Performance Assessment:
The Experience of Central Park East Secondary School

At Central Park East Secondary School (CPESS) in New York City, standardized testing has been replaced by a variety of performance-assessment approaches that make assessment a logical part of instruction. Within a curriculum theme, students explore "essential questions" surrounding that theme, then demonstrate their understanding and thinking about it through "exhibitions." For example, a year-long humanities study of non-Western civilizations focuses on four essential questions including "What is the relationship between culture and world view?" Students communicate their understanding of this question through exhibitions that respond to assignments such as:

- Discuss the relationship between the Mayan culture (myths, glyphs, artifacts, rituals) and how they view the world. Include areas such as good and evil, life and death, the universe, social structure, etc., in your essay.

- Write a myth for your own imaginary world. Discuss how your myth reflects your own world view and culture.

- Focusing on China up to the 1800s, which of the following was most important in developing China: Culture/ world view; government/ state; geography; family/ gender roles; economy/ social structure; technology. Use the material read in class and independently to develop your thesis. Be sure to include evidence and references to support your opinions and ideas.

- The women in *Their Eyes Were Watching God*, "Gold Flower's Story," *Daughter of Han*, and *Romeo and Juliet* help us to see the struggle in their societies. Compare and contrast these experiences and struggles using specific references to the books.

- Independent study: Research and present to the class information on one of the nations of Africa. Use the atlas, encyclopedia, almanacs, and periodicals to discuss the demography, geography, economics, and history of your country. Focus on the transitions from and effects of imperialism. Be sure to use proper footnotes; time-line pieces and bibliography are part of this exhibition.

At CPESS, assessment criteria in the humanities are organized into a grid reflecting expectations for student mastery in five areas: Viewpoint—Encompasses Wide Knowledge Base but Is Focused; Connections—The Whole Is Greater than the Sum of the Parts; Evidence—Credible/Convincing; Voice—Engaging; and Conventions—Legible and Intelligible. For each of these areas, the four or five concrete qualities that together define excellent work are specified for students.

For example, in the area of Connections students are expected to explain the nature of the problems discussed; conjecture, predict, and explain observations where appropriate; organize material so that all parts support the whole; use transitions effectively; and conclude in a satisfying way. For each area, standards define how students can produce work that "exceeds," "meets," "approaches," or "needs work to meet" mastery levels. For instance:

- A level of work that "exceeds" these requirements shows that "all parts support the whole and make connections beyond the scope of the paper."
- Performance "meets" acceptable levels when "most parts support the whole, resulting in a paper more significant than the information provided in the parts."
- Work "approaches" the requirements when "connections of parts to the whole are sometimes made."
- The effort "needs work" when the student is "not yet able to connect the parts to the whole."

Similar performance measures are presented for other categories. Four points are awarded for work that exceeds acceptable performance levels, three points for meeting those levels, two for approaching those levels, and one point when the effort needs work. Students can receive a maximum of twenty points, and "passing" requires "meeting" acceptable levels in at least three categories. These expectations apply to everyone, and students can continue to work with their teachers to improve their exhibitions for as long as they need to do so.

Because students know exactly what they have to do to meet acceptable standards, they have control over the degree of effort that they will make, and many *choose* to meet "exceeding" levels. Moreover, because expectations for performance closely reflect thinking skills emphasized in the school's approach to curriculum and instruction, students experience every possible chance for success. Ultimately, the final exhibition is presented to an assessment committee consisting of one teacher of humanities, one science/ math teacher, an adult of the student's own choosing, and one student from a lower grade. This "real" audience for student work is an additional source of motivation.

The Interface of Teaching and Assessment

Teaching and assessment innovations go hand in hand in untracking schools. As classroom learning becomes more personalized, so must assessment. As learning becomes deeper, centered on projects that involve interaction with others over longer periods of time, assessment focuses increasingly on the *process* of learning as well as the outcomes. Thus, in untracking schools, just as the focus on instruction shifts from the teacher to the student, assessment increasingly balances what students have learned with *how* they have learned.

The lessons regarding instruction and student assessment are clear. No longer can either teaching or evaluation be geared toward reinforcing classrooms organized according to levels of ability. Rather in heterogeneous classrooms, because neither the setting for learning nor the purpose of evaluating has to do with stratifying learning, teaching and assessment can work together to create powerful learning environments in which all students can succeed.

6 · *What about Math?*

> There has been a mentality that you have to be awfully special
> to be successful in mathematics, that you have to be the best
> and the brightest. Well, we're demystifying mathematics. We
> can no longer say that there is any segment of society that
> doesn't need mathematics.
>
> —Iris Carl, past president, National Council of Teachers
> of Mathematics

With higher mathematics increasingly recognized as a key tool
for all citizens of the twenty-first century, schools are on the spot
to ensure that *all* students learn this essential language. Yet
widespread tracking in mathematics in the middle grades
excludes large numbers of students from the skills and knowledge necessary for gaining access to future opportunities. Even
in untracking schools, math often remains the last outpost of
rigid grouping practices.

Successful heterogeneous grouping in math, as in other subjects, requires new approaches to curriculum, instruction, and
assessment and increased attention to professional development.
Perhaps most important, it calls for changes in fundamental
beliefs about the capacity to learn mathematics and about the
rights of all students to gain access to critical knowledge in this
field. A wealth of resources to support mixed-ability grouping in
middle-level math classes reflects a growing commitment both
to making mathematical knowledge available to previously
excluded students and to upgrading and enriching math learning
for everyone.

Mathematical Proficiency of Middle-Grade Students and Tracking in Public Schools

Assessments of mathematics achievement of American youth often suggest that they are not working hard enough in school. But tracking practices that limit access to knowledge and to settings where grade-level material is taught may contribute as much to depressed performance levels as students' study habits. Indeed, tracking in math is the norm in public schools, especially at the middle level. As Jomills Henry Braddock II of Johns Hopkins University reports, the percentage of young adolescents grouped homogeneously for math increases every year, growing from 57 percent in fifth grade to 94 percent in ninth grade. By seventh grade, students are more likely to be grouped by whole class in math than for any other subject.

These grouping patterns in turn institutionalize differences in the content of math instruction from class to class. For example, the National Assessment of Educational Progress (NAEP) reports that whereas 58 percent of eighth graders are enrolled in "eighth grade mathematics, which focuses on numbers and operations," 22 percent are in pre-algebra, and 16 percent are taking algebra. These differences allot the most meaningful curriculum to high-level students, with weaker ones most likely to be engaged in work-sheet activities. Moreover, as Ruth Eckstrom and Ana Maria Villegas learned in their study of urban middle-level math classes, even when the same type of content is offered at each level, teaching in high-level classes focuses on academics to a greater extent than in low-level classes which involve more time criticizing student behavior.

Reviewing national data, Jeannie Oakes and colleagues from the Rand Corporation further report that tracking practices across schools result in entire schools being dominated by a remedial curriculum—thus effectively denying many poor, African-American, Latino, and recent-immigrant students the opportunity to acquire higher-level knowledge. In schools with large African-American and Latino enrollments (50 percent or more), "advanced" classes make up only 12 percent of the math and science offerings; by comparison, in schools with an enrollment of 50 percent or more white students, "advanced" classes comprise 34 percent of all math and science courses. Oakes's data raise the possibility that perfectly capable students at low-income, high-minority schools may experience more limited access to valued knowledge than students of lesser capability at more advantaged schools. Because students can make academic progress only at the rate at which they are taught, depressed achievement inevitably results from schooling that offers few courses above a remedial level.

Educators in the middle grades are in a particular quandary in relation to tracking, especially in the area of mathematics—in part because elementary-school ability grouping practices may already have undermined the learning of some students. For example, Oakes's recent research relates that 65 percent of all elementary schools group their students into "high," "middle," and "low" groups. In *A Place Called School* John Goodlad explains the consequences:

> Since those comprising each group are taught as a group most of the time, it is difficult for any one child to move ahead and catch up with children in a more advanced group, especially in mathematics. It is not uncommon for a child in the most advanced group to have progressed five times as fast as a child in the least advanced group over the course of a year.

As a result, students may arrive at the middle level already disadvantaged by prior grouping practices that aggravate differences. in achievement. Yet despite these problems, untracking schools are beginning to demonstrate the power of approaches that improve access to mathematical knowledge for all students, both in individual classrooms and through schoolwide revamping of curriculum, instruction, and assessment.

Teaching Heterogeneous Math Classrooms

> A Umani lacrosse field is two miles long. A flag is placed every 6 3/4 feet. How many flags are placed on the Umani lacrosse field? Describe the steps you used to solve the problem, and explain why you made the decision to use those steps.

It is 8:05 A.M., and as twenty-one sixth graders file into their Tuesday math class, teacher Fred Gross reminds them to begin work right away in their groups of three or four with the "Problem of the Day," which is contained in a manila envelope resting on the shelf of the blackboard. With a little prompting, the groups begin work at the eight orange and yellow tables placed in a square around the room. Knowing how to think about the problem is important; there will be more like it on a quiz the next day. Over the year, these students have puzzled over similar Problems of the Day. For example:

> A softball pitcher's fastball was measured at .017 miles per second, and a hardball pitcher's fastball was measured at 86.4 miles per hour. Who threw faster and by what amount? Describe the steps you used...
>
> On the imaginary planet of Wrym, 1 glym = 50 krym, and 1 krym = 75 stym. Which unit is the larger? Which unit is the smaller? Find the missing numbers: (a) 8 glym = ____ krym; (b) 1 glym = ____ stym; (c) 900 stym = ____ krym....and explain why you used those steps.

Over the school year, students in heterogeneous groups will apply such problems to their understanding of operations with integers and rational numbers; the meaning and use of variables; beginning statistics; proportions, ratios, and percents; types of graphs; properties; classification of polygons; the metric system; and number theory. Curriculum will emphasize such themes as estimation, patterns and rules, communication, and applications. Methodology will stress problem solving and the use of calculators, computers, and manipulatives.

The commitment to offer this curriculum equally to all students reflects Gross's belief that schools should not be in the business of sorting children into groups designated as more or less capable of learning math. This belief, coupled with his observation that students deepen their learning when they work in cooperative teams with others who are both similar to and different from them, is fundamental to grouping practices in this math class.

This class, like a second combined math-science class that Gross teaches at the Brooks Middle School in Lincoln, Massachusetts, includes a diverse group of students. Although Lincoln is a mostly white, middle-class suburb of Boston, 20 percent of all classes include African-American students enrolled in a voluntary cross-district desegregation program; and of all the sixth graders in this first-period math class, seven have special education plans (IEPs) written to address particular learning disabilities. This class, like the second, is one designed both to teach math and to educate thinkers.

"The whole point of math is to give the world meaning," according to Gross who has taught in all the middle grades and leads staff development programs in math and heterogeneous grouping. His conviction that math is an essential language for understanding our environment shapes every feature of this classroom and its curriculum, including visual displays of math patterns found in the natural world, posters depicting the life stories of African-American scientists, and a first-day-of-school outdoor walk designed to orient students to "what mathematicians do." Through a variety of activities, "meaning" emerges as:

- Students take on assignments of polling their classmates on TV-watching habits and graphing their findings
- Students work together to apply what they have learned about fractions to the drawing of a blueprint of their own school building to scale
- Mixed-ability groups study charts and tables related to the environment, crime, and economic issues that appear in the daily newspaper and consider the questions "What do these tables tell us?" and "What else could they mean?"
- Groups come up with their own imaginary tables of equivalents and present symbolic illustrations of these tables on large poster paper for explanation to the whole class.

In the course of their year with Gross, all students will experience math as a way of communicating and thinking about the world. "If an estimate is a guess, how can an estimate ever be wrong?" asked an "average" student one day, prompting a wide-ranging philosophical discussion. The strong emphasis on "Why did you do this in this way?" and "Explain to me how you got to that answer" further reinforces that math is a form of communication, requiring logic and reasoning skills.

As students work together on their problem of the day, Gross moves from group to group, checking on their progress and identifying individuals who may need additional help. This day, in fact, one student says, "Please, I need help with word problems," and Gross responds that either he or the special education teacher who consults in the class will make time to go over some extra work with her later in the period.

Before the class moves on, Gross reacts to questions that some students have raised about team points. The first team to get 500 points earns a prize—a special "homework pass" or lunch with the teacher—and the point standing is of special interest as teams prepare for their next test. Point scores now range from 280 to 315 among the class's six teams. Individual students can win additional points for themselves and their team depending on their individual grade. But if every member of the team gets a grade of 90 or above, the team gets an additional 50 points, so everyone works hard to make sure that the whole group understands the material.

Today Gross does not plan to introduce any new math skills. Rather, his goal is to help students review content and apply study skills in preparation for their upcoming test. On the blackboard, he writes "T = Facilitator; E = Recorder; A = Checker; and M = Praiser." Students are familiar with each role, and they grin or groan as their teacher assigns the roles to each group. In the next five minutes, each group is asked to make two lists in response to two questions: "What do you think is going to be on the test tomorrow?" and "What resources do you have to help you study?" The lists are to be created in groups, then merged for everyone to work from.

"Operations of fractions, REDUCING, converting to proper fractions, inverting, word problems, common denominators, borrowing, cross multiplying, and converting measurements" are included in the first list. ("Do you really want to write 'reducing' big?" asks one student, and to Gross's reply that that's "what people struggle with," he confirms, "That's what I struggle with.") "Math book, individual folders with old problems, group members, parents ("Not always," says Gross), siblings, practice tests, the telephone, and flash cards" make up the second list.

Then students go to work in their groups. Some give one another original problems. Some work together on a set of practice tests. Some go to the folder box to pull their own files for review, some go to the blackboard and assume roles of teacher and learner. Gross travels around the room, responding to questions. At the same time, "Checkers" on each team are asking their peers, "Do you agree with that answer?" and "Do you understand that?" and "Why did you do that problem that way?" Although a few students appear to be more confident than the majority, all are engaged in learning. And although students clearly have different learning styles, it is, for the most part, impossible to distinguish differences in ability.

Because the class is scheduled with science in a double period of ninety minutes, Gross can give the students a little extra time to prepare. And as he calls the time to wind down, he reminds the students that they should study for one hour that night, emphasizing that effort does matter—a message reinforced by the "You can do it" sign on the door and above the blackboard. Before they end the lesson, Gross comments on students' effectiveness in assuming their group roles, noting especially their engagement with the work and their cooperative skills.

In many schools, untracking begins in individual classrooms where teachers are taking risks to employ math teaching techniques that engage all students. These include cooperative learning approaches, especially the Student Teams-Achievement Division and Team-Games-Tournaments models developed at Johns Hopkins University, instruction shaped by active learning and high expectations for everyone, and in-class cross-age tutoring support.

At the Bartlett School in Lowell, Massachusetts, Joanne Hatem begins the day by asking her twenty-three-member class—eighteen of whom are recent Latino or Cambodian immigrants to the city—to correct their own homework assignment at their desks, which are arranged in groups of four placed side by side and front to front. As she moves among the groups of students, she asks for answers, calling individuals by name.

Like many teachers in urban districts, Hatem is provided with a single, district-approved textbook. However, Hatem supplements this required text with her own ideas and materials that facilitate cooperative learning and critical thinking. In all her heterogeneously grouped classes, Hatem combines direct instruction with activities requiring sixth-, seventh-, and eighth-grade students to think problems through to their solutions, individually, in small groups, and at home.

In fact, the techniques that Hatem uses are appropriate not only for heterogeneous groups; they also constitute general good teaching for young adolescents. For example, Hatem:

- **Relates math problems to students' real life:**

    HATEM: "Have any of you been in business before?"
    FREDDY: "I've had a car wash.
    HATEM: "How much did you charge?"
    FREDDY: "Ten dollars—no matter what the size."
    HATEM: "How did you get the money for soap?
    FREDDY: "I saved money and bought the soap first."
    HATEM: "Did anyone ever have a lemonade stand? Good, a few of you. Well, you are all going to have a chance to set up a business. What kind of business would you like to set up...? All right, let's talk about a candy store."

Hatem uses her students' suggestion to explain the assignments related to fractions. She asks for three items that a candy store might sell and writes the answers on the board. Then she asks for estimates of the daily sales numbers for each item, and the class figures out a weekly sales total. All this information is charted for the whole class:

	Gum	Lollipops	Jellybeans	Total
Monday	50	25	75	150
Tuesday				
Wednesday				

After putting a partial chart on the board, Hatem asks the students: 1) Given this information, what kinds of questions would you want to ask? and 2) If you owned the store, what would be the advantage of using a similar chart? One student answers that she could figure out what part of the total sale was lollipops. Another answers that he would know what to buy when they were running out.

Hatem then asks the students to work in groups; with one working as a recorder, the groups are asked to come up with ideas for a group business. Later Hatem will select one group to explain its chosen business to the class. She will use this example to formulate questions based on the group problem and ask students to answer their own questions using the information that they provide.

• **Makes abstract problems concrete:**

When a student answers a problem incorrectly, Hatem reviews the problem on the blackboard: $7x + 5 + 4x = ?$ She then substitutes apples for the "x"s to see if this makes the problem more understandable. She explains, "You can't combine the five with the "x"s since 'five' doesn't mean apples; only "x"s mean apples."

- **Introduces new material in a nonthreatening but challenging way:**

"This is where it gets fun," Hatem tells the class. "Today is the day we're going to try using letters instead of numbers for the problems we've been doing." She asks the class to close their textbooks. When many look panic-stricken and ask if she is going to give them a test, she says no, that she just has a problem that she needs help in solving. She distributes a problem to each child:

> At a large Chinese party, sixty-five dishes were served all together. Every two guests shared a dish of rice between them; every three guests shared a dish of noodles, and every four guests shared a dish of meat. How many people were at the party?

- **Identifies ways in which some students can show others—both within the class and at home— a problem-solving process:**

After the students have discussed the problem in their groups, one student from one group suggests an answer. When Hatem asks the others if they agree, one student says she doesn't know how they got the answer, so Hatem suggests that they all put their heads together and help one another understand how they arrived at the answer.

With each group coming up with solutions, Hatem checks with each member of each group to make sure everyone has participated in the problem-solving process. Having done so, Hatem writes the answer on the blackboard, evoking cheers from the group that has reached that answer. She then asks one of the students in the "winning" group to explain to the entire class how his group came up with that particular solution.

When the bell rings to end the class, Hatem suggests that they take their problem sheet home and try it on their friends or teach it to their family.

- **Provides a context that challenges students to think about how math relates to their future lives:**

HATEM: "Now I want you to close your books. We're going to talk about triangles. Does anyone plan to be an architect? Does anyone know what an architect does…? We're going to take a walk around the neighborhood for one of our classes and observe the different designs of buildings. Has anyone notices anything architecturally different in this neighborhood?"

("A castle…" "A perfectly round house…")

HATEM: "I know a woman who won the Megabucks lottery. She decided to build a modern house with the money she won. She would set up some specifications for architects who wanted to compete to design her house, and she would add a 10 percent commission for the winning design. The specifications required the house to have at least six geometric shapes. It could be drawn or built as a model. This is *your* assignment. You'll need to use your greatest imagination."

Hatem reviews the various shapes with the students: "What is a five-sided figure," she asks. "What is a hundred-sided figure?" asks a student, while someone else guesses "a centagon," prompting Hatem to appoint a third student to look that word up in the dictionary.

- **Provides problems in a context that taps into students' curiosity about the lives of their teachers:**

Here we have Bernie, Terry, Ethel, and Maureen. These people are all teachers. They teach math, English, phys. ed., and biology, but not necessarily in this order. The phys. ed. teacher's wife is the math teacher. Maureen hates numbers and bugs. Terry is a confirmed bachelor. Who teaches what course?

("What is a bachelor, Ms. Hatem?")

*High
Expectations
for Low-
Achieving
Math Students*

In exploring alternatives to ability grouping in math, many middle-grade educators have found that, for a variety of reasons, complete untracking cannot happen overnight. Even if schools make the decision to keep differentiated classes, however, they can still create positive learning conditions and offer their students excellent teaching guided by high expectations.

Many beginning algebra students learn the old mnemonic trick for following the proper order in solving equations: "Please pity (excuse) my dear Aunt Sally"—parentheses, power (exponents), multiply, divide, add, subtract. Wellesley Middle School math teacher Judy O'Rourke describes how she introduced her thirteen below-grade-level students to this trick and other concepts necessary for later success in algebra:

> *What I Did:* I taught three algebraic concepts to a low-level pre-algebra class according to the following schedule:
>
> - Day 1—Combining like terms (addition, positive numbers)
> - Days 2 and 3—Combining like terms and evaluating the resulting algebraic expression (addition, subtraction, positive and negative numbers)
> - Day 4—Pretest, review, and practice
> - Day 5—Quiz with questions on work of days 1 and 2 and cumulative review questions.
>
> *How It Went:* I gave a "pep talk" about the importance of the algebraic concept that we were going to learn. I stressed the fact that it was one of the tools we needed (like operations with signed numbers) to continue to move ahead in pre-algebra.
>
> I taught students to handle $2x + 3y + 5x + 9 + y$ by first discussing these situations: (a) 6 dogs + 5 dogs; (b) 1 dog + 7 cats + 3 dogs; and (c) 2 flippety-gibbets + 10 flippety-gibbets + 17 corks. I then stressed the importance of doing the work in steps. My coteacher and I constantly had to circulate as some students resisted doing the algebraic steps. We encouraged, insisted, praised, and finally exclaimed over the beautifully done algebraic work by everyone in class. Days 2 and 3 were a buildup and continuation of day 1.

What I Learned: It was essential that I stress the importance
of what we were doing. I needed to restate this often over
the week in the most positive, confident way I could.

1. My low-level students can do pre-algebra, but I need to:
   - Start out as concretely as I can
   - Do several examples broken down into the
     simplest steps
   - Explain clearly and repeatedly until students
     verbalize the example for me and I become the
     "secretary"
   - Insist that algebraic steps be followed and accept
     nothing else.

2. I learned that these students tire of lengthy examples very
   quickly, so I have to plan different activities and change
   gears every fifteen minutes or so.

3. From past experience, I know I will move on to new
   material in the next class. However, I'll need to provide
   practice in these concepts (maintenance problems at the
   beginning of class each day) two or three times a week.
   For several weeks I'll include questions on these concepts
   in the quiz, and then I'll do it sporadically.

4. Friday quiz results: There were five examples on the quiz
   relating to the work of days 1 and 2. These were the
   results: All correct = eight students; four correct = three
   students; three correct = two students—and no one
   missed more than two!

O'Rourke predicts that every one of these students, many of
whom have severe emotional and learning disabilities, can enter
algebra-1 in ninth grade, perhaps in a program that stretches
content over two years. Because she does not equate quickness
with capacity to learn, she is persistent but not impatient in
working with students' resistance and fears. Her teaching is
founded on the beliefs that all students can learn algebra regardless of varying learning paces and that all students can and must
have a foundation in algebra in order to take advantage of later,
post-secondary educational opportunities.

*Saturating
Algebra
Classrooms
with Support*

Twenty-four years of public-school teaching, most of which involved teaching low-track high school students, was enough to convince math teacher Jim Reisinger of Ponderosa High School in Parker, Colorado, that tracking is detrimental to all students. As he explains, "The policy of tracking is inconsistent with the value of equal opportunity in our educational system." After attending a workshop with Jeff Howard of the Efficacy Institute, Reisinger was even more persuaded that with effective effort, *everyone* could excel. From his perspective, all students deserve equal access to high-level math from their first year in high school.

To put his beliefs into practice, Reisinger instituted an innovative approach to ensure that all students would be exposed to a rigorous math curriculum that balances skills and concepts at high levels. He explains how this has worked:

> In August 1991, I was again given the two lowest-track math courses. Unwilling to once again teach elementary and junior-high-level math to sophomores, I began teaching them the same algebra course offered to the other students in the school. Acknowledging their inferior mathematical background (a result of earlier tracking), I used cross-age tutoring (CAT) for extra support. The CAT program, consisting of older students acting in a mentor capacity to tutor younger students, has been extremely effective. There is no inferior status attached to receiving help from an older student as with peer tutoring. The older student is, in fact, a positive, motivating role model for the younger student. The CAT program also has the beneficial side effect of steering our most motivated students into a teaching career.

Reisinger explains in more detail how coordination with other algebra-1 classes and extra support has led to expanded access to higher mathematics:

> We have four algebra-1 classes, two of which are my pilot classes. The other two are taught by Bret Crock as a regular algebra-1 class. We both started with about sixty students each (thirty in each class). If a student had trouble in the regular class, he or she could transfer (if we agreed) to the pilot classes. Students who did well in the pilot class were transferred to the regular class. (About twenty students were switched.) All algebra-1 classes are on the same page of Saxon's algebra-1 text at the same time. They have the same tests, too.

> The only difference between the pilot and the regular classes is that my pilot class has a lot of help. In the classroom with me are a special education teacher and two special education adult aides. In addition, I presently have six student aides who are seniors (one junior) who work with the students, and I could use more. If a student is having a lot of trouble with the pilot, I have him or her assigned to me for another class period, and one of the student aides works with them on their homework. (About five students are doubled up.)
>
> The experiment was a success. Students who had always been told that they were inferior to those on the higher track were suddenly proudly carrying the same book as every one of their peers. These students now have not only the academic background, but also the confidence and self-esteem to meet the higher standards required for success in our society.

With an emphasis on pacing and regular, challenging homework, Reisinger sees positive results for students who, in other years, would have been relegated to basic math. As the school expands to include the ninth grade, Ponderosa will enroll all entering students in algebra. Says Reisinger, "We're trying to make sure that *all* kids get the benefits of algebra when it counts—at the beginning of high school!"

Introducing Schoolwide Changes in Math Curriculum and Instruction

> Achieving equity requires, for starters, a program in which heterogeneous groups can succeed in mathematics, in which problem solving is the focus and manipulative materials are used through all grade levels, where alternative assessment is intermingled with instruction, and where cooperation and communication are as important as the mathematical skills themselves. None of these conditions is simple to achieve, and all require a rethinking of one's methods and materials.
>
> —Nancy Kreinberg, director, EQUALS

Although math is often seen as the least appropriate subject area for untracking, regrouping of students into more heterogeneous classes is both possible and desirable when coupled with innovative approaches to teaching, redefined curriculum objectives, and more diverse assessment procedures. These changes are more likely to take hold when planning precedes a change to heterogeneous grouping. Fred Gross advises a process that includes these steps:

1. Begin focused staff discussions about questions regarding the nature of mathematics itself: What is mathematics? Why study mathematics? What is the role of mathematics in schools?

2. Consider curriculum design: What are the concepts you want to teach? How do you introduce skills that relate to these concepts? How do you teach concepts and skills within a context that is meaningful to the world of your students?

3. Consider teaching methodology: How will your teaching approaches reflect a belief in the capacity of all children to learn mathematics? To what extent will you depend on cooperative-learning activities to help students learn and improve motivation? How will you introduce reading, writing, and articulation of math concepts? What sorts of thematic units lend themselves to the skills and concepts you want students to learn? What activities can you adopt that extend math concepts into other disciplines?

Discussion of these questions sets the stage for the elimination of leveled classes, and a school can then implement heterogeneous grouping with interdisciplinary pairing of teachers as appropriate.

Frick Junior High School's Math Demonstration Program

Frick Junior High School in Oakland, California, could be seen as a tough inner-city school. Enrollment at the school is 97 percent African-American and Latino, and students enter Frick's seventh grade from elementary schools in low-income, urban neighborhoods having typically achieved an average mathematics level of fourth grade. In the face of significant hurdles, however, Frick teachers have undertaken a focused five-year campaign to expand access to mathematical knowledge for all students with a minimum of sorting.

Setting Goals and Assessing School Placement Data

Having decided to move from a tracked mathematics program to a heterogeneous classroom structure, teachers first articulated six major goals:

1. To maximize the number of students taking algebra, or an alternative college preparatory course, by ninth grade
2. To minimize the number of students leaving Frick's ninth grade and enrolling in general or remedial math in their high-school tenth grade
3. To have students realize that the pursuit of mathematical understanding is a cooperative enterprise

4. To introduce all students to the wide range of concepts and ideas that fall under the umbrella of mathematics
5. To instill in all students the willingness to try something when they come to a problem that might not be familiar, and to give them as large a bag of tricks as they can carry to approach these problems
6. To have students enjoy mathematics

When teachers began to consider these goals, it became increasingly clear that the existing math program would not be adequate to achieve the program's new objectives. Reviewing the school's course-placement data, for example, teachers realized that students who began seventh grade in general math rarely left that track and that those at the higher levels actually lost ground over their three years in the school. Moreover, 78 percent of Frick's graduates wound up in tenth-grade general math, a placement that was, according to district statistics, powerfully associated with later dropping out.

Changing Curriculum, Instruction, and Groupings

In the 1987–88 school year, Frick introduced its first changes in math curriculum and class structure. In all grades, remedial math was simply eliminated. In the ninth grade, general-math courses were also eliminated, with all Frick ninth graders enrolled in either algebra-1 or pre-algebra. This change resulted in doubling the number of students who graduated from Frick and enrolled in algebra or higher-level math courses in high school.

The next year, while Frick continued to group seventh and eighth graders into three levels—high pre-algebra, pre-algebra, and general math—staff also shifted the orientation of the curriculum from rote calculation to problem solving. That same year, the school introduced the algebra-A option, stretching algebra content over two years, at the ninth-grade level. This change allowed greater access to a formal algebra curriculum and resulted in 85 percent of students entering algebra-1 in tenth grade and receiving a grade of "C" or better.

By 1989–90, all seventh- and eighth-grade math classes were grouped heterogeneously. At first, this worried teachers who had not made changes in their traditional lessons and realized that about half of their teaching went "over the heads of most students" while the strongest students were "bored silly." In reaction, teachers began to implement new instructional approaches. All Frick math classes now use cooperative groups for the majority of their lessons, and staff estimate that most lessons work for all students at different levels. In the 1990–91 year, Frick teachers continued to develop their program with assessment changes ranging from portfolios to group-performance assessments under consideration.

Results and Future Directions

New math curriculum and heterogeneous grouping have opened access to knowledge for many Frick students who were formerly closed out of high-level course offerings. By 1990–91, 54 percent of Frick's students were in the algebra-1 or algebra-A programs, and 82 percent of ninth graders leaving the school after the 1989–90 academic year went into algebra-1 or beyond. High-school teachers in Oakland have reported that their best prepared students came to them from Frick.

Well into the middle of the second year of heterogeneous grouping, Frick's math teachers reflected on their experience, noting:

- Traditional textbooks don't work well in heterogeneous classrooms. We discovered this in 1989–90 and didn't even issue textbooks this year.

- Heterogeneous lessons and goals of instruction must be thought of differently. Traditional lessons are aimed at students at certain levels, but heterogeneous lessons must reach students at a variety of levels. All students will not get the same things from all lessons. Flexibility is a key word. A variety of ways of looking at a topic is a key concept. Students in heterogeneous classes must write, draw, design, and create as well as calculate.

- Class structure must be modified. Why group students heterogeneously, and then not let them take advantage of one another? The move toward cooperative learning fits hand in glove with heterogeneous classrooms.

- Homework must be done differently. You cannot change the structure of the classrooms and continue to give the same old homework. Currently we are using problems of the week, portfolios, writing assignments, drawing, and other types of mathematical exploration to revamp our homework program.

- Assessment needs to be rethought. Grading students in the same old way is unfair, but grading students in a way that reflects changes in the class needs to be thought through.

- Classroom management is different. A heterogeneous classroom is often a noisier classroom. Students need to talk with one another, they need to explain things and ask questions. Manipulatives are used often. There are as many different solutions to management as there are teachers, but rule one is that management headaches stem from curriculum and lesson-plan deficiencies. A lesson that bores or frustrates students will often produce unacceptable behavior. As our lessons become more interesting, and more multilevel, many management problems disappear.

By its own admission, Frick has not solved all its problems by introducing the new math program. For example, students are slow in accepting their new homework program, and staff believe that too many of them are only halfheartedly attempting to solve problems that would enhance learning. Clearly, a new math program alone does not solve other problems that frequently haunt inner-city schools. At the same time, Frick teachers now claim:

> Students who come into a Frick classroom and want to do some mathematics, can. They get to explore, examine, create. They get to write, draw, calculate. They get to solve problems. Today, any student at Frick who wants to gets to do mathematics, every day. That clearly could not have been said five years ago.

Math Curriculum for the Twenty-first Century

> Some people's view is that all we have to do is make the kids work harder. That's simply the first tier of the problem, a question of paper and pencil skills. At the root of the issue is the curriculum.
>
> —Kenneth Hoffman, Joint Policy Board of Mathematics; professor, Massachusetts Institute of Technology

If Fred Gross's math class is a far cry from the chalk-and-talk approach of the past, it is not far from current recommendations for sixth-grade mathematics learning proposed by the National Council of Teachers of Mathematics (NCTM). Outlining expectations for what students in the middle grades should learn in grades five through eight in *Curriculum and Evaluation Standards for School Mathematics*, NCTM calls for increased attention to math as problem solving, communication, and reasoning; mathematical connections; number relationships; number systems and number theory; computation and estimation;

patterns and functions; algebra; statistics and probability; geometry; and measurement.

Overall, the *Standards* call for an emphasis on mathematical reasoning, real-world applications, and communication about mathematics. They highlight the need for classrooms in which all students have access to calculators and a computer for individual and group work and in which genuine problems can be experienced on a regular basis. Problem solving, NCTM insists, *develops* the ability to compute; computational skills should *not* be a prerequisite for working with word problems. The Mathematical Association of America and the Mathematical Sciences Education Board have also called for a small group-oriented math curriculum that requires students to solve problems using mathematical evidence as verification, employ technology, and connect mathematical ideas to everyday situations. They also advocate changes in evaluation, assessment, and the training of mathematics teachers.

The Algebra Discussion: Acceleration or Enrichment?

> The collective wisdom of our time indicates that algebra is without question the most important subject in high-school mathematics, and to substitute less-important stuff is giving our students a weaker education. That is, enrich eighth graders by giving them algebra.
>
> —Zalman Usiskin, University of Chicago
> School Mathematics Project

If our students are lagging in math achievement, shouldn't we encourage them to take algebra earlier, perhaps making it standard fare in seventh rather than ninth grade? The question is open to debate. For example, several studies cited in a 1988 article by Fernand J. Prevost in the *Middle School Journal* suggest that the gains we might make by offering more students algebra earlier in their schooling may be lost later when 60 percent or more drop math prior to enrolling in pre-calculus.

Researcher James Flanders analyzed three different math textbook series to determine the amount of new material that children were exposed to as they progressed through the grades. He found that whereas kindergarten children are exposed to 100 percent new math content, the amount of new material offered by the textbooks decreases steadily through the grades until it reaches a low of about 30 percent in eighth grade, with most of it found only in the last 100 pages of the text. No wonder many

middle-grade students feel bored by and disengaged from
their math work: they've been doing the same thing for years
and years!

Then in ninth grade, students are hit with 90 percent new
material again as they are exposed to algebra for the first time.
Not surprisingly, many experience difficulty and failure, not from
the new material *per se*, but from the rate at which they are
introduced to it. Or, if in an effort to ease them into algebra, they
are placed in "basic" courses below grade level, the lull simply
continues.

Instead of adhering to existing curriculum, say some educators, let's restructure the curriculum itself so that algebra is not a
"sudden death" experience but instead becomes a part of all students' learning beginning in the fifth grade. On this basis, then,
curriculum innovation has focused on developing transitional
approaches designed to make algebra accessible to more students in the middle grades. Introduced gradually through the
intermediate years, these approaches both allow more students
to pass through the gate to valued mathematical knowledge and
help all of them stay in the mathematical ball park through high
school. As Usiskin argues, if students are exposed to content in
variables, expressions, equations, formulas, and graphing in the
sixth and seventh grades, elementary algebra *can* be an eighth-
grade subject for more than the 9 percent of eighth graders currently receiving credit for it.

Indeed, a number of untracking middle-grade schools are
drawing on several approaches to achieve the twin objectives
of reducing tracking in middle-grade math and upgrading content for all students. These approaches include the Algebra
Project, the University of Chicago School Mathematics Project,
the University of Hawaii Transitional Algebra Project, and
Algebridge. In addition, ongoing research and development in
new math curricula offer resources to enrich math instruction
particularly in urban schools.

The Algebra Project

Along with new curriculum standards has come the realization that all students must have equal access to the mathematical knowledge embodied in them. The Algebra Project is one effort designed to offer a meaningful curriculum to minority students who have long been underrepresented in math courses that lead to advanced study and expanded opportunity in the next century.

The walls outside the algebra classroom at the Martin Luther King, Jr., School in Cambridge, Massachusetts, are covered with student-designed murals detailing stations of the city's subway system visited by sixth graders enrolled in the school's Algebra Project. These murals, along with displayed written descriptions of the trip that students take during the early weeks of the program, are part of an introduction to positive and negative integers and other new and complicated concepts.

In the King School's classrooms, The Algebra Project is in full swing. At midyear, sixth- and seventh-grade students are practicing the skills that they have learned while mastering concepts in small groups, pairs, or on their own, with the teacher acting as "coach." The walls of Lynn Godfrey's sixth-grade classroom are decorated with pictures of train number lines, products of the beginning lessons in the Algebra Project workbook. Today, however, Godfrey's students are well into their textbook, concentrating on data collection, frequency tables, and relative-frequency tables.

Discussion of the day's assignment begins the day before students break into cooperative work groups. Today, students are preparing year-of-birth tables based on the zodiac system, and each group is taking an extra ten minutes to collect their data. Before they go off to interview members of the population sample that they have selected, Godfrey asks them to repeat the rules for behavior: "No running," "No yelling," and "Say 'thank you' to those you interview."

One group returns quickly, and Godfrey reviews the next steps in their assignment. She quizzes them about the difference between a frequency table and a relative-frequency table. She reminds them that the relative-frequency tables need to be completed with fractions, decimals, and percents. "And for this assignment, no calculators, and show me your work, please," she says.

This first group then goes off to their desks to share information that they have gathered from different people within the population sample, and they begin construction of their frequency tables. The second and third groups arrive, and Godfrey reviews her instructions with them.

In the seventh grade, Yolanda Rodriguez's students are working independently on the assignment for the day. The classroom is large enough so that students can work where they wish, and Rodriguez encourages certain ones to work together. In one corner of the room, a student works with a student teacher on an algebraic problem from previous homework. In another corner, two pupils work semi-independently, occasionally asking each other for help.

The class has two computers available, and Rodriguez assigns two girls to work together on one of them. The computer is running a new algebra program that provides opportunities to practice manipulating algebraic equations. Working with this program, the children familiarize themselves with the terminology of algebra, become more comfortable with equations, and understand how to manipulate the variables without having other processes, such as arithmetic operations, interfere. Students continue to work on the math of their problems assigned from the textbook, but the computer is key to helping them solve tricky algebra problems without worrying about tricky math—much as a word processor's "spelling check" function allows language-arts students to develop their writing skills without worrying about spelling errors.

Marcel, one of Rodriguez's students, types in the linear equation $7x - 10 = 2x$. He then tells the computer to subtract $2x$ from each side, stopping momentarily to double-check that it is indeed "positive $2x$" that he wants to subtract. The program then shows him the next two steps:

$7x - 10 - 2x = 2x - 2x$;

$5x - 10 = 0$.

Marcel then tells the computer to add a "positive 10" to each side, with the steps appearing as:

$5x - 10 + 10 = 0 + 10$;

$5x = 10$.

Marcel knows that he has almost finished the problem now and tells the computer to divide both sides by 5. He is then shown:

$x = 10/5$.

Finally, he highlights the fraction with his mouse and tells the computer to divide those numbers, saying to himself, "$X = 2....$"

The Algebra Project is a unique approach to teaching mathematical concepts in an order designed to take students from the concrete to the abstract—a design particularly well suited to the cognitive development of young adolescents who often require a concrete base from which to grasp more abstract concepts. As project founder Robert Moses explains:

> My goal was math literacy, and I began thinking about it like English literacy…wanting students to know enough math so that they would have access to what is written in the language of math. I was particularly concerned about when they hit college they would have access to a full curriculum, so that if they wanted to study science, economics, statistics, or physics, they would know the mathematical language for that curriculum.

To develop math literacy, or "numeracy," the project's curricular process exposes students to new ideas in the following sequence:

1. The physical event, such as the subway trip
2. The visual picture of the event, expressed through hallway murals, three-dimensional models, or graphs
3. Intuitive, "ordinary" English, involving students in describing the experience in their own words
4. Structured English, the formal writing of the experience
5. Symbolic representation, the rewriting of the experience as an algebraic equation

Throughout, interesting group activities introduce students to new concepts such as displacements or equivalences. For example, sixth graders participate in an African trading market during which they price items that they bring in for sale or trade—Nintendo game cartridges, scarves, or combs—and discover that different items are equivalent if they have the same price. The results of this approach are promising. As a result of the implementation of The Algebra Project at the King School, all students entering ninth grade are prepared for algebra 1, with some of them "testing out" of algebra 1 and entering geometry.

*University
of Chicago
School
Mathematics
Project*

Unlike many traditional mathematics materials, textbooks developed under the auspices of the School Mathematics Project at the University of Chicago (UCSMP) treat seventh- and eighth-grade math curriculum as an introduction to high-school mathematics, rather than a review of elementary arithmetic. The project's director Zalman Usiskin notes that "by teaching skills without a context, students do not know why they are studying what they are studying." He endorses a shift from a curricular emphasis on computational skills alone to one that stresses math as a tool for solving real-world problems. Noting that all students need algebra, his work both strengthens the argument against tracking and supports efforts to upgrade mathematics education for all students.

Testing of the project's transitional algebra materials has demonstrated the value of slowly including algebraic concepts at least by seventh grade. As a result, more students may remain engaged and successful in mathematics over their subsequent high-school years. The commercial publication of the project's materials by Scott, Foresman as textbooks for teaching seventh-grade transition mathematics and eighth-grade algebra makes implementing NCTM's new curriculum standards more feasible for more schools.

In practice, some teachers working with heterogeneous classes in untracking schools prefer to balance the complex material presented in this curriculum with hands-on activities borrowed from other curricula or from materials that they develop themselves. In addition, in a paper citing the Chicago curriculum as exemplary, staff at the University of Arizona note that one district has reported offering reading workshops for mathematics teachers "because UCSMP requires students to read beyond the levels typically presented in mathematics texts." Although publisher Scott, Foresman provides staff orientation to the materials, many districts offer additional in-service training to aid in the transition process.

University of Hawaii Transitional Algebra Project

Like other innovative approaches, the basic premise of the Hawaii Algebra Learning Process (HALP), developed by Sidney Rachlin of the University of Hawaii, is that all students can learn algebra. Defining algebra as a problem-solving process, HALP goes beyond the level of rote memorization of formulas and algorithms. Instead, curriculum focuses on teaching students to understand a problem, devise a plan for solving the problem, carry out the plan, and assess the process.

Through "Process Algebra," key concepts of reversibility, generalization, and flexibility are learned. An open-ended inquiry process challenges students in heterogeneous classrooms to give increasingly complicated solutions. Above-average students stretch to increase the range of acceptable solutions; others follow this lead by creating new examples of the enlarged generalizations.

HALP represents an alternative to a "rule-driven" curriculum. It allows students to look at mathematics in a different way and reduces the frustration of learning math that can come from the extreme inflexibility of approaches that emphasize rules over thinking. Rather than focusing on "right" or "wrong" answers, the HALP curriculum allows time for the development of algebraic concepts through three to eight days of problem-solving experiences and class discussion. After each concept or generalization has been developed, students spend three to five additional days developing skills on the topic. Periodically, teaching reinforces these skills throughout the course.

Curriculum developer and researcher Rachlin points out that this approach emphasizes the scaffolding of algebra. Rather than focusing on a single topic in isolation for forty-five minutes in one day, concepts are taught for a total of about forty-five minutes over a five-day period. This approach allows all children access to the material within each one's "zone of proximal development," with instruction leading the development, not following it.

HALP is currently being used in seven states. Sometimes, as in the case of North Carolina, the curriculum has been adopted in response to a state-level "Algebra for All" mandate which requires that all ninth graders entering that grade in 1992 complete and pass at least one year of algebra before graduating. Steps to fulfill this mandate have begun in many districts including in North Carolina's 67,000-student Wake County School District where Barbara Moore, Secondary Math Program Specialist, believes that a process approach to algebra will play a crucial role in helping district schools meet that mandate. Moore explains:

You can't undo your tracking procedures all of a sudden. But Process Algebra is a real tool to help you get there. In a typical math class, if you're not an auditory learner, you've had it. Process Algebra has manipulatives; it allows for tactile and kinesthetic learning, so it lends itself to heterogeneous classrooms where lots of kids can have success.

Those familiar with the program report that intensive teacher preparation is essential to successful adoption of HALP. Indeed, the University of Hawaii's HALP group offers a thirty-five staff development program in which teachers work on the questioning and coaching skills that are at the core of the program.

Supplemental Curriculum Resources for Urban and Minority Students

Finally, untracking schools with large enrollments of African-American and Latino students can benefit from additional resources designed to promote math competence among minorites. For example, Algebridge, a supplementary curriculum designed to bridge the gap between the concrete operations of arithmetic and the abstract concepts of algebra, is specifically targeted to schools with a minority enrollment of over 40 percent. The approach combines concept-based instruction with ongoing assessment targeting the meaning of negative numbers; the concept of equality and inequality; the construction of numerical equations; pattern recognition and proportional reasoning; fractions in expressions and equations; operations on equations and inequalities; the concept of the variable; and approaches to word problems. The results of the program are promising in terms of student and teacher enthusiasm and acceptance. Says Marilyn LaCount, Algebridge Coordinator at Arizona State University:

A big plus is there's a lot of interaction with students. You have to talk with students to find out which concepts they need to work on. Then you discuss the misunderstandings, instruct to fill in the gaps, and then reassess. [Algebridge] works fine with mixed-ability groups.

In addition, the Quantitative Understanding and Amplifying Student Achievement and Reasoning (QUASAR) Project of the University of Pittsburgh's Learning Research and Development Center focuses on the development of new math curricula and its impact on the learning of students in urban districts. Projects include implementation of Summermath, at the Magnet Middle School in Holyoke, Massachusetts; Visual Mathematics and Math in the Mind's Eye, curricula that use manipulatives, models, and diagrams as tools for teaching key math concepts, at the Portsmouth Middle School in Portland, Oregon; Transition

Mathematics, a program of the University of Chicago School Mathematics Project, at the Sulzberger Middle School in Philadelphia, Pennsylvania; and efforts to enhance existing math curricula through application of research findings on students' intuitive knowledge and reasoning toward the math curriculum at the Edison Middle School in Milwaukee. In addition, QUASAR is researching strategies to make algebra accessible to all students at the Thurgood Marshall Middle School in Atlanta and exploring the integration of middle-level math and science at the Spurgeon Intermediate School in Santa Ana, California. By targeting schools with large numbers of African-American and Latino students, these projects promise to enrich mathematics curricula for urban students and inform schoolwide strategies for implementing heterogeneous grouping and closing gaps in mathematical learning.

Assessment Strategies for Heterogeneous Math Classes

> We have reached into this bag of blocks six times and have pulled out three red blocks, one green block, and two blue blocks. If you reached into the bag and pulled out another block, what color do you think it would be? Explain why you think it would be that color. How could you get more information?

If one goal of teaching mathematics is to develop thinking skills, then assessment in mathematics will require far more than a determination of whether students have arrived at the "right" answer to a problem. Assessment must also include an examination of *how* students are working on a problem, exploring such questions as whether they have a systematic way of organizing and recording information, how they relate one problem to other similar problems, how they express their ideas orally or in writing, and whether they can come up with ways to expand their information. Several resources are available to assist schools with new assessment approaches that both measure student progress and strengthen instruction.

EQUALS

In 1989, EQUALS, a project of the University of California at Berkeley, and the Assessment Committee of the California Mathematics Council's Campaign for Mathematics published *Assessment Alternatives in Mathematics.* A compendium of "instruction-embedded" assessment techniques, this handbook is rich with examples of evaluation approaches designed to support instruction in heterogeneous classrooms where students conduct projects and investigations in small groups; use manipulative materials, calculators, computers, assorted textbooks and reference books; consult with one another and the teacher; keep journals and written reports of their work; and work with the whole class on large and small problems.

The handbook details innovative strategies including student portfolios, journal writing in mathematics, open-ended questions, investigations, interviews, observations, performance assessments, and student self-assessments, all grounded in the view of mathematics as an essential tool for effective global citizenship. As the guide notes:

> In the world of work, people are valued for the tasks or projects they do, their ability to work with others, and their responses to problem situations. To prepare students for future success, both curriculum and assessment must promote this kind of performance.... We present in this booklet some ways to bring about assessment of authentic achievement. The implications are that students should be working on worthwhile investigations or tasks and that their success should be evaluated in ways that make sense.... We want to make it possible for all students (and their teachers) to show their best work, and to be so proud of their assessment results that they are eager to continue learning.

National Council of Teachers of Mathematics

Like the materials published by EQUALS, NCTM's *Mathematics Assessment: Myths, Models, Good Questions, and Practical Suggestions* is an essential resource for practical suggestions on assessing student progress at all levels. Included are successful models and prototypes for math assessment that follow the recommendations in the *Curriculum and Evaluation Standards for School Mathematics.* NCTM also offers a free bibliography of "Selected Assessment Resources" and copies of the February 1992 issue of *Arithmetic Teacher,* devoted entirely to assessment issues.

Professional Development for New Mathematics Curriculum and Instruction

Recommendations proposed by the Mathematical Association of America and NCTM highlight the need for mathematics teachers of the 1990s to be able to communicate mathematical ideas easily and clearly; organize and analyze information, solve problems, and construct logical arguments; understand math at deeper levels than required by the level being taught; enjoy math and appreciate its "power and beauty"; understand how math informs our current everyday world; and use technology in the learning, teaching, and doing of math. These expectations suggest that staff development for mathematics teachers in the middle grades must be a high priority in the untracking effort. Several approaches to staff development can hasten the adoption of new teaching and curriculum approaches.

Summer School

In Philadelphia public schools, a unique summer program has a dual purpose: to redirect students slated for general math in ninth grade into algebra 1 instead, and to provide staff development in new instructional strategies for selected eighth- and ninth-grade teachers. This approach succeeds in offering students curriculum that reflects NCTM recommendations and has also introduced participating teachers to nontraditional instruction using the University of Chicago Transition Mathematics materials. Beginning in the summer of 1990, participating teachers were asked to attend professional-development seminars, change their pedagogy to implement the program, and teach the same students in both the summer program and during the school year.

With funding from the Pew Charitable Trusts, the program, known as the Algebra Transition Project, has invested heavily in teacher-based decision making. At the start, according to Susan Stetzer of Philadelphia public schools, teachers selected the University of Chicago's *Transition Mathematics* as the basis for the summer text and UCSMP's *Algebra* as the follow-up school-year text. In shaping the summer curriculum, teachers also identified topics deemed essential preparation for algebra 1.

Recognizing that a new curriculum demanded different instructional approaches, teachers themselves generated a list of topics for staff development. Their suggestions formed the basis for a twenty-five-hour program conducted during two full-day Saturday sessions and six after-school sessions. The topics focused on using the Chicago materials; a discussion of algebra in light of NCTM standards; the use of manipulatives; reading in mathematics; critical thinking; and the technology of calculators and computers.

In addition, at the top of the list of selected topics was cooperative learning. As Stetzer reports, "Many teachers wanted to know more about the range of cooperative-learning approaches available and how to incorporate them into their classes. An introductory session on cooperative learning was scheduled, followed by an all-day workshop in which teachers worked in groups, modeling cooperative learning as they learned specific techniques for its implementation."

With this preparation, teachers worked in the three-hour-per-day summer session to put their newly acquired skills into practice. An additional hour and forty-five minutes each day of peer discussions, planning, curriculum development, and administrative tasks supported their increased confidence and sense of success. Most important, the entire experience formed the basis for introducing changes in curriculum and instruction into the regular school year as teachers saw their students experience success at higher rates than comparable students citywide. Indeed, Philadelphia's success suggests that the summer school model could serve as a vehicle for professional development in many local school districts.

The Middle-Grades Mathematics Project

Supporting local district efforts, the Middle Grades Mathematics Project (MGMP) at Michigan State University works to develop teachers' skills, self-confidence, and understanding of effective curriculum and instruction for heterogeneous classrooms through national dissemination of curriculum and teacher development materials. As a Johns Hopkins University review noted:

> Staff development is central to MGMP. Teachers are defined first as "mathematicians" and are helped to operate as such. This is an important and provocative component of many promising programs in all subjects. The goal is for teachers to feel that they are members and leaders of a community of active learners at school. They are not only "tellers" of information, but also thinkers, scholars, and workers. With their roles clarified, teachers are then provided clear guidelines on how to teach challenging middle-grades math concepts to their students. The teachers are taught using the same methods they will use to teach students—another promising approach to staff development in several programs.

Glenda Lappan of Michigan State explains how the project's approach dovetails with support for heterogeneous grouping. Units of curriculum, she says, are "built around mathematical situations that give students access at many different levels. We try to help the teacher by providing extension questions that can be used to stimulate students of different levels." In addition to

MGMP-made materials, the project recommends that teachers consider using curricula from Oregon's Math Learning Center, especially *Visual Mathematics* and *Math in the Mind's Eye*.

The Math Solution Materials

In addition, MGMP recommends the Math Solution, packaged materials developed by Marilyn Burns and available through Cuisenaire. Burns's staff-development videotape series, *Mathematics for Middle School*, demonstrates the teaching of problem-solving lessons in actual middle-school classroom settings. Drawing from content in geometry, measurement, probability and statistics, logical reasoning, patterns and functions, and algebra, the lessons present the fundamental elements of effective mathematics teaching. *A Collection of Math Lessons From Grades 6 Through 8*, a text by Burns and Cathy McLaughlin, also suggests ways in which math teachers can organize their classes into small cooperative groups, use concrete materials in instruction, and integrate writing into the math curriculum.

In the New York City public schools, Susan Zakaluk, Director of Mathematics for the district, reports that almost all middle-grades teachers have access to Burns's materials. Zakaluk notes that teachers in staff training sessions "fell in love with the book," and they saw from the videotapes how students who would otherwise have been placed in below-average classes both benefited from and contributed to heterogeneously grouped classes structured around small-group problem solving.

School-Based Study Groups

Even with new materials now available, where are the middle-grades teachers of today—many with twenty years or more remaining until retirement—going to acquire the characteristics cited by the MAA and NCTM? One educator seeking answers to this question is Herbert Rosenfeld of the Bank Street College of Education in New York City. A co-founder, along with Deborah Meier, of the acclaimed Central Park East Secondary School in New York, Rosenfeld continues to work with teachers at that school and elsewhere to develop innovative mathematics and science curricula and strengthen pedagogy with a focus on helping teachers broaden curriculum content. He asks:

> Why is it that despite wide acceptance of some of the
> mechanisms of restructured and untracked schools—
> a reorganized daily schedule or cooperative learning, for
> example—we still see our students working on the same
> kinds of tasks? How can teachers develop a math curriculum
> that is nonsequential and nonhierarchical? How can teachers
> begin to broaden their perspective of what is possible in
> a mathematics curriculum beyond seeking solutions to
> equations or learning geometric proofs?

Rosenfeld suggests that staff development designed to address these questions should take place in reading discussion groups for mathematics teachers, with teachers allowed time within the school day to study general-interest works such as *Innumeracy: Mathematical Illiteracy and Its Consequences* or *Beyond Numeracy: Ruminations of a Numbers Man,* by John Allen Paulos. Other reading focuses on stimulating a math curriculum that includes a wide range of mathematical content. In the process of considering how specific math concepts might translate into curriculum, says Rosenfeld, teachers create their own opportunities to develop as learners themselves and continue to grow as mathematicians.

Making Math Available for All

If the current technological revolution demands new standards of mathematics and science literacy, will all citizens be given equal access to the new skills, or will some be left behind, denied participation in the unfolding economic and political era? Those who are concerned about the life chances for historically oppressed people in the United States must not allow math-science education to be addressed as if it were purely a matter of technical instruction.

—Robert P. Moses, founder, The Algebra Project

Although mathematics may appear to represent the most difficult subject to untrack, the success of increasing numbers of schools that have implemented heterogeneous grouping coupled with innovative curriculum, instruction, and assessment approaches suggests that mixed-ability grouping in math is not impossible. Moreover, schools' experiences indicate that untracking in math can promote the complementary goals of expanding access to valued knowledge for students most often excluded from such knowledge and strengthening learning in mathematics for all young adolescents.

7 · Student Aspirations and Untracking

"Malcolm, you ought to be thinking about a career. Have you been giving it thought?

"Well yes, sir. I've been thinking I'd like to be a lawyer."

Mr. Ostrowski looked surprised, I remember, and leaned back in his chair and clasped his hands behind his head. He kind of half-smiled and said, "Malcolm, one of life's first needs is for us to be realistic. Don't misunderstand me now. We all like you here, you know that. But you've got to be realistic about being a nigger. A lawyer—that's no realistic goal for a nigger. You need to think about something you *can* be. You're good with your hands—making things. Everybody admires your carpentry shop work. Why don't you plan on carpentry? People like you as a person—you'd get all kinds of work."

—The Autobiography of Malcolm X, p. 36

In tracked schools, differences in learning conditions and school responses to perceived differences in ability frequently work together to undermine students' aspirations for future success. In some cases, a discussion of aspirations is simply not part of a school's routine. In other cases, tracking practices may directly close students off from access to opportunities that would help them turn their dreams into reality.

Young adolescents do have dreams of higher education. However, whether they realize it or not, many students will be limited in their access to further education as the result of certain school conditions—particularly course placement and lack of guidance. For example:

- According to data gathered from the U.S. Department of Education's National Educational Longitudinal Survey of 1988 eighth graders (NELS:88), a majority of eighth graders plan to attend college, but only 29 percent intend to take college-preparatory courses in high school.

- A study by California's Department of Education found that although two-thirds of the state's sophomores aspired to a goal requiring at least four years of college, many were not enrolled in courses that would prepare them for college. In fact, nearly half of all students taking general-education courses rather than college-preparatory ones had career goals that required a college degree.

- In a study of tracking in Boston public schools, interviews with middle-grades students revealed that many had future aspirations that called for post-secondary education. However, only the "top track" students had been directly encouraged to pursue options in higher education.

Schools can reinforce the purposes of heterogeneous grouping by expanding their mission to include the nurturing of the aspirations of *all* students, and the middle level is the place where this guidance may matter most. Specifically, schools can assess students' knowledge of post-secondary opportunities, redefine the role of the guidance staff, infuse related content into classroom instruction, and build awareness activities into every aspect of school life. Finally, because high-school course selection can powerfully determine future options, a renewed, opportunity-oriented mission also requires schools to ensure that all students enter high school with a course plan that clearly corresponds to their future goals.

Student Aspirations and the School Mission

In untracking schools, reorganization of grouping practices in and of itself can spark heightened student aspirations. As staff at Newport, Rhode Island's Thompson Junior High have observed, when certain students no longer see themselves as the "dumb group," they begin to imagine new plans for themselves. Staff from the Plainfield, Connecticut, Central School agree that as untracking proceeds, more students begin to discuss college as a possibility. At the Walnut Hill Middle School in Shreveport, Louisiana, untracking has inspired more students to express interest in the high-school magnet program; and at the Reid Middle School in Pittsfield, Massachusetts, in the wake of untracking fewer students are talking about dropping out.

Untracking schools understand that some form of post-secondary education beyond a high-school diploma—whether technical or commercial school, community college, four-year college, or university—is a necessity for anyone who will enter adulthood at the turn of the century. How, then, can schools best organize themselves to prepare nearly all students to pursue some form of post-secondary education?

To help answer this question, The Edna McConnell Clark Foundation has proposed a self-assessment approach for tailoring school structures and routines to expand higher-education opportunities for all students. The foundation's questions can help schools develop a solid schoolwide precollege guidance plan:

1. Why should this school transform itself so that its mission is to prepare nearly all students to enter and complete some form of post-secondary education?

2. What percentage of this current school year's students enrolled at the highest grade level (eighth grade? ninth grade?) of the school are likely to pursue post-secondary education after completing high school?

3. How would this school phrase a *goal* that responds to the following question: What percentage of the cohort group that enters the lowest grade level (sixth grade? seventh grade?) of the school in the next year *should* be enrolled in post-secondary institutions by at least the year 2001?

4. How would this school phrase an *objective* that responds to the following question: What percentage of the cohort group that enters the lowest grade level of the school currently *will*, within at least four years, be enrolled in high-school courses leading to post-secondary education?

5. How must this school change to prepare nearly all students to seek post-secondary education?

6. How can this school give equal attention and emphasis to all levels of post-secondary education?

7. What transition activities can this school or school system initiate with the receiving high schools to ensure that middle-level students are appropriately placed and counseled to continue their preparation for some form of post-secondary education? Who will be responsible for planning and ensuring the effective implementation of these activities?

8. Who at the building level will be responsible for coordinating the many activities designed to encourage, support, and enable nearly all students to pursue some form of post-secondary education?

9. What commitments can be obtained from post-secondary education institutions, business partners, and community-based organizations to assist this school in carrying out the activities designed to encourage post-secondary enrollment?

10. What kind of advisory/oversight group can this school create to advise on the implementation of the school's initiatives, and to assess periodically the progress and results of the school's efforts to fulfill its new mission? How, and to whom, will this group annually report on the school's progress and results? (The advisory group may be an existing group, or a new and expanded subcommittee of such a group.)

11. How can this school system monitor and follow students through high school to determine what percentage remain in school, successfully complete college-preparatory courses, and pursue post-secondary education? Who, in what office within the school system, will be responsible for this monitoring? To whom will the results be reported on an annual basis? How will this information be made public?

In some schools, self-assessment based on these questions may suggest changes both in the expectations that staff hold for students and in curriculum and classroom instruction. It may also suggest the need for new directions in leadership, resource development, and relationships with other institutions, both within and outside of the district.

Broadening Students' Aspirations: Turning Dreams into Goals

I was [fifteen and] throwing batting practice, and Howie
Kaplan told me, 'Kid, you're going to pitch in the big leagues.'
It was the first time I'd ever heard it, and I never forgot it.
Howie made my dream my goal.

— Tony Fossas, pitcher, Boston Red Sox

Early adolescence is not too soon to bring up the subject of "life-
after-school" with students. Indeed, if young adolescents are
beginning to develop a consciousness of their future options,
why should their teachers and counselors not use students' own
ambitions to fuel the motivation to reach the high levels of education and training necessary for the most potentially rewarding
opportunities of the future? At the very least, teachers and counselors need to understand what their students believe about the
opportunities available to them.

In 1989, Anita Rassias, a teacher at Eastern Junior High
School in Lynn, Massachusetts, decided to do an informal survey
of her students to assess their perceptions of post-secondary educational opportunities. She asked eighty-three of them, all from
low-income families, these questions:

1. How does a student get into college?
2. If you don't have a lot of money, can you still go to college?
3. Are there any colleges within a bus ride of this school?
4. Will any colleges take students who do not have good grades?

What Rassias learned was how little students actually knew
about their own potential and their possible future participation
in educational programs beyond high school. Almost all believed
that college admission required students to be "very smart"
with "straight 'A's" all through school. All believed that college
entrance was impossible without "lots of money," and only seventeen even knew that one public community college was
located virtually down the street from their school.

These findings jolted Eastern's staff members into launching a
comprehensive campaign designed to raise the awareness of
their students about post-secondary educational opportunities.
Key to the program was a formal partnership with the local community college and opportunities for everyone—not just
"honors" students—to visit the campus and attend classes there.
The partnership also created a pool of volunteer interns from the
college to serve as mentors and tutors for Eastern's students.
College fairs and other informational activities rounded out the
school-college offerings.

Eastern students were not alone in their lack of access to information about post-secondary opportunities. According to NELS:88 data, 64 percent of eighth graders have never discussed their future high-school program with a counselor, and only half of all eighth graders have discussed their high-school plans with a teacher. It makes sense, then, that efforts to engage young adolescent students and their parents in discussions about post-high-school educational opportunities begin in classrooms where teachers introduce and reinforce the concept of education as a key to success. Ultimately, however, the school must mobilize all its resources to ensure that the encouragement and information necessary for realizing dreams and ambitions are built into every student's school experience.

Classroom Instruction

The nurturing of aspirations begins in the classroom, and Carolyn Cole, a sixth-grade literature teacher at the West Baltimore Middle School, does not like to let a good opportunity to broaden students' thinking about their futures pass her by. Her class has been reading a Chinese folktale about a young woman of humble background named Precious Jade. The class begins to discuss the story:

> COLE: Who was called a peasant in the story?…Why was she called a peasant?…As the story went on, was Precious Jade still a peasant?…What happened to her?…What is the theme, the main idea, the meaning, the message the author wants to get across?

Cole's voice becomes very soft, and she walks around the room among her students. She holds up a wide, wound-up satin ribbon, and as she speaks just above a whisper to her group of twenty-four enthralled students, she slowly unwinds the ribbon.

> COLE: The theme unwinds through the story…it runs through every part of the story just like this ribbon. The theme is the message, the lesson, of the story. Concentrate now, and watch this ribbon unwind, and think about the theme, the message. Now I want you to imagine this: What if Precious Jade were living in today's world, with all the kinds of troubles we have? What jobs could she do best and why? What would she need to know? And what do *you* need to know about Precious Jade? You need to know *everything* about Precious Jade, *everything*.

Cole's questioning sets the stage for a discussion about Precious Jade's qualities. She is wise. She is honest. She is clever, say the students, giving examples of how Precious Jade has demonstrated these traits. Cole wants to know how these qualities would translate into the world today. She asks her students to form their regular groups of four to list all the jobs that would allow Precious Jade to use her cleverness. The lists are long: "Lawyer, teacher, doctor, scientist, architect, antique-shop owner, police detective, journalist, fashion designer, financial counselor, judge, FBI worker, banker, nurse..."

Cole responds to the lists, noting qualities needed for each. She remarks that all her students who have read "Precious Jade" have thought that Precious Jade could have been a lawyer. She tells a story:

> COLE: You know, when I finished college and started teaching, I thought I might want to be a lawyer one day. But what do you think held me back? ("Ms. Cole, you loved children too much," respond several students.) I did love children, and I couldn't wait to teach, but I also didn't want to go to law school for three more years. But a friend of mine went into teaching, and she also went to law school part-time. She became a lawyer, and just three weeks ago, she was appointed a judge in Baltimore City Court! One day I'm going to ask her to come in to talk with you.
>
> Yes, you do have to be very clever to do many things. You have to use your head, and you have to think. But your hands are extremely important to you, too. Now, for your homework, listen: I want you to pretend that you are a television reporter, and you must prepare an interview for Precious Jade. You have to think and come up with five *good* questions for Precious Jade....

Broader student aspirations, in many ways, go hand in hand with higher teacher expectations. When teachers communicate to students that a world of possibilities is open to them, students can begin to think concretely about the personal qualities necessary for certain roles and understand that social background need not necessarily limit their own potential to fill those roles.

*School-Based
Counseling*

At the same time, although higher teacher expectations support higher student aspirations, students also need systematic access to guidance resources to help them plan concretely for their futures. The story of Banning High School illustrates how guidance can be reorganized to support student aspirations.

Phyllis Hart was a guidance counselor at Banning, the fifth largest high school in Los Angeles, when she learned from a survey of former students who had gone on to post-secondary education that many had found that they did not have the necessary skills to make it in their new situation. Even some of the "top track" students from Banning were on probation in college, and many had dropped out. Hart was puzzled and angry. She knew that college could make all the difference to these students, and she knew that they could succeed in post-secondary institutions.

Hart decided to change this pattern, and, with the support of the principal and a few additional staff members, Banning began to offer opportunities that matched students' real aspirations. First, counselors visited the eighth and ninth grades in feeder junior high schools to discuss students' personal goals. As Hart suspected, most students dreamed of jobs that offered interest, status, and financial rewards. But when she asked which students had college plans, few raised their hands. They changed their minds, however, when Hart pointed out that the jobs they wanted required post-secondary education. This was the information these students needed to connect their own ambitions to a commitment to enroll in college-preparatory courses that could make their dreams real.

Hart next described Banning's College Core Curriculum to the students, explaining that courses were rigorous and required regular study, completed homework, and careful time management. Banning set no minimum standards for admission to the program; students had only to express their desire to go to college and sign a contract indicating their commitment. To support all students in the heterogeneous classrooms generated from this "open admission" policy, the school promised not only challenging academic preparation but also individual tutorial support and counseling.

Back at Banning, Hart's next step was to report to the six teachers assigned to the program that their incoming students all had plans to go to college, and that they should be prepared to teach a college-preparatory curriculum. But everything did not go smoothly. Shortly after school started, the six teachers called on Hart. "We thought these students were going to college," they said. "Well, they don't have a chance. They're not even doing their homework."

So Hart went back to the students. "How many of you are going to college?" she asked. All of them raised their hands. "Then why aren't you doing your homework? Have you forgotten your contracts? Do you realize you have to put in some effort to get yourselves to college?"

Through the ensuing years, these conversations continued. Some students who had not been challenged for years struggled with new expectations. Some teachers accustomed to teaching "traditional" college-bound students resisted the presence of these "untraditional" students. But Hart and her colleague Helen Monahan coached, badgered, and cajoled the students into keeping their dreams alive. They organized an Academic Boosters Club to recognize academic performance at special events attended by students from Banning's feeder schools. They sought out opportunities to reward students for working hard, requesting help, taking college-entrance examinations, and enrolling in courses that would give them access to higher education.

It was never easy, but Hart insisted on defining her role as counselor in terms of furthering students' *academic* needs and goals. Her conversations with students and teachers alike inevitably began with a focus on what graduating students should know in order to gain access to further educational opportunities. Then together they worked backwards, figuring out how to get to that point. In the end, students at Banning beat the odds, dodging the low-track courses in favor of others that offered meaningful opportunity for future success.

The first step in adopting alternatives to tracking, says Hart, involves "killing the myth that underrepresented ethnic and poor students can't succeed in higher education." She adds, "The school community must be dissatisfied with the status quo and be prepared to work hard to achieve change." Reviewing school data, including comparisons with other schools; visiting schools with similar student populations but better college-preparation results; and hearing about parallel efforts from staff in more successful schools can create a necessary belief in the need to change, she emphasizes.

Redefining the Counseling Role in Untracked Schools

Hart's story illustrates how changes in a school's counseling program can leverage change throughout an entire school. Key to this change is a shift in the role of the counseling staff from sorting students to motivating everyone to achieve academically. For example, counselors should:

- Actively target and enroll poor and underrepresented ethnic students for recruitment into college-prep courses
- Play a central role as part of a planning team to improve student achievement
- Assist in setting up a monitoring system to assess student performance and provide services where needed
- Use data on a regular basis to analyze and improve learning
- Involve parents in academic planning, selecting courses, and reviewing post-secondary opportunities

Administrators can support counselors by making educational guidance a priority and by monitoring progress as schools increase the number of poor and underrepresented ethnic students who enter college.

The Role of School Counselors: Creating Conditions for Dreams to Come True

Access to guidance resources can make a significant difference in the lives of students. School counselors provide information and assistance to students about high-school course enrollment, and in some settings, counselors themselves may assign students to particular "gatekeeping" courses that determine their track throughout high school. Unfortunately, course-placement decisions may be made *for* students without consideration of personal goals. For example, California's study of student aspirations found that although 81 percent of the sophomores surveyed indicated that school counselors had helped them plan their schedules, only half said that a counselor had discussed college or career plans with them.

To the extent that school counseling in the middle grades provides access to critical information that links placement in college-preparatory courses to post-secondary opportunities, guidance itself is a critical "gatekeeping resource." However, according to the College Entrance Examination Board, vital post-secondary counseling resources are not equally distributed among all students. The College Board reports, for example, that:

- Middle-level students from low-income families, rural as well as urban, are less likely than their more advantaged peers to have access to appropriate guidance in considering course selection in high school.

- The less access to counseling students have, the more likely they are to be placed in nonacademic curricular tracks with the result that they take fewer academic courses.

In *Keeping the Options Open*, The College Board emphasizes that counselors must work with students to enhance their academic performance and assist them in making choices to widen their opportunities. The report's major recommendations urge schools to take four critical steps for action:

1. **Establish a broad-based process in each local school district for determining the particular guidance and counseling needs of the students within each school and for planning how best to meet those needs.** Planning should involve a broad spectrum of representatives who will implement the plan and be affected by it. One outcome of this planning process should be to establish the goals of precollege guidance and counseling for the district.

2. **Develop a program under the leadership of each school principal that emphasizes the importance of the guidance counselor as a monitor and promoter of student potential, as well as coordinator of the school's guidance plan.** Under such a plan, the role of the guidance counselor may shift from provider of direct services to mobilizer and coordinator of services at the school level. The counselor's activities may broaden to include putting into place new resources such as computer-assisted guidance, supervising paraprofessional aides, supporting teachers, and planning awareness activities.

3. **Mount programs to inform and involve parents and other influential members of the family in the planning, decision making, and learning activities of the student.** Students are more likely to talk with their parents than with any other adult about their future goals, but sometimes parents know little about the concrete steps necessary to realize those goals. Involving parents can harness support for the extra effort required of students.

4. **Provide a program of guidance and counseling during the early and middle years of schooling, especially for students who traditionally have not been served well by the schools.** In particular, direct extra attention to the 40 percent of eighth graders who have no plans regarding their high-school course enrollments and those who plan to enroll in a "general" program.

These recommendations can guide schools' efforts to raise the aspirations of all students. As the role of the guidance counselor shifts from providing services to coordinating services, the guidance counselor becomes a critical part of the academic team, rather than an adjunct to it.

School Counseling, Improved Student Outcomes, and Heterogeneous Grouping

A key step in reforming a school to support the aspirations of all students is the creation of a vision for the school. Shaping this vision involves answering the question: "In terms of preparing students to enter and graduate from college, where do you want to be in five years' time?"

At Pioneer Valley Regional School, which virtually eliminated tracking in 1985, counselor Dona Cadwell can tell you exactly how the school's expectations for everyone to excel have translated into students' leaving school with greater potential for realizing their own aspirations. The changes that occurred at Pioneer Valley as a result of untracking have been dramatic, beginning with many more students enrolling in foreign language and advanced science and math courses. Shifts in course enrollments have, in turn, translated into more focused post-secondary plans. For example, between 1982 and 1990:

- The percentage of seniors going on to further education increased from 37 to 80 percent.
- The percentage in students entering four-year colleges increased from 17 to 45 percent.
- Fifty-five percent of all students now take Scholastic Aptitude Tests (SATs).
- The percentage of seniors going directly to work dropped from 26 to 8 percent.
- The percentage of seniors enlisting in the military has declined from 17 percent to zero.

At Pioneer Valley, heterogeneous grouping itself focused the sights of many students on further education. As one student noted, "I had never dreamed of going to college until we started having mixed classes and I got to know people who were going to go to Greenfield Community College." Moreover, Cadwell reports, college-attending students are now entering a wider variety of colleges of higher quality.

As the school as a whole worked on untracking, counselors decided that they could take specific steps to support success in heterogeneous groups, communicate high expectations, and stimulate students to take advantage of future opportunities. For example, Cadwell recommends:

- Expect that every eighth grader will eventually go to college; provide students with information to help them identify with people similar to them in skills and interests who have gone on to college and ended up in interesting occupations.

- Reiterate college admissions requirements in every grade. Ask questions that communicate the expectation that students will consider college, such as "Which language did you choose?," "Are you ready for algebra now?," or "Will you start a foreign language this year or next year?"

- Tell students about how particular graduates' high-school experiences contributed to their post-secondary success: "Most of our students who have gone on to college tell me how much they use computers…"

- Bring in resource people who are able to inspire and relay information about occupations and their requirements for further education.

- Work with teachers on career-investigation projects.

- Introduce students to guidance resources such as Career Explorer.

- Share newspaper clippings about successful people and how they reached their goals.

- Publicize college video screenings in empty classrooms during study halls or lend videos to students to take home.

- Run parent workshops to let them know about options and opportunities for their children.

Cadwell knows well how former tracking practices closed students out of opportunities that might have appealed to their interests. She remembers:

> Being responsible for placing students in different levels in grades seven through nine felt extremely uncomfortable. It was like playing God with so many unknowns, unopened minds, unexplored options, and lack of knowledge of the world. The kids usually trusted us. Parents wanted the best, even if students were not recommended for the high levels, and students would be made to feel inferior if they couldn't handle the work in the particular group. Often the difference in work was amount rather than difficulty. The very act of labeling was repulsive.

Counseling in an untracked setting, in contrast, creates a climate that is more compatible with honoring students' ambitions and plans for the future. "Now some decisions need to be made regarding math and science," she says. "Still, many students choose more difficult courses and feel confident or ready to take a risk. Most succeed."

Making Aspirations Real Through Planning and Early Awareness Activities

At our school it's not an option *not* to plan. We tell the students what their choices mean. If they set their sights low, we tell them the consequences.

—Ronald Allen and Debbie Hart, Counselors,
Crete-Monee Junior High School, 1991

Expanding opportunities to acquire knowledge and extending high expectations to all students *could* stop with the middle-level academic program and fulfill the mission of untracking. But the real test of this approach is in the concrete plans that students develop and follow in subsequent years. Individual plans and early awareness activities are two strategies that strengthen the potential of students to act on their dreams once they have left the middle grades.

Individual Plans

At Crete-Monee, the spirit of the untracking mission extends to helping all students develop a written short- and long-range educational plan to realize their ambitions. In experiential, classroom-based guidance meetings, students learn basic information to help them identify personal strengths, values, and interests. They also learn decision-making strategies designed to help them make informed choices about their futures. The overriding objective of the program is to help students coordinate their academic program with career goals.

Counselors Ronald Allen and Debbie Hart developed "Pathways to Success: Individualized Educational and Career Plan" along with other counselors from the school district. As part of a continuous program for grades seven through twelve, the course helps students explore career and educational opportunities. Seventh- and eighth-grade activities provide information about projected occupational choices of the future, connect particular jobs to school courses, and help students clarify their own personal interests and the value of work. Parents are involved at key points during each year, and computer-assisted activities supplement the curriculum.

Key to the planning process is the expectation that students will leave Crete-Monee having made a four-year plan to guide their high-school careers; indeed, the main message Allen and Hart deliver is that students should *plan* to graduate from high school and *plan* for post-secondary training, whether through on-the-job training, apprenticeships, trade school, community college, or four-year college. "Keep your options open!" counselors emphasize over and over.

A major activity for all students during the eighth grade second semester is a high-school planning program that emphasizes effort more than ability for achieving success in school and in life. The program, combined with the elimination of all "low" classes at the school, has encouraged many students to risk new challenges. Compared with a few years ago, the number of Crete-Monee's graduating eighth graders entering low-level language-arts/English courses at the high school has dropped by more than half, broadening access to improved opportunities for many more students.

Early Awareness of Post-Secondary Education

In poor school districts, in particular, students need information about how to realize their own educational goals. In Massachusetts, the Massachusetts Higher Education Information Center's Statewide Youth Awareness Program promotes materials and activities to stimulate concrete planning by students and parents. The center's multilingual publications, workshops, videos, motivational speakers, field trips to college campuses, and interest inventories not only highlight the importance of college and the steps needed to prepare for it, they also introduce students to all forms of post-secondary education including two-year community colleges, technical schools, and commercial schools.

But do these activities make a difference in the lives of low-income and minority students who are underrepresented in meaningful post-secondary educational programs? In 1991, the center surveyed some 900 eighth graders in four urban school districts in the state to find out. In these districts, four out of five eighth graders believed that they would continue their education beyond high school, but four-year high-school dropout rates ranging from 30 to 50 percent suggested that, for many, this would not be the case. In each of the districts, four schools had conducted early-awareness activities with their eighth graders; four had done little or nothing in this area. The center's intention was to compare the plans of students who had experienced these activities with those who had not.

Study findings supported the center's hypothesis that early-awareness activities could have a positive impact on the plans of middle-level students. Specifically, the center found that:

- Significantly more students who participated in early-educational-awareness activities planned to enroll in college-preparatory programs than those who did not.

- Benefits of intervention were especially significant for Latino students, with significantly more students who participated in early-awareness activities aspiring to graduate from college and attain college-level occupations than Latino students who were not involved in such activities.

- Students participating in early-awareness programs believed that their teachers had significantly higher expectations for their achievement than did those students not involved.

Intervention to help students put their goals into action, although requiring consistency and coherence, does not have to be extensive. In fact, some schools that demonstrated an impact on students' plans offered a series of activities during class time as infrequently as once a week for four to six weeks during the winter prior to selecting high school courses. Even minimal allocation of time for these activities makes a significant difference for many students.

Early intervention, then, can influence students' futures first by helping individuals take steps to bring their high school plans in line with their aspirations. As important, by reducing differences between the aspirations of minority students and those of white students and contributing to a climate of higher expectations, early-awareness activities may foster a stronger sense of shared purpose among all members of the school community.

The initiatives schools can take to prepare students to pursue post-secondary options are many. They are fundamental to communicating high expectations to everyone. The most popular of these activities are organized visits to colleges, and the early middle grades years are not too soon to begin. For example, at the Holyoke Magnet Middle School, all sixth graders grouped with their school "family" make day-long visits to neighboring Mount Holyoke College. With extended time on the campus, students may spend the first half of the day working with the chemistry faculty in the science laboratories to make silly putty and the second half using the sports facilities under the supervision of the college's physical-education staff. Likewise, all seventh graders from the Central Park East Secondary School in East Harlem, New York City, take weekend field trips to visit colleges and universities, sometimes spending the night in the dormitories of the institutions they visit.

When all is said and done, making post-secondary education a viable option for all students in the middle grades is one key to unlocking rigid tracking in later grades. By building on the understanding that nearly all students can and should consider formal education beyond high school, middle-level staff can encourage greater numbers of students to envision improved life options for themselves and help them enter critical gatekeeping courses that provide entry to meaningful opportunities.

Reorganizing School Routines to Strengthen Student Aspirations

In addition to strengthening the role of school counselors, establishing school-college partnerships, visiting post-secondary institutions, and preparing all students for high-school courses required for post-secondary education, schools may consider the following suggestions developed by the Edna McConnell Clark Foundation's Program for Disadvantaged Youth:

- Develop and implement a system to monitor, analyze, and report on how and why students enroll in specific courses. Involve parents by utilizing the Parents and Counselors Together (PACT) curriculum of the National Association of College Admission Counselors.

- Ensure that all members of the school staff believe that most students can and should pursue post-secondary education, and that staff consistently communicate these expectations to students.

- Within content areas, encourage students to conduct research projects on post-secondary institutions, write reports, and make oral presentations to their classmates on what they have learned about the institutions and the courses that they require for admissions.

- Ensure that most students take a Preparing for Post-Secondary Education exploratory course.

- Seek locally funded programs that guarantee tuition for all economically disadvantaged students accepted by post-secondary-education institutions.

- Persuade post-secondary-education institutions to establish on their campuses summer-enrichment programs for middle-level students.

- Seek high-school students preparing for post-secondary education to come to the middle-level school and participate in small group discussions on what to expect in and how to prepare for high school.

- Seek frequent, consistent visits to the school by representatives of post-secondary institutions. Include alumni as well as staff.

- Host teachers from post-secondary institutions to discuss, by content area, issues of mutual interest with teachers from the middle-school level.

- Utilize students from post-secondary institutions to mentor and tutor students, focusing on helping middle-level students learn about the institutions from which the mentors/tutors come.

- Prominently display throughout the school posters and other visual materials from post-secondary institutions.

- Arrange for post-secondary institutions to donate shirts, binders, pens/pencils, posters, and tickets to sports and cultural events which the school can distribute as incentives for improved academic performance and academic achievement.

Activities like these, when implemented in a coherent way, can form the foundation of a schoolwide plan for building on student aspirations for a productive future. To the extent that they touch on teacher and parent roles, curriculum, and instruction, these activities can make concrete the commitment to high expectations for all students.

Opening Doors Through Mathematics Enrichment

ITEM: In a study presented in 1989 to the Mathematical Sciences Education Board, a branch of the National Academy of Sciences, researchers from the U.S. Department of Education reported that the more math you take in school, the more money you earn in later life.

ITEM: According to the National Action Council for Minorities in Engineering, as of 1986, only 2.5 percent of all engineers in the United States were African-American; and only 2.1 percent were Latino.

The field of mathematics offers particular opportunities for broadening students' aspirations, and these deserve special mention. Indeed, for students with a burgeoning interest in math or science, these opportunities can open doors otherwise unimagined by many students, especially minorities and females. The Mathematics, Engineering, and Science Achievement Project (MESA), the National Action Council for Minorities in Engineering (NACME), and the Southeast Consortium for Minorities in Engineering (SECME) are three examples of organizations committed to helping African-American, Latino, and Native American students understand that higher mathematical knowledge offers the potential for expanded future life opportunities.

MESA

Applying math to solving problems can motivate many students to think about future opportunities. For example, how would you approach this problem?

> **Problem:** To design and construct a protective packaging that will protect a raw egg from damage (cracking or breakage) when the packaged egg is dropped from a second-story window or any other equivalent specified height onto a concrete slab.

> **Specifications:** The container must allow insertion and removal of a single grade-A medium chicken egg. The construction materials are limited to plastic straws, masking tape, and glue.

> **Design and construction tips:** Consider a variety of ideas. Be creative and innovative with the materials. Would it help if you had some information about the properties of triangles? Or if you had a diagram of an egg and understood the location of the air cell? What if you knew that "$F = m$ times a" ("Force is equaled to mass multiplied by acceleration")?

In some middle schools committed to offering students tools for realizing their aspirations, teachers organize after-school clubs to introduce fields that appear to hold special promise for future opportunities. At the West Baltimore Middle School, Science Department chairperson Trezeline Brooks believes that a Mathematics, Engineering, and Science Achievement Club for students interested in applying math concepts to practical problems meets this goal. The club, an affiliate of its parent group MESA, a project based at the University of California at Berkeley, attracts some thirty active minority and female youngsters whose interest in math surmounts the inconvenience of walking home after the regular school busses have left.

The club offers opportunities for small work groups of sixth to eighth graders to solve selected mathematical problems and develop critical thinking skills by practicing an "engineering method" that replicates problem solving in the real world. For every problem posed, students first define the problem in concise terms, assemble and analyze all data pertinent to the problem, and bring together all the factors involved to form a solution, including the most likely solutions. They then decide on the best course of action to take and complete the design. As the opportunity arises, students enter their designs in open competition. A project researching, designing, and building a container crane built from straws won West Baltimore students $450 in prize money along with a new sense of pride and confidence in their work.

Brooks uses the engineering method in her regular science classes and finds that it works well with students at all levels. For example, in the case of one underachieving child, the experience of working with two engineers "on loan" from local corporations sparked new interests and turned around his attitude toward classroom activities. As Brooks points out, "This club is a way of getting students to accomplish challenging tasks without scaring them in the process."

National Action Council for Minorities in Engineering (NACME)

Complementing the work of MESA, the National Action Council for Minorities in Engineering (NACME) has a dual commitment to explore the best models in the country for teaching with technology and to recruit and retain minority engineering students. NACME's resources are designed to open doors of opportunity to African-American, Latino, and Native American students and strengthen their interest and aspirations in math. For example, *Chaos at the Construction Site! The Amazing Spider-Man vs. Dr. Octopus* is a comic book that leads the Amazing Spider-Man, an engineer, and three minority students through an exciting story which advises readers to take algebra 1 rather than general math in junior high school. An annual conference provides a continuing source of ideas for generating minority-student interest in math-related fields.

Southeast Consortium for Minorities in Engineering (SECME)

Similar to NACME, the Southeast Consortium for Minorities in Engineering (SECME), a regional coalition organized to qualify more minority students to enter and complete studies in engineering, mathematics, and science, promotes increased access to math through intensive teacher training and student activities emphasizing interest rather than ability. According to Phyllis McLaughlin of SECME, "We try to impress upon teachers that we're about broadening the pool of potential engineers so that students who may not be readily identified as 'gifted' can have opportunities for achievement they would not have had otherwise." These students might have an entrepreneurial bent with a wish to sell things and make money; they might love projects—manipulating materials to make models at home or school, repairing a bike or an appliance, building things such as a skateboard, or taking things apart and rebuilding them. SECME's activities are designed to reach out both to these students, who might never have imagined themselves in math-related fields, and to the important adults in their lives.

Using Real-World Experiences to Broaden Student Aspirations

Many students proceed with plans for higher education on the strength of school counseling that links post-secondary education and higher earnings. Others, however, may find it difficult to plan on the basis of an abstract idea alone, unrelated either to their interests or practical experience. Yet opportunities for learning about the world of work are limited for many young adolescents. For example, according to a Brandeis University report, 74 percent of young-adolescent students are learning very little about people's work activities in the next century, and one-third have little knowledge of the world of work even in their own communities.

Helping students make concrete choices about future goals requires defining the possibilities for further education within the context of occupational awareness. For example, Philadelphia's Public/Private Ventures (P/PV) has found that intensive personal relationships with elderly mentors add a personal dimension to more formal youth programs and provide a window for students onto adult life, including the world of work and its requirements. When implemented in combination with experienced-based programs, these relationships can enhance the aspirations of all students, especially those who might not otherwise consider post-secondary education. For example:

- A partnership between the Timilty Middle School and the Massachusetts General Hospital (MGH) in Boston, Massachusetts, includes several activities designed to help students make connections between their studies and the job responsibilities that they might want to pursue in the future. With some 11,000 employees in hundreds of different job classifications, the hospital stretches students' imaginations about their future through a speakers' bureau of MGH employees who are prepared to visit classes to relate their personal and career history, describe their present position, and demonstrate how students' current school activities are relevant to future success. In addition, any child can apply to become a Timilty Explorer and have a hospital employee as a mentor who hosts students on the job, allows students to observe them at work, and helps students develop job-awareness. In another MGH-Timilty project, 25 students of all academic backgrounds are paired with an MGH employee to develop a Science Fair project, ranging from building a refrigerator with a refrigerator mechanic to designing a study of baseball team averages with a computer specialist. At the same time, staff from the hospital's training department work with all the students to help them practice and hone their presentation skills. Finally, the hospital provides training for teachers on changes and new developments in the work force and summer internships to familiarize them with the hospital environment.

- At the Butler Junior High School in Lowell, Massachusetts, engineers and scientists who work at M/A-Com Corporation spend up to five days a month with students working on projects designed to show them how their classroom learning can translate into the real world. Projects include teaching students how to build weather equipment, design kites from triangles, and run a T-shirt business. According to science teacher Bill Gianoulis, the corporate guests provide real-life role models for the students, helping them to consider careers in scientific and manufacturing industries.

- Louisville's Western Middle School made the best of the annoying necessity for extensive school renovations to fashion a partnership program involving students and skilled workers engaged in physical plant rehabilitation activities. Dubbed Side-by-Side, this program fostered personal connections between students and engineers, heating and cooling mechanics, electricians, and construction supervisors working at the school site. Paired students learned firsthand that the skilled trades often require training beyond high school. Says teacher Patricia Futch, "The kids certainly found out they can't just leave school in eighth grade."

Activities like these can expand all students' awareness of future life possibilities. They can make it clear that the future favors those who are prepared to learn throughout their lives, and that planning for education beyond high school will pay off in expanded opportunities.

Keeping Student Goals and Needs at the Center of Tracking Reform

Young adolescents harbor aspirations no less ambitious than those of the generations that preceded them. But finding themselves in tracked schools, many of these students begin to suspect that the opportunities offered them hold little promise for realizing these ambitions. Over time, their dreams narrow and may disappear.

One of the less obvious but no-less-real outcomes in untracking schools is a perceptible heightening of student aspirations. These aspirations represent the beginning steps in the process of preparing for responsible adulthood, however far in the future that may seem. They are a crucial part of the adolescent world of imagining oneself as an adult, considering oneself in future roles.

In untracking schools, educators make extra efforts to avoid foreclosing on opportunities for their students. Most important, in the middle grades, untracking schools take active steps to ensure that the transition to the high-school level will "keep the options open" so that students' plans are not prematurely curtailed. To do this, they implement classroom practices, teacher-based counseling, early-awareness activities, and mentoring programs designed to help students form concrete plans to make their dreams come true. Finally, it is the comprehensive package of heterogeneous grouping, active learning, meaningful curriculum, and activist guidance programs that builds the strongest bridge between student aspirations and opportunity.

Conclusion

At the root of the movement for untracking in public schools lie a passion for excellence and equity and the belief that all children are entitled to the best education that the country can offer. This movement is one that responds to research documenting the harm of tracking. It is a response to the increasing availability of research-based innovations in curriculum, teaching, assessment, and counseling and to the academic, developmental, and social needs of students who are enrolled in the nation's schools.

Most of all, untracking is a manifestation of the deeply held belief on the part of many educators, parents, and citizens that American public schools have a special responsibility for putting into practice the values of democracy and equal educational opportunity for all students. The stories told by untracking schools about their experiences are stories of schools stretching their imaginations and resources to implement their commitment to educate all students for life in the twenty-first century. These schools are preparing their students for life in a democracy not just by talking about it, but by living it.

Although the stories that these schools tell are unique, they reveal a set of common themes and suggest lessons for school change efforts everywhere. These include:

- The importance of grounding change in a climate of high expectations and participatory learning for all

- The need to articulate goals for excellence and equity in ways that win the support of all constituencies in a school

- The need for school and district leadership that nurtures teachers' readiness for change and willingness to take risks

- The need for change in organizational structures to allow for flexibility and innovation in classroom teaching

- The need for rich, high-level curriculum that reflects the goal of preparing students for a multiplicity of productive adult roles

- The need for coordinating all school resources to expand equal educational opportunity for all students

Changes in all these aspects of schooling are taking place in untracking schools. They are taking place despite rather than because of national policy. This policy currently pays lip service to improved education but rarely expands the definition of school improvement to include the day-to-day school practices that weaken student motivation and engagement, undermine teacher morale, and, ultimately, erode the sense of a school community committed to the success of everyone. The movement for untracking arises now in part because of an understanding that these practices, including ability grouping of students, fall short of what many educators and parents want for all children.

The challenge of untracking is before us now because it has also become clear that the health and well-being of future generations depends on developing every mind that we have. Imagine, for example, what would happen if we viewed every mind as a source of genius. Imagine what our schools might be like if we resolved to offer all students the intellectual and social tools that they need to take on the great issues of our time. Imagine what our classrooms might be like if we began to ensure that every one of our students was equipped to play a role in discovering a cure for AIDS or Alzheimer's Disease, negotiating a lasting peace in the Middle East, redesigning our urban and rural communities for environmental safety and economic prosperity, eradicating homelessness in America and starvation in the Sahara, or writing the great symphonies, dramas, or poetry of the twenty-first century.

Untracking schools have created academic communities founded on a moral vision of all students learning together at high levels with the understanding that they are engaged in the first stages of a process of lifelong learning. Every day more schools turn to alternatives to tracking to make this vision a reality in the lives of their students. Their doing so in the face of great odds merits widespread recognition, appreciation, and support.

The process of untracking is still young. It is still fragile. But as this movement gains momentum, we can look forward to learning more about the process and the vision of democratic schooling that it promotes through more detailed school histories. It is our hope that this report will be a first step in acknowledging the importance of this movement for our children and our society. We await further stories from schools themselves in the expectation that their experiences will deepen our understanding of how we can shape our institutions to meet the needs of all the young people who put their faith in us.

Resources

For further information about schools, programs, or references cited in each chapter, readers may refer to the following:

Part I: Introduction

Braddock, Jomills Henry. "Tracking the Middle Grades: National Patterns of Grouping for Instruction." *Phi Delta Kappan* 71, no. 6 (February 1990).

Buttenwieser, Peter. "Notes from the Field." Unpublished paper prepared for the Ford Foundation, 1985.

Carnegie Council on Adolescent Development. *Turning Points: Preparing American Youth for the 21st Century.* Washington, D.C.: Carnegie Corporation, June 1989.

George, Paul S. "Tracking and Ability Grouping: Which Way for the Middle School?" *Middle School Journal* (September 1988).

Goodlad, John I. *A Place Called School: Prospects for the Future.* New York: McGraw-Hill, 1984.

Kearns, David T., and Denis P. Doyle. *Winning the Brain Race.* San Francisco: ICS Press, 1988.

Kozol, Jonathan. *Savage Inequalities: Children in America's Schools.* New York: Crown, 1991.

Lipsitz, Joan. *Successful Schools for Young Adolescents.* New Brunswick, N.J.: Transaction Books, 1984.

Lounsbury, John H., and Donald C. Clark. *Inside Grade Eight: From Apathy to Excitement.* Reston, Va.: National Association of Secondary School Principals, 1990. Available from NASSP, 11904 Association Drive, Reston, VA 22091; (703) 860-0200.

Massachusetts Advocacy Center. *Locked In/Locked Out: Tracking and Placement Practices in Boston Public Schools.* Boston: Massachusetts Advocacy Center, 1990.

McDonnell, Lorraine M., Leigh Burstein, Tor Ormseth, James Catterall, and David Moody. *Discovering What Schools Really Teach: Designing Improved Coursework Indicators.* Report prepared for the Office of Educational Research and Improvement, United States Department of Education, June 1990.

McLaren, Peter. *Life in Schools.* New York: Longman, 1989.

Milwaukee Public Schools, 5225 West Vliet St., Milwaukee, WI; (414) 475-8393; Howard Fuller, Ph.D., Superintendent of Schools.

National Center for Educational Statistics, National Educational Longitudinal Survey (NELS:88), (NCES no. 91-460), Washington, D.C.: Office of Educational Research and Improvement, April 1991. Available from United States Department of Education, 555 New Jersey Ave., N.W., Washington, DC 20208-5641; (800) 424-1616.

National Center on Education and the Economy. *America's Choice: High Skills or Low Wages.* Rochester, N.Y.: National Center on Education and the Economy, 1990. Available from NCEE, 39 State St., Suite 500, Rochester, NY 14614; (716) 546-7620.

National Commission on the Role of the School and the Community in Improving Adolescent Health. *CODE BLUE: Uniting for Healthier Youth.* Washington, D.C.: American Medical Association/National Association of State Boards of Education, 1990. Available from NASBE, 1012 Cameron St., Alexandria, VA 22314; (703) 684-4000.

Nieto, Sonia. *Affirming Diversity: The Socio-Political Context of Multicultural Education.* White Plains, N.Y.: Longman, 1992.

Oakes, Jeannie. *Keeping Track: How Schools Structure Inequality.* New Haven: Yale University Press, 1985.

Smith, Mary Lee, and Lorrie A. Shepard, eds. *Flunking Grades: Research and Policies on Retention.* New York: Falmer Press, 1989.

Solomon, Jolie. "As Cultural Diversity of Workers Grows, Experts Urge Appreciation of Differences." *Wall Street Journal,* 14 September 1990.

Spring, Joel. *The Sorting Machine: National Educational Policy Since 1945.* New York: David McKay, 1976.

Weis, Lois, and Michelle Fine, eds. *Silenced Voices: Issues of Class, Race, and Gender in U.S. Schools.* Albany: SUNY Press, 1992.

Part II: Conditions for Untracking

Accelerated Schools Project, 402 S CERAS, Stanford University, Stanford, CA 94305-3084; (415) 723-3095; Henry M. Levin, Director; Wendy S. Hopfenberg, Middle School Project Director; Dr. Jane McCarthy, Newsletter Editor.

Altersitz, Janet. "Successfully Eliminating Tracking…The Principal's Role." *Early Adolescence Magazine* 5, no. 5 (May–June 1991).

Association for Illinois Middle-Level Schools (AIMS), 810 W. Springfield Ave., Suite 205, Champaign, IL 61820-4764; (217) 356-7982.

Association for Supervision and Curriculum Development, 1250 N. Pitt St., Alexandria, VA 22314-1403; (703) 549-9110.

Berger, Ron. "Building A School Culture of High Standards: A Teacher's Perspective." In *Expanding Student Assessment,* edited by Vito Perrone. Alexandria, Va.: Association for Supervision and Curriculum Development, 1991.

Jake Burks, Associate Superintendent for Curriculum and Instruction, Harford County Public Schools, 45 E. Gordan St., Bel Air, MD 21014; (410) 838-7300, ext. 230.

Burlington Public Schools, 150 Colchester St., Burlington, VT 05401; (802) 864-8461; Paul Daniel, Superintendent; Monica Nelson, Director of Curriculum.

California State Department of Education, Superintendent's Middle Grade Task Force. *Caught in the Middle: Educational Reform for Young Adolescents in California Public Schools.* Sacramento, Calif.: California State Department of Education, 1987. Available from Bureau of Publications, California State Department of Education, Box 271, Sacramento, CA 95802-0271; (916) 445-1260.

Center of Education for the Young Adolescent, University of Wisconsin-Platteville, 1 University Plaza, Platteville, WI 53818-3099; (608) 342-1276; Martin Tadlock, Director.

Central Park East Secondary Schools, 1573 Madison Ave., New York, NY 10029; (212) 860-8935; Deborah Meier, Principal.

ChartHouse International Learning Corporation, 221 River Ridge Circle, Burnsville, MN 55337; (800) 328-3789; (612) 890-1800. Call for information about special offers for schools and educational organizations.

Coalition of Essential Schools, Brown University, Box 1969, Providence, RI 02912; (401) 863-3384; Theodore Sizer, Chairman.

Crete-Monee Junior High School, 1500 Sangamon St., Crete, IL 60417; (708) 672-2700; J.T. Crawford, Principal.

Cummins, Jim. "Empowering Minority Students: A Framework for Intervention." *Harvard Educational Review* 56, no. 1 (February 1986).

Cushman, Kathleen. "The Essential Conversation: Getting It Started, Keeping It Going." *HORACE* 8, no. 2 (November 1991).

George, Paul. "Tracking and Ability Grouping: Which Way for the Middle School?" *Middle School Journal,* September 1988.

George, Paul. "What's the Truth About Tracking and Ability Grouping—Really???" Available from Paul George, Teacher Education Resources, P.O. Box 206, Gainesville FL 32602; (904) 378-7267; (904) 392-2391, ext. 268.

Goodlad, John I. *A Place Called School: Prospects for the Future.* New York: McGraw-Hill, 1984.

Goodlad, John I. "Linking Schools and Universities: Symbiotic Partnerships." Occasional Paper No. 1. Seattle, Wash.: Center for Educational Renewal, 1987.

Hergert, Leslie F., Janet M. Phlegar, and Marla E. Perez-Selles. *Kindle the Spark: An Action Guide for Schools Committed to the Success of Every Child.* Andover, Mass.: Regional Laboratory for Educational Improvement of the Northeast and Islands, 1991. Available from the Regional Laboratory for the Northeast and Islands, 300 Brickstone Sq., Suite 900, Andover, MA 01810; (800) 347-4200.

Islander Middle School, 8225 S.E. 72nd St., Mercer Island, WA 98040; (206) 236-3413; Susan Galletti, Principal.

Jericho Middle School, Cedar Swamp Rd., Jericho, NY 11753; (516) 681-4215; Anna Hunderfund, Principal.

Levine, Daniel U., and Lawrence W. Lezotte. *Unusually Effective Schools: A Review and Analysis of Research and Practice*. Madison, Wis.: National Center for Effective Schools, 1990.

Lipsitz, Joan. *Successful Schools for Young Adolescents*. New Brunswick, N.J.: Transaction Books, 1984.

Brenda R. Lyons, Ed.D., Director, Secondary Education and Communications, Edmond Public Schools, 1216 South Rankin, Edmond, OK; (405) 340-2800.

Maryland Task Force on the Middle Learning Years. *What Matters in the Middle Grades: Recommendations for Maryland Middle Grades Education*. Baltimore: Maryland State Department of Education, 1989. Available from Maryland State Department of Education, Bureau of Educational Development, Division of Instruction, 200 W. Baltimore St., Baltimore, MD 21201-2595; (301) 333-2352.

Massachusetts Board of Education. *Structuring Schools for Student Success: A Focus on Ability Grouping*. Quincy, Mass.: Massachusetts Department of Education, 1990. Available from Massachusetts Department of Education, 1385 Hancock St., Quincy, MA 02169; (617) 770-7589.

McCulloch Middle School, 3520 Normandy, Dallas TX 75205; (214) 521-7840; Cecil Floyd, Principal.

Meier, Deborah. "Central Park East: An Alternative Story." *Phi Delta Kappan*, June 1987.

Meier, Deborah W. "The Little Schools That Could." *The Nation*, 23 September 1991.

Middle School of the Kennebunks, 87 Fletcher St., Kennebunk, ME 04043-1997; (207) 985-2912; Sandra Caldwell, Principal.

National Association of Secondary School Principals, Council on Middle Level Education. *Developing a Mission Statement for the Middle Level School*. Reston, Va.: NASSP, 1987. Available from NASSP, 1904 Association Dr., Reston, VA 22091; (703) 860-0200.

National Center on Effective Schools, 1025 W. Johnson St., Suite 570, Madison, WI 53706; (608) 263-7575.

National Education Association. *Academic Tracking*. Washington, D.C.: National Education Association, 1990. Available from NEA, 1201 Sixteenth St., N.W., Washington, DC 20036; (202) 822-7350.

National Middle School Association, 4807 Evanswood Dr., Columbus, OH 43229-6292; (614) 848-8211; Denis D. Smith, Executive Director.

National Network (of School-University Partnerships) for Educatonal Renewal, Center for Educational Renewal, Institute for the Study of Educational Policy, College of Education DQ-12, University of Washington, Seattle, WA 98195; (206) 543-6230; John I. Goodlad, Director.

National Resource Center for Middle Grades Education, University of South Florida, College of Education, EDU-115, Tampa, FL 33620-5650; (813) 974-2530.

Nevada State Board of Education, Middle School Task Force. *Right in the Middle: Today's Young Adolescents; Nevada's Future.* Carson City: Nevada Department of Education, 1990. Available from Nevada Department of Education, Capitol Complex, Carson City, NV 89710.

New England League of Middle Schools (NELMS), 460 Boston St., #4, Topsfield, MA 01983-1223; (508) 887-6263.

New York State Department of Education, Office of General and Occupational Education, Middle Level Education Program, Room 212 EB, Albany, NY 12234; (518) 474-8224; David Payton, Director of Middle Level Education.

Outcomes-Driven Developmental Model: A Program for Comprehensive School Improvement, Johnson City Central School District, 666 Reynolds Rd., Johnson City, NY 13790; (607) 770-1200; Dr. Frank V. Alessi, ODDM Project Director.

Powell, Arthur G., Eleanor Farrar, and David K. Cohen. *The Shopping Mall High School: Winners and Losers in the Educational Marketplace.* Boston: Houghton Mifflin, 1985.

Rosenfeld, Herb. "Reflections From a Workplace for Cognitive Apprenticeship." In *Teaching Advanced Skills to Educationally Disadvantaged Students,* edited by Barbara Means and Michael S. Knapp. Menlo Park, Calif.: SRI International and Policy Studies Associates, March 1991. Report prepared for the U.S. Department of Education.

Sizer, Theodore. "Diverse Practice, Shared Ideas: The Essential School." In *Organizing for Learning: Toward the 21st Century,* edited by Herbert J. Walberg and John J. Lane. Reston, Va.: National Association of Secondary School Principals, 1989.

Sizer, Theodore. *Horace's School: Redesigning the American High School.* New York: Houghton Mifflin, 1992.

Slavin, Robert. "Are Cooperative Learning and 'Untracking' Harmful to the Gifted?" *Educational Leadership,* March 1991.

Valley Park Middle School, 130 Overlea Blvd., Toronto, Ontario, Canada M3C 1B2; (416) 396-2465; Phyllis Hill, Principal.

Vickery, Tom Rusk. "ODDM: A Workable Model for Total School Improvement." *Educational Leadership,* April 1990.

Wellesley Middle School, 50 Kingsbury St., Wellesley, MA 02181; (617) 446-6235; John D'Auria, Principal.

Part III: Strategies and Tools for Reform

1: Involving Parents and the Community

The Achievement Council, 4055 Wilshire Blvd., Suite 350, Los Angeles, CA 90010; (213) 487-3194; Linda Wong, Executive Director; Jean Adenika, Southern California Director; Phyllis Hart, Manager of School Services.

Albany Citizens for Education (ACE), P.O. Box 6934, Fort Orange Station, 450 Central Ave., Albany, NY 12206; (518) 447-5877.

BEST Education Support Team, P.O. Box 1305, Selma, AL 36702.

Educational Testing Service, Princeton, NJ 08541-0001; (609) 734-5308.

Hispanic Policy Development Project, 36 E. 22nd St., New York, NY
    10010; (212) 529-9323; Siobhan Nicolau, Executive Director.
Kammerer Middle School, 7315 Wesboro Rd., Louisville, KY 40222;
    (502) 473-8279; Nancy A. Weber, Principal.
Kreinberg, Nancy, and Harriet Nathan, eds. *Teachers' Voices, Teachers'
    Wisdom: Seven Adventurous Teachers Think Aloud.* Berkeley, Calif.:
    EQUALS, 1991. Available from EQUALS, Lawrence Hall of Science,
    University of California, Berkeley, CA 94720; (510) 642-1823.
Levine, David. "Selma Confronts Tracking." *Rethinking Schools* 4, no. 3
    (March/April 1990).
National Association for the Advancement of Colored People (NAACP),
    Eastern Long Island Branch, P.O. Box 338, East Hampton, NY 11937;
    Louis Ware, President; Lyla Hoffman, Education Committee.
National Coalition of Advocates for Students, 100 Boylston St., Boston,
    MA 02116; (617) 357-8507.
National Coalition of Education Activists, P.O. Box 405, Rosendale,
    NY 12472; (914) 658-8115; Debi Duke, Executive Director.
National Urban League, 500 East 62nd St., New York, NY 10021;
    (212) 310-9000.
Oakes, Jeannie, and Martin Lipton. *Making the Best of Schools:
    A Handbook for Parents, Teachers, and Policymakers.* New Haven:
    Yale University Press, 1990.
"On the Right Track: What Can Parents Do to Help Their Children
    Succeed in School?" Available from the National Urban League.
"On the Right Track: What Students Should Know To Succeed In
    School." Available from the National Urban League.
People About Changing Schools (PACE), 79 Leonard St., New York,
    NY 10013.
Quality Education for Minorities Network, 1818 N St., NW, Suite 350,
    Washington, DC 20036; (202) 659-1818.
Rethinking Schools, 1001 E. Keefe Ave., Milwaukee, WI 53212;
    (414) 964-9646.
Rose, Mike. *Lives on the Boundary: The Struggles and Achievements
    of America's Underprepared.* New York: Free Press, 1989.
Schools Are for Everyone (SAFE), P.O. Box 583, Syracuse, NY 13210.
School Voices, 79 Leonard St., New York, NY 10013.
The Right Question Project, Inc., 167 Holland St., Somerville, MA 02144;
    (617) 628-4070; Dan Rothstein, Director.
Useem, Elizabeth L. "'You're Good, But You're Not Good Enough':
    Tracking Students Out of Advanced Mathematics." *American
    Educator,* Fall 1990.
Wellesley Middle School, 50 Kingsbury St., Wellesley, MA 02181; (617)
    446-6235; John D'Auria, Principal.
Williamson, Ron, and J. Howard Johnston. *Planning for Success:
    Successful Implementation of Middle Level Reorganization.* Reston, Va.:
    National Association of Secondary School Principals, 1991

2: Expecting the Best

Joseph H. Capelluti, College of Education, 221 Bailey Hall, University of
    Southern Maine, Gorham, ME 04038; (207) 780-5077, (207) 780-5300.
deLone, Richard, for the Carnegie Council on Children. *Small Futures:
    Children, Inequality, and the Limits of Liberal Reform.* New York:
    Harcourt Brace Jovanovich, 1979.
Eckstrom, Ruth B., and Ana Maria Villegas. "Ability Grouping in Middle
    Grade Mathematics: Process and Consequences." *Research in Middle
    Level Education* 15, no. 1 (Fall 1991).
Edmonds, Ronald. "Effective Schools for the Urban Poor." *Educational
    Leadership,* October 1979.
Edmonds, Ronald. "School Effects and Teacher Effects." *Social Policy,*
    Fall 1984.
Edna McConnell Clark Foundation, Program for Disadvantaged Youth.
    Program Statement, June 1988. Available from the Edna McConnell
    Clark Foundation, 250 Park Ave., Suite 900, New York, NY 10017.
Efficacy Institute, 99 Hayden St., Lexington, MA 02173; (617) 862-4390;
    Dr. Jeffrey P. Howard, President.
Forbes, Roy H., and Gina E. Burkhardt. *A Staff Development Model
    (Featuring the TESA Program in Decatur Township, Indiana).*
    Bloomington, IN: Phi Delta Kappa, 1988.
Good, Thomas L., and Jere E. Brophy. *Looking in Classrooms,* New
    York: Harper and Row, 1987.
Hispanic Policy Development Project, 36 E. 22nd St., New York, NY
    10010; (212) 529-9323; Siobhan Nicolau, Executive Director.
Kerman, Sam. "Teacher Expectations and Student Achievement: "Why
    Did You Call on Me? I Didn't Have My Hand Up!" *Phi Delta Kappan,*
    June 1979.
Matthews, Jay. *Escalante: The Best Teacher in America.* New York:
    Henry Holt, 1988.
Oakes, Jeannie, and Martin Lipton. *Making the Best of Schools:
    A Handbook for Parents, Teachers, and Policymakers.* New Haven:
    Yale University Press, 1990.
Nancy Peck, Associate Director, Southeastern Desegregation Assistance
    Center, Kendall One Plaza, 8603 S. Dixie Hwy., Suite 304, Miami,
    FL 33143; (305) 669-0114.
Silvernail, David L., and Joseph Capelluti. "An Examination of the
    Relationship Between Middle Level School Teachers' Grouping
    Preferences and Their Sense of Responsibility for Student Outcomes."
    Research in Middle Level Education 15, no. 1 (Fall 1991).
Sizer, Theodore. "Diverse Practice, Shared Ideas: The Essential School."
    In *Organizing for Learning: Toward the 21st Century,* edited by Herbert
    J. Walberg and John J. Lane. Reston, Va.: National Association of
    Secondary School Principals, 1989.
Smey-Richman, Barbara. *Teacher Expectations and Low-Achieving
    Students.* Philadelphia: Research for Better Schools, 1989.
    Available from RSB, 444 North Third St., Philadelphia, PA 19123;
    (215) 574-9300.

Teacher Expectations, Student Achievement (TESA), Kerman
  Associates, 23965 Minnequa Dr., P.O. Box 5738, Diamond Bar,
  CA 91765; (714) 598-7561; Sam Kerman, Director.
Valley Park Middle School, 130 Overlea Blvd., Toronto, Ontario, Canada
  M3C 1B2; (416) 396-2465; Phyllis Hill, Principal.
Charles A. Weed, Coordinator, Curriculum and Instruction, Albany-
  Schoharie-Schenectady Counties Board of Cooperative Educational
  Services, 47 Cornell Road, Latham, NY 12110-1402; (518) 786-3211.

3: Organizing and Grouping for Diversity

Appalachia Educational Laboratory. "Teaching Combined Grade
  Classes: Real Problems and Promising Practices." Appalachia
  Educational Laboratory, P.O. Box 1348, Charleston, West Virginia
  25325.
Bennett Park Public Montessori School, 342 Clinton St., Buffalo,
  NY 14204-1797; (716) 852-3033; Jan Dombkowski, Principal.
Castle High School, 45–386 Kaneohe Bay Drive, Kaneohe, Hawaii
  96744; (808) 235-4591; Robert Ginlack, Principal.
Cohen, Elizabeth G., Edward DeAvila, and Jo Ann Intili. "Multi-Cultural
  Improvement of Cognitive Ability." Executive summary of findings of
  a three-year study of *Finding Out/Descubrimiento.* State of California,
  Department of Education, Contract #9372.
Crete-Monee Junior High School, 1500 Sangamon St., Crete, IL 60417;
  (708) 672-2700; J.T. Crawford, Principal.
Davidson Middle School, 280 Woodland Ave., San Rafael, CA 94901;
  (415) 485-2400; Robert Vasser, Principal.
Gardner, Howard, and Thomas Hatch. "Multiple Intelligences Go to
  School: Educational Implications of the Theory of Multiple
  Intelligences." *Educational Researcher* 18, no. 8 (November 1989).
Gartner, Alan, and Dorothy Kerzner Lipsky. "Beyond Special Education:
  Toward a Quality System for All Students." *Harvard Educational
  Review* 57, no. 4 (November 1987).
Holsing, Addie. "A Core Curriculum Classroom." Berkeley: Willard
  Junior High School, n.d.
Holsing, Addie. "A Core Curriculum Classroom: Grouping." Berkeley:
  Willard Junior High School, n.d.
Jericho Middle School, Cedar Swamp Rd., Jericho, NY 11753; (516) 681-
  5829; Anna Hunderfund, Principal.
King, Arthur R., and Thomas G. Stone. "Teacher Teams: The Key to
  Success in a Large Secondary School." Unpublished paper, February
  1991. University of Hawaii at Manoa, College of Education,
  Curriculum Research and Development Group, Castle Memorial Hall
  132, 1776 University Ave., Honolulu, HI 96822; (808) 956-7961.
Louis Armstrong Middle School, 32-02 Junction Blvd., East Elmhurst,
  Queens, NY 11369 (718) 335-7500; Dr. Mary Ellen Levin, Principal.
MacIver, Douglas J. "Meeting the Needs of Young Adolescents: Advisory
  Groups, Interdisciplinary Teaching Teams, and School Transition
  Programs." *Phi Delta Kappan,* February 1990.

MacMagic Partnership, Lucasfilm Learning, P. O. Box 2009, San Rafael, CA 94912; (415) 662-1794; Contact: Karla Kelly, Project Manager/ Senior Curriculum Designer.

Middle School of the Kennebunks, 87 Fletcher St., Kennebunk, ME 04043-1997; (207) 985-2912; Sandra Caldwell, Principal.

National Education Association. *Academic Tracking.* Washington, D.C.: National Education Association, 1990. Available from NEA, 1201 Sixteenth St., N.W., Washington, DC 20036; (202) 822-7350.

Pardo, Elly B. "Cooperative Education and Technology: Preparing Culturally Diverse Youth for Today's Challenges." An Interim Evaluation of Language-Minority Students in the Davidson Middle School's MacMagic Program, May 1991. Contact: Elly Pardo, Ph.D., Consultant in Evaluation, Research, and Bilingual Education, 3616 Lake Shore Ave., Oakland, CA 94610; (510) 465-9312.

Pratt, David. "On the Merits of Multiage Classrooms." *Research in Rural Education* 3, no. 3 (1986).

Project Zero, Longfellow Hall, Harvard Graduate School of Education, Cambridge, MA 02138; (617) 495-4342; Howard Gardner, Co-Director.

Rachlin, Jill. "The Label That Sticks." *U.S. News and World Report,* 3 July 1989.

Rundlett Junior High School, Conant Dr., Concord, NH 03301; (603) 225-0862; Pam Melanson, Principal.

Sapon-Shevin, Mara. "Initial Steps for Developing a Caring School." In *Support Networks for Inclusive Schools,* edited by Susan Stainback and William Stainback. Baltimore: Paul H. Brooks, 1990.

Sapon-Shevin, Mara. "Celebrating Diversity, Creating Community: Curriculum that Honors and Builds on Differences." In *Adapting the Regular Class Curriculum: Enhancing Student Success in Inclusive Classrooms,* edited by Susan Stainback and William Stainback. Baltimore: Paul H. Brooks, 1991.

Slavin, Robert E., and Nancy A. Madden. "What Works for Students At Risk: A Research Synthesis." *Educational Leadership* 46, no. 5 (February 1989).

Wellesley Middle School, 50 Kingsbury St., Wellesley, MA 02181; (617) 446-6235; John D'Auria, Principal.

Western Middle School, 2001 West Main St., Louisville, Kentucky 40212; (502) 454-8345; Ron Barber, Principal; Chris Corbin, Chapter 1 Coordinator.

Willard Junior High School, 2425 Stuart St., Berkeley, CA 94705; (415) 644-6330, 644-6231; Chris Lim, Principal.

Woodruff School, Cleburne St., West Helena, Arkansas 72390; (501) 572-7864; Kenneth Murphree, Principal.

4: High-Level Curriculum for Heterogeneous Groups

Alvino, James. "Building Better Thinkers: A Blueprint for Instruction." *Learning,* February 1990. A major portion of this issue is devoted to articles about curriculum and instruction for thinking skills.

Arnold, John. "Towards a Middle Level Curriculum Rich in Meaning." *Middle School Journal* 23, no. 1 (November 1991).

Association for Supervision and Curriculum Development, 1250 N. Pitt St., Alexandria, VA 22314-1403; (703) 549-9110.

Beane, James A. *A Middle School Curriculum: From Rhetoric to Reality.* Columbus, Ohio: National Middle School Association, 1990.

Beyer, Barry K. *Practical Strategies for the Teaching of Thinking.* Needham, Mass.: Allyn and Bacon, 1987.

Bloom, Benjamin S. *Human Characteristics and School Learning.* New York: McGraw-Hill, 1976.

Bloom, Benjamin S., ed. *Taxonomy of Educational Objectives Handbook I: Cognitive Domain.* New York: David McKay, 1956.

Brandt, Ron. "On Philosophy in the Curriculum: A Conversation with Matthew Lipman." *Educational Leadership,* September 1988.

Brown, Rexford. "Schooling and Thoughtfulness." *Basic Education: Issues, Answers, and Facts* 3, no. 3 (Spring 1988).

Bruner, Jerome S. *The Relevance of Education.* New York: W.W. Norton, 1973.

Cambridge Rindge and Latin School, 459 Broadway, Cambridge, MA 02138; (617) 349-6630, (617) 349-6751; Larry Rosenstock, Director, School of Technical Arts.

Center for Teaching Thinking, The Regional Laboratory for Educational Improvement of the Northeast and Islands, 300 Brickstone Square, #900, Andover, MA 01810; (800) 347-4200; Jill Mirman Owen, Robert Swartz, Co-directors.

Central Park East Secondary School, 1573 Madison Ave., New York, NY 10029; (212) 860-8935; Deborah Meier, Director.

Children's Museum of Boston, Museum Wharf, Boston, MA 02110; (617) 426-6500; Bernie Zubrowski, Middle Grades Science Curriculum Project Leader.

Arthur L. Costa, Search Models Unlimited, 950 Fulton Ave., #245, Sacramento, CA 95825; (916) 489-2106.

Costa, Arthur L. "What Human Beings Do When They Behave Intelligently and How They Can Become More So." In *Developing Minds,* rev. ed., edited by Arthur L. Costa. Alexandria, Va.: Association for Supervision and Curriculum Development, 1991.

Council for Basic Education. "Off the Tracks." *Perspective,* Summer 1989. Available from the Council for Basic Education, 725 Fifteenth St., N.W., Washington, DC 20005; (202) 347-4171.

Council of Chief State School Officers. *Higher Order Learning for All.* Washington, D.C.: CCSSO, November 1990. Available from Council of Chief State School Officers, One Massachusetts Ave., NW, Suite 700, Washington, DC 20001; (202) 408-5515.

Davis, Albie, and Kit Porter. "Tales of Schoolyard Mediation." *UPDATE on Law-Related Educaton* 9 (Winter 1985).

Dewey, John. *The School and Society,* rev. ed. Chicago: University of Chicago Press, 1989.

Dudley Street Neighborhood Initiative, 513 Dudley St., Roxbury, MA 02119; (617) 442-9670.

Early Adolescent Helper Program, Center for Advanced Study in Education, City University of New York, 25 West 43d St., New York, NY l0036; (212) 642-2947; Joan Schine, Director.

Educational Development Center, 55 Chapel St., Newton, MA 02160; (800) 225-4276; (617) 969-7100, ext. 430; Carolee Matsumoto, Principal Investigator, Improving Urban Middle School Science Project.

Eisner, Elliot W. "Should America Have a National Curriculum?" *Educational Leadership* 49, no. 2 (October 1991).

Epstein, Joyce L., and Karen Clark Salinas. *Promising Practices in Major Academic Subjects in the Middle Grades,* Report No. 4. Baltimore: Center for Research on Effective Schooling for Disadvantaged Students, Johns Hopkins University, May 1990.

Facing History and Ourselves National Foundation, Inc., 25 Kennard Rd., Brookline, MA 02146; (617) 232-1595; Margot Stern Strom, Executive Director.

Food First, Institute for Food and Development Policy, 145 Ninth St., San Francisco, CA 94103; (415) 864-8555; For ordering materials: (800) 888-3314; Walden Bello, Executive Director.

Foundational Approaches in Science Teaching (FAST), University of Hawaii, Curriculum Research and Development Group, 1776 University Ave., Honolulu, HI 96822; (808) 956-7863; Donald B. Young.

John Glenn Middle School, McMahon Rd., Bedford, MA 01730; (617) 275-1700; Dr. Laurence Aronstein, Principal.

Gursky, Daniel. "The Unschooled Mind." An Interview with Howard Gardner. *Teacher Magazine,* November/December 1991.

Holyoke Magnet Middle School, 325 Pine St., Holyoke, MA 01040; (413) 534-2010; J. Efrain Martinez, Principal.

"Higher Level Thinking Activities Boost Retention," *NewsLeader* 38, no. 7 (March 1991). Newsletter of the National Association of Secondary School Principals,

Higher Order Thinking Skills (HOTS) Project, College of Education, Division of Edcuational Foundations and Administration, University of Arizona, Tucson, AZ 85721; (602) 621-1305; Stanley Pogrow, Director.

Human Biology Middle Grades Life Sciences Project, Building 80, Quad, Stanford University, Stanford, CA 94305-2160; (415) 723-3693; Craig Heller, Professor of Human Biology and Herant Katchadourian, Professor of Psychiatry and Human Biology, Directors; Mary Kiely, Associate Director.

Institute for the Advancement of Philosophy for Children, Montclair State College, Upper Montclair, NJ 07043; (201) 893-4277. Matthew Lipman, Director.

Junior Great Books Program, The Great Books Foundation, 35 E. Wacker Dr., Suite 2300, Chicago, IL 60601-2298; (800) 222-5870. The program offers a newsletter, *Leader Notes,* as well as a basic overview for teachers, *An Introduction to Shared Inquiry* (Chicago: The Great Books Foundation, 1987).

Lewis, Barbara A. *The Kids' Guide to Social Action.* Minneapolis, Minn.: Free Spirit Publishing, 1991. Available from Free Spirit Publishing, Inc., 400 First Ave. North, #616, Minneapolis, MN 55401; (612) 338-2068; (800) 735-7323.

Lipman, Matthew. "Thinking Skills Fostered by Philosophy for Children." In *Thinking and Learning Skills. Vol. 1, Relating Instruction to Research,* edited by Judith W. Segal, Susan F. Chipman, and Robert Glaser. Hillsdale, N.J.: Lawrence Earlbaum Associates, 1985.

Livermore Falls Middle School, 1 Highland Ave., Livermore Falls, ME 04254; (207) 897-2121; Robert Miller, Principal.

Mann, Amy. "A Dynamic Approach to Teaching Literature." *The Pioneering Practitioner* 1, no. 1 (Fall 1990).

McDonough, Lee. "Middle Level Curriculum: The Search for Self and Social Meaning." *Middle School Journal,* November 1991.

Middle School of the Kennebunks, 87 Fletcher St., Kennebunk, ME 04043-1997; (207) 985-2912; Roger Twitchell, Science Department Chair.

National Asociation for Mediation in Education (NAME), 425 Amity St., Amherst, MA 01002; (413) 545-2462; Annette Townley, Executive Director.

National Resource Center for Middle Grades Education, University of South Florida, College of Education, EDU-115, Tampa, FL 33620-5650; (813) 974-2530; Dick Puglisi, Director; Sandra Schurr, Associate Director.

Oakes, Jeannie, and Martin Lipton. *Making the Best of Schools: A Handbook for Parents, Teachers, and Policymakers.* New Haven: Yale University Press, 1990.

Parker Middle School, 45 Temple St., Reading, MA 01867; (617) 944-0768; Jeff Cryan, English Department Chairperson.

Pioneer Valley Regional School, Route 10, Northfield, MA 01360; (413) 498-2931; Evrett Masters, Principal.

Pogrow, Stanley. "Challenging At-Risk Students: Findings from the HOTS Program." *Phi Delta Kappan,* January 1990.

Pogrow, Stanley. "Converting Students Who Have Been Placed At-Risk into Reflective Learners." In *Mind Matters,* edited by Arthur Costa and James Bellanca. Palatine, Ill.: Skylight Publishing, 1992.

Project Public Life, Humphrey Center, 301 19th Ave. South, Minneapolis, MN 55455; (612) 625-0142.

Sleeper, Martin, Margot Stern Strom, and Henry C. Zabierek. "Facing History and Ourselves." *Educational Leadership* 48, no. 3 (November 1990).

Teaching Tolerance, 400 Washington Ave., Montgomery, AL 36104; (205) 264-0286; Sara Bullard, Editor.

Technical Education Research Centers (TERC), 2067 Massachusetts Ave., Cambridge, MA 02140; (617) 547-0430; Candace Julyan, Project Director for "Kids' Network."

"Voyage of the *Mimi.*" Available from Wings for Learning, 1600 Green Hills Rd., P.O. Box 66002, Scotts Valley, CA 95067-0002; (800) 321-7511.

West Windsor-Plainsboro Middle School, 55 Grovers Mill Rd., #410, Plainsboro, NJ 08536; (609) 799-9600; Kay Goerss, Principal.

5: Instruction and Assessment for Heterogeneous Classrooms

Instruction for Heterogeneous Groups

"Big Kids Teach Little Kids: What We Know About Cross-Age Tutoring."
Harvard Education Letter 3, no. 2 (March 1987).

Carrel, Sue. "What's Good for Gifted Is Good for All." Letters.
Educational Leadership 49, no. 1 (September 1991).

Central Park East Secondary School, 1573 Madison Ave., New York,
NY 10029; (212) 860-8935; Deborah Meier, Director.

Cohen, Elizabeth, and M. Beatriz Arias. "Accelerating the Education of
Language Minority At-Risk Students. Paper presented at Conference
on Accelerating the Education of At-Risk Students, Stanford
University, November 17–18, 1988.

Cohen, Elizabeth. *Designing Groupwork: Strategies for Heterogeneous
Classrooms.* New York: Teachers College Press, 1986.

Complex Instruction News, a newsletter published three times a year
of interest to "all who believe that cooperative groupwork is an
educational approach whose time has come;" Michael Chatfield,
Editor. Available from the Program for Complex Instruction, Stanford
University School of Education, Stanford, CA 94305; (415) 723-5992.

Cone, Joan Kernan. "Untracking Advanced Placement English: Creating
Opportunity Is Not Enough." *Phi Delta Kappan* 73, no. 9 (May 1992).

Cooperative Learning, The Magazine for Cooperation in Education,
published by the International Association for Cooperation in
Education. Editorial Office: 136 Liberty St., Santa Cruz, CA 95060;
(408) 429-6550; Nan and Ted Graves, Executive Editors.

Council of Chief State School Officers. *Principles to Support Higher
Order Learning in the Middle Grades.* Washington, D.C.: CCSSO,
1991. Available from the Council of Chief State School Officers,
One Massachusetts Ave., NW, Suite 700, Washington, DC 20001;
(202) 408-5505.

Cross-Age Structured Tutoring Program for Math, Boise Public Schools,
1207 Fort St., Boise, ID 83702; Dr. Geri Plumb.

Allan Dittmer, Foxfire Network, Urban Studies Team, School of
Education, University of Louisville, Louisville, KY 40258;
(502) 588-0590.

Foxfire Teacher Outreach, P.O. Box B, Rabun Gap, GA 30568; (404) 746-
5318; Hilton Smith, Coordinator.

Intercultural Development Research Association, 5835 Callaghan Rd.,
Suite 305, San Antonio, TX 78228-1125; (512) 684-8180; José
Cardenas, Executive Director.

International Association for the Study of Cooperation in Education
(IASCE), Box 1582, Santa Cruz, CA 95061-1582; (408) 426-7926.

Johns Hopkins University, Center for Research on Effective Schooling
for Disadvantaged Students, 3505 North Charles St., Baltimore, MD
21218; (301) 338-7570; Robert Stevens, Middle Grades Reading and
Writing Project.

Johnson, David W., Roger T. Johnson, and Edythe Johnson Holubec.
Cooperation in the Classroom. Edina, Minn.: Interaction Book
Company, 1988.

Joyce, Bruce, and Marsha Weil. *Models of Teaching*. Englewood Cliffs, N.J.: Prentice-Hall, 1986. Available for order from Skylight Publishing, 200 E. Wood St., Suite 250, Palatine, IL 60067; (800) 348-4474 or (708) 991-6300 in Northern Illinois.

Kagan, Spencer. *Cooperative Learning: A Resource for Teachers*. San Juan Capistrano, Calif.: Resources for Teachers, 1989.

Levin, Henry M., Gene V. Glass, and Gail R Meister. "Cost-Effectiveness of Computer-Assisted Instruction." *Evaluation Review* 11, no. 1 (February 1987).

Louis Armstrong Middle School, 32-02 Junction Blvd., East Elmhurst, Queens, NY 11369; (718) 335-7500; Fran Corvasce, English teacher.

Lounsbury, John. "A Fresh Start for the Middle School Curriculum." *Middle School Journal* 23, no. 1 (November 1991).

MacLeod, Jay. "BLOODLINES: A Case Study of Educational Empowerment." Lexington, MS: Rural Organizing and Cultural Center, December 1990.

Means, Barbara, and Michael S. Knapp, eds. *Teaching Advanced Skills to Educationally Disadvantaged Students*. Menlo Park, Calif.: SRI International and Policy Studies Associates, March 1991. Report prepared for the U.S. Department of Education.

Nystrand, Martin. "High School English Students in Low-Achieving Classes." In *Tracking and Ability Grouping* (Newsletter of the National Center for Effective Secondary Schools) 5, no. 1 (Spring 1990). Available from NCESS, 1025 W. Johnson St., Madison, WI 53706 (608) 263-7575.

Parkman Middle School, 3620 North 18th St., Milwaukee, WI 53206; (414) 445-9930; Kenneth Holt, Principal.

Pioneering Practitioner: A Journal on Heterogeneous Grouping, Cooperative Learning, and School Change, a teacher-directed, biannual journal including descriptions of curriculum and instruction that works with heterogeneous groups in grades seven through twelve and reviews of books and articles promoting innovative teaching. Available from Pioneer Valley Regional School.

Pioneer Valley Regional School, Route 10, Northfield, MA 01360; (413) 498-2931; Roger Genest, English Department Chairperson.

Program for Complex Instruction, School of Education, Stanford University, Stanford, CA 94305; (415) 723-4661; Dr. Elizabeth Cohen, Director.

Resources for Teachers, 27134 Paseo Espada, #202, San Juan Capistrano, CA 92675; (800) 933-2667; Spencer Kagan, Director.

Rural Organizing and Cultural Center, 103 Swinney Lane, Lexington, MS 39095; (601) 834-3080.

Dan Sharkovitz. "Crossing the Tracks: Literacy and Liberation." *Bread Loaf and the Schools*. Summer 1989.

Slavin, Robert E. *School and Classroom Organization*. Hillsdale, N.J.: Lawrence Erlbaum Associates, 1989.

Slavin, Robert E. *Cooperative Learning: Theory, Research, and Practice*. Englewood Cliffs, N.J.: Prentice-Hall, 1990.

Tate's Creek Middle School, Centre Parkway, Lexington, KY 40517; (606) 272-3452; Dorie Combs, Elizabeth Barrett, Julia Robbins, Seventh Grade Team teachers.

Teachers' Curriculum Institute, 4149 El Camino Way, Suite B, Palo Alto, CA 94306; (415) 858-2228; (800) 287-0654 (inside California); Bert Bower, Executive Director.

Teachers Networking, a newsletter focusing on classroom strategies for using whole language instruction with heterogeneous groups. A $15 subscription includes four issues. Available from Richard Owen Publishers, 135 Katonah Ave., Katonah, NY 10536; (800) 336-5588; FAX (914) 232-3977.

University of Minnesota, Cooperative Learning Center, 202 Pattee Hall, 150 Pillsbury Dr., S.E., Minneapolis, MN 55455; (616) 624-7031; David Johnson and Roger Johnson, Directors.

West Baltimore Middle School, 201 North Bend Rd., Baltimore, MD 21229; (301) 396-0700; Sheila Kolman, Principal.

Wigginton, Eliot. *Sometimes a Shining Moment: The Foxfire Experience.* Garden City, N.Y.: Doubleday, 1985.

Youth of the Rural Organizing and Cultural Center. *Minds Stayed on Freedom: The Civil Rights Struggle in the Rural South.* Boulder, Colo.: Westview Press, 1991.

Assessment for Heterogeneous Groups

Arter, Judy. "Performance Assessment: What's Out There and How Useful Is It Really?" Paper presented at the annual meeting of the American Educational Research Association, Chicago, 1991.

Arter, Judith A., and Vicki Spandel. "Using Portfolios of Student Work in Instruction and Assessment," June 1991. A training module with a built-in "self-test" to facilitate thoughtful planning for introduction of performance-assessment strategies. Available from Northwest Regional Educational Laboratory.

Authentic Assessment Network of the Association for Supervision and Curriculum Development allows educators to exchange ideas and solve problems related to developing assessment strategies. Contact Albert Koshiyama, Administrator, School Intervention; California Department of Education, 502 J St., Sacramento, CA 95814; (916) 324-4933.

Clara Barton Open School, 4237 Colfax Ave. South, Minneapolis, MN 55409; (612) 627-2373; Yvonne Beseler, Principal; Launa Ellison, Middle Grades Coordinator.

Costa, Arthur. "Re-assessing Assessment." *Educational Leadership* 46, no. 7 (April 1989).

FairTest, National Center for Fair and Open Testing, provides a regular flow of information on a wide range of national and state-level policy-development activities related to different kinds of performance assessment. The *FairTest Examiner* offers analysis of testing policies and reflects the organization's commitment to raising issues concerning equity and bias in testing and assessment. Contact FairTest, National Center for Fair and Open Testing, 342 Broadway, Cambridge, MA 02139-1802; (617) 864-4810.

Harman, Susan. "Appropriate Evaluation." *School Voices* 1, no. 1
   (Winter 1991). Available from Susan Harman, 889 Pacific St.,
   Brooklyn, NY 11238; (718) 857-2130.
Mitchell, Ruth. *Testing for Learning: How New Approaches to Evaluation
   Can Improve American Schools.* New York: Free Press, 1992.
National Resource Center for Middle Grades Education, University of
   South Florida, College of Education, Room 118, Tampa, FL 33620-
   5650; (813) 974-2530; Dr. Dick J. Puglisi, Director.
Northwest Regional Education Laboratory, 101 S.W. Main St., Suite 500,
   Portland, OR 97204; (503) 275-9500 (inside Oregon), (800) 275-9500
   (outside Oregon). Contact Judy Arter or Richard Stiggins for
   information about performance assessments.
Perrone, Vito, ed. *Expanding Student Assessment.* Alexandria, Va.:
   Association for Supervision and Curriculum Development, 1991.
Portfolio Assessment Newsletter is published three times each year by
   the Northwest Evaluation Association (NWEA). The association's
   goal is to promote an information network for educators interested
   in portfolios and portfolio assessment. In addition, NWEA, in close
   collaboration with the Northwest Regional Educational Laboratory,
   hosts conferences and institutes for teachers, instructional leaders,
   assessment specialists, and administrators to explore and plan
   alternatives for classroom and program assessment. Contact
   Northwest Evaluation Association, P.O. Box 2122, 5 Centerpointe
   Dr., Suite 100, Lake Oswego, OR 97035; (503) 624-1951; Allan Olson,
   Editor.
"Portfolio Bibliography." An extensive annotated bibliography updated
   regularly by The Test Center, Northwest Regional Educational
   Laboratory. Included are contact names and addresses of developers
   and practitioners of materials, papers, articles, and portfolio samples.
   Other annotated bibliographies available on assessment include
   "Assessment Alternatives in Science," "Reading Assessment
   Alternatives," and "Math Assessment Alternatives."
Portfolio News is a quarterly publication of the Portfolio Assessment
   Clearinghouse, a network of educators involved in portfolio
   assessment. Each issue contains reports of individual projects and
   discussion of issues of concern in portfolio assessment. For example,
   contents might include brief reports from practitioners about the use
   of portfolios in language arts and math, perspectives on portfolios
   as a basis for grading, and a description of students' responses to
   portfolios. In addition, the newsletter published a directory of
   projects, located in individual schools and at the state and university
   levels, involving portfolio assessment. Contact *Portfolio News*,
   Portfolio Assessment Clearinghouse, c/o San Dieguito Union High
   School District, 710 Encinitas Blvd., Encinitas, CA 92024. $25/year.
Project Zero is engaged in documenting how thematic project work
   and complex assessment can involve students in their own learning,
   promote reflective thinking, and help students use their strengths
   to develop areas of intelligence that do not come naturally. Contact
   Project Zero, Longfellow Hall, Harvard Graduate School of Education,
   Appian Way, Cambridge, MA 02l38-3752; (800) 235-2132; (617) 495-4342.

6: What about Math?

Algebridge: Contact Janson Publications, Inc., 222 Richmond St., Suite 105, Providence, RI 02903; (800) 322-MATH; (401) 272-0090.

The Algebra Project, 22 Wheatland Ave., Boston, MA 02124; (617) 287-1508; Cynthia Silva, Project Coordinator.

Bartlett School, 79 Wannalancit St., Lowell, MA 01854; (508) 937-8968; Lisa Bryant, Principal.

Bay Area Mathematics Project, Lawrence Hall of Science, University of California at Berkeley, Berkeley, CA; (510) 642-3167.

Braddock, Jomills Henry. "Tracking the Middle Grades: National Patterns of Grouping for Instruction." *Phi Delta Kappan* 71, no. 6 (February 1990).

Brooks Middle School, Ballfield Rd., Lincoln, MA 01773; (617) 259-9408; Fred Gross, Teacher.

Burns, Marilyn, and Cathy McLaughlin. *A Collection of Math Lessons From Grades 6 Through 8* and Marilyn Burns, *Mathematics for Middle School.* Available from Cuisenaire Co. of America, Inc., 12 Church St., Box D, New Rochelle, NY 10802; (800) 237-3142.

Callahan, Phil, Stanley Pogrow, and Kay Gore. "Middle School Exemplary Curricula: Mathematics," College of Education, Division of Educational Foundations and Administration, University of Arizona, Tucson, AZ 85721; (602) 621-1305.

Eckstrom, Ruth B., and Ana María Villegas. "Ability Grouping in Middle Grade Mathematics: Process and Consequences." *Research in Middle Level Education,* 1991.

Education Development Center, Inc., 55 Chapel St., Newton, MA 02160; (617) 969-7100.

Educational Testing Service. *A World of Differences.* Princeton, N.J.: Educational Testing Service, 1989.

EQUALS, Lawrence Hall of Science, University of California, Berkeley, CA 94720; (510) 642-1823.

Flanders, James R. "How Much of the Content in Mathematics Textbooks Is New?" *Arithmetic Teacher,* September 1987.

Frick Junior High School, 2845 64th Ave., Oakland, CA 94605; (415) 562-6565; Murphy Taylor, Principal.

Goodlad, John I. *A Place Called School: Prospects for the Future.* New York: McGraw-Hill, 1984.

Kreinberg, Nancy. *I'm Madly in Love with Electricity and Other Comments About Their Work by Women in Science and Engineering,* 1983. Available from EQUALS, Lawrence Hall of Science, University of California, Berkeley, CA 94720; (510) 642-1823.

Mathematical Association of America, 1529 18th St. NW, Washington, DC 20036; (202) 334-2000.

Mathematical Sciences Education Board, 2101 Constitution Ave. NW, Washington, DC 20418; (202) 334-3294.

Math Learning Center, P.O. Box 3226, 2590 Pringle Rd. S.E., Salem, OR 79302.

Middle Grades Mathematics Project, Michigan State University, Department of Mathematics, Wells Hall, East Lansing, MI 48824-1027.

Moses, Robert P., et al. "The Algebra Project: Organizing in the Spirit of Ella." *Harvard Educational Review* 59, no. 4 (November 1989).

National Assessment of Educational Progress (1990). *Mathematics Report Card: Are We Measuring Up?* NAEP, P.O. Box 6710, Princeton, NJ 08541-6710.

National Assessment of Educational Progress (1991). *The State of Mathematics Achievement.* Available from Educational Information Branch, Office of Educational Research and Improvement, U.S. Department of Education, 555 New Jersey Ave., N.W., Washington, DC 20208-5641; (800) 424-1616.

National Council of Teachers of Mathematics, 1906 Association Drive, Reston, VA 22090; (703) 620-9840. For publications and periodicals: (800) 235-7566.

National Research Council. *Everybody Counts: A Report to the Nation on the Future of Mathematics Education.* Washington, D.C.: NRC, 1989. Available from NRC, 2101 Constitution Ave. NW, Washington, DC 20418; (202) 334-2000.

New York City Public Schools, 110 Livingston St., Brooklyn, NY 11201; (718) 935-5301; Susan Zakaluk, Director of Mathematics.

Oakes, Jeannie. *Multiplying Inequalities: The Effects of Race, Social Class, and Tracking on Opportunities to Learn Mathematics and Science Education,* 1990. Report #R-3928-NSF, Available from RAND Publications Department, 1700 Main Street, P.O. Box 2138, Santa Monica, CA 90406-2138.

Paulos, John Allen. *Beyond Numeracy: Ruminations of a Numbers Man.* New York: Alfred A. Knopf, 1991.

Paulos, John Allen. *Innumeracy: Mathematical Illiteracy and Its Consequences.* New York: Hill and Wang, 1989.

Philadelphia Public Schools, 21st Street So. of the Parkway, Philadelphia, PA 19103-1090; (215) 299-7797; Susan A. Stetzer, Director, Algebra Transition Project.

Ponderosa High School, 7007 E. Bayou Rd., Douglas County Schools, Parker, CO 80134; (719) 841-2770; Jim Reisinger, Math Department.

Prevost, Fernand J. "Are We Accelerating Able Students Out of Mathematics?" *Middle School Journal,* February 1988.

Project PRIME, Algebridge Project, Arizona State University, Downtown Center, 502 E. Monroe St., Phoenix, AZ 85004-2337; (602) 965-8510; Marilyn LaCount, Instructional Specialist.

QUASAR, Learning Research and Development Center, University of Pittsburgh, 3939 O'Hara Street, Pittsburgh, PA 15260; (412) 624-7485.

Dr. Herbert Rosenfeld, Consultant; 711 Amsterdam Ave., #17L, New York, NY 10025; (212) 666-7025.

Rothman, Robert. "First State-Level Assessment Finds Wide Variations: But Math Performance Remains Low Overall." *Education Week* 10, no. 38 (12 June 1991).

University of Chicago School Mathematics Project, 5835 S. Kimbark Ave., Chicago, IL 60637; (312) 702-1130; or Scott, Foresman and Company, 1900 East Lake Ave., Glenview, IL 60025; (800) 554-4411.

University of Hawaii, Hawaii Algebra Learning Project (HALP), College of Education, Castle Memorial Hall 132, 1776 University Ave., Honolulu, HI 96822; (808) 948-7962.

Usiskin, Zalman. "Why Elementary Algebra Can, Should, and Must Be an Eighth Grade Course for Average Students." *Mathematics Teacher*, September 1987.

Wellesley Middle School, 50 Kingsbury St., Wellesley, MA 02181; (617) 446-6235; John D'Auria, Principal.

Working Group on Mathematics Education. *Mathematics Education in New York City: What It Is and What It Should Be.* Brooklyn, N.Y.: New York City Public Schools, June 1990.

7: Student Aspirations and Untracking

Butler Junior High School, 864 Gorham St., Lowell, MA 01852; (508) 937-8973; Harry Koulogeras, Principal.

The College Entrance Examination Board, Commission on Precollege Guidance and Counseling. *Keeping The Options Open.* New York: The College Board, 1986. Available from The College Board, 45 Columbus Ave., New York, NY 10023-6917.

Eastern Junior High School, 19 Porter St., Lynn, MA 01902; (617) 592-3444.

Edna McConnell Clark Foundation, Program for Disadvantaged Youth, "Transforming Your Middle Level School to Prepare Nearly All Students to Pursue Some Form of Post-Secondary Education: Questions and Examples," 250 Park Avenue, Suite 900, New York, NY 10177-0026; (212) 986-4558.

Future Options Education: *"Not Another Handbook" Handbook on How to Help Young People in the Middle Grades Aspire and Achieve.* Brandeis University, Heller School, Center for Human Resources, Waltham, MA 02254; (617) 736-3774.

Graham and Parks School, 15 Upton St., Cambridge, MA 02139; (617) 349-9612; Len Solo, Principal.

Higher Education Information Center, a division of The Educational Resources Institute, Boston Public Library, 666 Boylston Street, Boston, MA 02116; (617) 426-0681; Ann Coles, Executive Director.

Massachusetts General Hospital/Timilty Partnership, 32 Fruit St., Boston, MA 02114; (617) 726-5055; Thomas R. Marcussen, Partnership Coordinator.

Mathematics, Engineering, and Science Achievement (MESA), Lawrence Hall of Science, University of California, Berkeley, CA 94720.

Mayer, Daniel. "Do Early Awareness Programs Increase the Chances of Eighth Graders Reaching Higher Education?" Evaluation Report, July 1991. Available from Higher Education Information Center, 330 Stuart St., Boston, MA 02116; (617) 426-0681.

National Action Council for Minorities in Engineering, 3 West 35th St., New York, NY 10001; (212) 279-2626.

National Association of College Admissions Counselors, 1800 Diagonal
Rd., Suite 430, Alexandria, VA 22314; (703) 836-2222; Frank Burtnett,
Executive Director.

"Pathways to Success: Individualized Educational and Career Plan,"
Part I—Grades 7,8, Crete-Monee Junior High School, 1500 Sangamon
St., Crete, IL 60417; (708) 672-2700; J.T. Crawford, Principal.

Pioneer Valley Regional School, Route 10, Northfield, MA 01360;
(413) 498-2931; Dona Cadwell, Counselor.

Public/Private Ventures, 399 Market St., Philadelphia, PA 19106-2178;
(215) 592-9099.

Southeastern Consortium for Minorities in Engineering, c/o Georgia
Institute of Technology, Atlanta, GA 30332-0270; (404) 894-3314.

Timilty Middle School, 205 Roxbury St., Boston, MA 02119;
(617) 445-3114; Roger Harris, Principal.

Walker, Reagan. "California Study Documents Mismatch Between
Student Goals, Course-Taking." *Education Week,* 21 March 1990.

West Baltimore Middle School, 201 North Bend Rd., Baltimore,
MD 21229; (301) 396-0700; Sheila Kolman, Principal.

Western Middle School, 2201 West Main St., Louisville, KY 40212;
(502) 454-8345; Ron Barber, Principal.

Appendix:
Untracking Schools

The following schools have indicated their willingness to entertain inquiries and visits from interested educators and citizens.

Arizona

Cholla Middle School
3120 W. Cholla
Phoenix, AZ 85029
(602) 866-5151
Principal: Gary A. Batsell

Sierra Middle School
5801 S. Del Moral
Tucson, AZ 85706
(602) 741-2656
Principal: Susan Masek

Desert Sky Middle School
5130 W. Grovers Ave.
Glendale, AZ 85308
(602) 866-5821
Principal: Janet K. Altersitz

California

Valley Jr. High
801 Pine Ave.
Carlsbad, CA 92008
(619) 434-0602
Principal: Donald A. LeMay

Willis Jepson Middle School
580 Elder St.
Vacaville, CA 95688
(707) 446-6829
Principal: Shereene D. Wilkers

Muirlands Middle School
1056 Nautilus St.
La Jolla, CA 92037
(619) 459-4211
Principal: Cassandra Countryman

Ray A. Kroc Middle School
5050 Conrad Ave.
San Diego, CA 92117
(619) 496-8150
Principal: Isabelle Skidmore

National City Jr. High
1701 D Ave.
San Diego, CA 92118
(619) 691-5710
Principal: Gloria Samson

Willard Jr. High School
2425 Stuart St.
Berkeley, CA 94705
(415) 644-6330
Principal: Chris Lim
Contact: Chris Lim
  or Ann Hiyakumoto

Colorado

Isaac Newton Middle School
4001 E. Arapahoe Rd.
Littleton, CO 80122
(303) 771-5540
Principal: Florence Bullock

Connecticut

Plainfield Central School
75 Canterbury Rd.
Plainfield, CT 06374
(203) 774-4447
Principal: Maryanne T. Dumas

Delaware

Seaford Middle School
Stein Highway
Seaford, DE 19973
(302) 629-4586
Principal: George Stone
Contact: Cynthia Spicer

Hawaii

J. B. Castle High School
45-386 Kaneohe Bay Drive
Kaneohe, HI 96744
(808) 235-4591
Principal: Robert Ginlack

Illinois

Crete-Monee Jr. High
1500 Sangamon St.
Crete, IL 60417
(708) 672-2700
Principal: J.T. Crawford

Iowa

Harding Middle School
4801 Golf St., NE
Cedar Rapids, IA 52402
(319) 398-2254
Principal: Sandra Ledford

Kansas

Felten Middle School
301 W. 29th St.
Hays, Kansas 67601
(913) 625-6563
Principal: Will Roth

Kentucky

Noe Middle School
121 W. Lee St.
Louisville, KY 40208
(502) 499-1998
Principal: Linda Compton
Contact: Kathy Sayre

South Jr. High
800 S. Alves
Henderson, KY 42420
(502) 826-9568
Principal: David Jordan

Louisiana

Walnut Hill Elementary/
  Middle School
9360 Woolworth Rd.
Shreveport, LA 71129
(318) 687-6610
Principal: Albert Hardison
Contact: Lucian Cloud,
  Albert Hardison

Prescott Middle School
4055 Prescott Rd.
Baton Rouge, LA 70805
(504) 357-6481
Principal: Anna Bernard

Massachusetts

Johnson Middle School
Robbins Rd.
Walpole, MA 02081
(508) 668-5400 ext. 242
Principal: Stephen R. Driscoll

W.S. Parker Middle School
45 Temple St.
Reading, MA 01867
(617) 944-1236
Principal: John Delaney

Leicester Memorial
Memorial School Dr.
Leicester, MA 01524
(508) 892-3469
Principal: John P. Hartnett

Wellesley Middle School
50 Kingsbury St.
Wellesley, MA 02180
(617) 446-6235
Principal: John D'Auria

Graham and Parks School
15 Upton St.
Cambridge, MA 02139
(617) 349-6612
Principal: Leonard Solo
Contact: Kathy Greeley,
    Ellen Gaies, Steve Barkin

Swampscott Middle School
71 Greenwood Avenue
Swampscott, MA 01907
(617) 596-8820
Principal: Ronald Landman

Bartlett School
79 Wannalancit St.
Lowell, MA 01854
(508) 937-8968
Principal: Lisa Bryant

Chestnut St. Jr. High School
495 Chestnut St.
Springfield, MA 01107
(413) 787-7285
Principal: Virginia O. Anderson

John T. Reid Middle School
950 North St.
Pittsfield, MA 01201
(413) 499-1512
Principal: Douglas McNally

Maryland

Col. Richardson Middle School
Route 2, Box 340A
Federalsberg, MD 12632
(301) 754-9922
Principal: Steve Garner

Riverview Middle School
207 Lockermain St.
Denton, MD 21629
(301) 479-2760
Principal: Harry Martin

Maine

Deer Isle-Stonington
    Jr./Sr. High School
RR1 Box 81
Deer Isle, ME 04627
(207) 348-2303
Principal: George Marnik

Minnesota

Clara Barton Open School
4237 Colfax Ave. South
Minneapolis, MN 55409
(612) 627-2373
Principal: Yvonne Beseler
Contact: Launa Ellison,
    Middle Grades Program

Maplewood Middle School
    (Science Dept. only)
2410 Holloway Ave.
Maplewood, MN 55109
(612) 770-4690
Principal: Mary Leary
Contact: John Stangl,
    Science Dept.

Montana

Havre Middle School
Box 7791
Havre, MT 59501
(406) 265-9613
Principal: Jeff Pratt

Helena Middle School
1029 N. Rodney
Helena, MT 59601
(406) 442-5720
Principal: Pep Jewell

Nevada

Kingsbury Middle School
P.O. Box 648
Zephyr Cove, NV 89448
(702) 588-6281
Principal: Klaire Pirtle

New Hampshire

Rundlett Jr. High
Conant Drive
Concord, NH 03301
(603) 225-0862
Principal: Pam Melanson

New York

Columbus Academy
100 West 77th St.
New York, NY 10024
(212) 678-2923
Principal: Esther Forrest

Louis Armstrong Middle School
32-02 Junction Blvd.
E. Elmhurst, Queens, NY 11369
(718) 335-7500
Principal: Mary Ellen Levin

Oakdale-Bohemia Jr. High School
Oakdale-Bohemia Rd.
Oakdale, NY 11769
(516) 244-2267
Principal: Richard Cantin
Contact: Terry Earley

Oceanside Middle School
Alice and Beatrice Avenues
Oceanside, NY 11572
(516) 678-1200, ext. 261
Principal: Mrs. Enid D'Arrigo

Bennett Park Public
   Montessori School
342 Clinton St.
Buffalo, NY 14204-1797
(716) 852-3033
Principal: Jan Dombkowski

North Carolina

Ferndale Middle School
701 Ferndale Blvd.
High Point, NC 27262
(919) 841-2366
Principal: Dr. Margaret Bray

Rhode Island

Thompson Jr. High School
39 Broadway
Newport, RI 02840
(401) 847-1493
Principal: Brian G. Abdallah
Contact: Rodgero Borgueta

Joseph H. Gaudet Middle School
Aquidneck Avenue
Middletown, RI 02840
(401) 874-6395
Principal: Vincent J. Guiliano

South Carolina

Bell Street Middle School
Rt. 3, Box 1031
Clinton, SC 29325
(803) 833-0807
Principal: Claude Underwood

Campus R/Irmo Middle School
6051 Wescott Rd.
Columbia, SC 29212
(803) 732-8200
Principal: Phyllis W. Pendarvi

Vermont

Rutland Jr. High
Library Ave.
Rutland, VT 05701
(802) 773-1960
Principal: Sanford A. Bassett

Washington

College Place Middle School
7501 208th St. SW
Lynnwood, WA 98036
(206) 670-7451
Principal: Ann E. Foley

Finn Hill Jr. High
8040 NE 132nd
Kirkland, WA 98034
(206) 821-6544
Principal: Robert Strode

Islander Middle School
8225 S.E. 72nd
Mercer Island, WA 98040
(206) 236-3413
Principal: Wayne Hashiguchi

Wisconsin

Van Hise Middle School
4801 Waukesha St.
Madison, WI 53711
(608) 267-4295
Principal: Dr. Marvin Meissen

Glen Hills Middle School
2600 W. Mill Rd.
Glendale, WI 53209
(414) 351-7160
Principal: Don Behrens

About the Author

Anne Wheelock has eleven years experience as a child policy analyst at the Massachusetts Advocacy Center. She is the author of several books on dropout prevention and public school reform.